Weinerface
Stories

by Joel Samberg

Black Rose Writing | Texas

The author grants the final approval for this literary material.

First printing

The author has tried to recreate events, locales and conversations from his/her memories. In order to maintain anonymity in some instances, the author may have changed the names of individuals and places. The author may have changed some identifying characteristics and details such as physical properties, occupations and places of residence.

ISBN: 978-1-68513-184-5
PUBLISHED BY BLACK ROSE WRITING
www.blackrosewriting.com

Printed in the United States of America
Suggested Retail Price (SRP) $23.95

Weinerface is printed in Book Antiqua

*As a planet-friendly publisher, Black Rose Writing does its best to eliminate unnecessary waste to reduce paper usage and energy costs, while never compromising the reading experience. As a result, the final word count vs. page count may not meet common expectations.

For Bob Buono, Linda Wright, Marc Feingold, Bill Freytag, Tom Truitt, Gary Alt, and Bonnie June.

"Winter, spring, summer or fall,
all you've got to do is call
and I'll be there.
You've got a friend."
—Carole King

Thanks, Colin
Stay well.
Be safe.
Have fun.

Joel Smirkig

3/27/23

Weinerface
Stories

Table of Contents

Foreword & Acknowledgements

Yes. Okay. It's true. I admit it. When I was in junior high school I saw a chubby bully standing on the steps of a house across the street and, with the safety of my own front door right behind me, decided to hurl at him the kind of insults to which I had been subjected for years. You know—the orangey red hair, the face full of freckles, the fact that I knew a lot about Y. A. books, but nothing about Y. A. Tittle.

In other words, while this book is officially labeled fiction, a dozen stories in *Weinerface* are based in some measure on things that really happened either to me or to people I know. The other twenty-three stories are based on ideas sparked by random sightings, comments that were overheard, extrapolations on various what-if situations, expansions of conversations with friends, maybe even a dream or two.

I was compelled to create these stories for a dual purpose. The first is to share with anyone I can the literary musings that often take over the greater part of my days and nights. (I often state that the *only* reason I write is to share.) The second is to do my part, as insignificant as it may be, to help us weather this storm called Life on Planet Earth These Days. It can be a little crazy. So while *Weinerface* may not actually un-shake this already shook-up world, maybe it can provide a brief diversion.

Many authors include an Acknowledgements page in their books. Like a handful of characters in *Weinerface* (there are more than a dozen who yearn for success in the arts—literature, theatre, movies, music), I expect to become rich and famous one day, and when that happens more people might read my stuff, and when *that* happens more people will yell at me for leaving them out of the Acknowledgements. So let me apologize for that in advance. If I do become rich as famous one day, I promise to mention everyone else (though not necessarily in print).

I'd like to thank Celia Stangarone and Kate Buffone, who actually said or did something that gave me the concepts for "The One" and "Molly in the Morning"; Dan Samberg, whose 'Squaad' shoutout at Sunset Beach in a roundabout way turned into "A Story With No Ending"; Bonnie Samberg, whose casual and sincere comment at the West Hartford Reservoir gave me the title for "The Tale of the Magic Pause Button"; the late Benny Bell, without whose experience on a Brooklyn street, "Davening on Avenue Y" would never have been written; Irene Levine, who offered proofing assistance and is also proof that a certain mother really talked about riding on the trees, which in turn led to "Riding on the Trees"; Renèe and Jerry Samberg, both departed and sorely missed, whose fateful meeting in the Catskill Mountains (for which you must ride on the trees to get to) blossomed into a "Manhattan Moon"; Jeff Bass, who helped my promotional effort by posting what he'd bring with him on an endless trip to outer space, like the astronaut in "One-Hundred-Fifty-Nine Pounds Max" (just don't mention it to his dogs, who would exceed the maximum anyway); the late Jesse Wilkes, an Olympian mentor who shared an experience that made me say "Bingo!"; Michelle Traub for some valiosa ayuda en el diálogo Español in "Selective Emory"; and all my friends who consistently support my crazy endeavors, literary and otherwise. I mention most of them on the dedication page. Speaking of which, maybe someday there will be a follow-up book with stories about mentally triggered contraception devices, special messages hidden in fortune cookies, and other friend-sparked memories.

Several beta readers have my deepest gratitude, especially Owen O'Farrell ("There is no tongue that moves, none, so soon as yours could win me," Act I, Scene II), for his additional feedback. The crew at Black Rose Writing, who agreed to move ahead even with a rather chaotic first draft, also has my thanks.

And finally, so does that chubby bully.

How Deep is Your Love?

Larry and Susan had to choose between Intercourse, Blue Ball, and Mount Joy. When it came time to plan their annual bed-and-breakfast vacation, they concentrated on Pennsylvania Dutch country. Last year it had been the Jersey Shore; the year before that, Martha's Vineyard. They narrowed it down to Intercourse, Blue Ball, and Mount Joy based on recommendations from friends, Wikipedia, and nightly room rates. Larry liked the fact that he had three unusual names from which to choose, because he knew that unusual town names sometimes spark unusual short stories, and one of his oldest and most ardent professional goals is to one day publish a book of short stories.

Susan preferred Blue Ball. Larry said it sounded painful, and he wanted his vacation to be without discomfort, imagined or otherwise.

"How about Mount Joy, then?" Susan asked.

"Sounds too much like a porn star," Larry protested. "I don't want to look at you in our bed at the B&B and wonder how many movies you've been in."

That left Intercourse.

When he researched the town online, Larry found a 1970s-themed bed-and-breakfast that had the oddest name for a B&B that he had ever heard—the Night Fever Inn—as well as the lowest rates. He liked its unusual name because that, too, might be good for a short story, and he appreciated its affordable rate. Money was always a concern.

The ride down from Massachusetts was pleasantly uneventful. As Larry and Susan pulled out of the driveway, they talked about Sarah and Eli, both now young teenagers, and how much fun they would have with Susan's fun-loving parents over the long weekend. Then they listened to the radio and during commercials talked about their hopes and goals. At one point, *Pinball Wizard* played on the air, which reminded Larry of his lifelong dream to own a classic 1960s pinball machine. It was the second time that week he was reminded of pinball; a few days earlier, he had to write a review of a new novel called *A Trip Down Pinball Lane*. Much to his frustration, that assignment reminded him of another related and unrealized dream—to one day have a novel published.

"Reviewing other people's books just isn't the same thing as publishing one of your own," Larry said to Susan as they crossed the border into Connecticut. "Actually, it's kind of depressing."

"Well, if it's any help, I can't stand my job, either," Susan said a few minutes later. She worked for a small advertising and public relations firm and hoped to open her own agency one day. She had just seen a highway billboard for Indeed.com, which is what prompted her to complain about her current position.

In New York they talked about how important it is not to veer too far from hopes and goals, despite the constant strenuous challenges of domestic life, homeownership, parenting, all that...

In New Jersey, they admitted to each other that while neither of them had yet reached the big Four Oh, both were talking as if they already faced retirement age.

By the time they crossed into Pennsylvania, Larry and Susan agreed that Intercourse was just what they needed.

• • •

The Night Fever Inn stood unassumingly at the end of East Newport Road. A single row of eastern hemlock trees separated East Newport from a smaller dirt road that ran parallel to it. Every few minutes a horse-drawn carriage steered by an Amish man would pass by on that small country road, often with two or three Amish passengers. The inn was a simple long ranch, which disappointed Susan, for most of the B&Bs in which she and Larry had stayed were glorious old Victorians or chic modernized farm houses; still, the Night Fever looked exceedingly well kept. Its green paint was fresh, the front porch railing in excellent condition, the gardens well attended. There was a gazebo on the lawn to the left of the house. A handful of wind chimes that hung on tree branches clanged lightly in the breeze.

In the dirt parking lot, Larry pulled into an empty spot and shifted into park. He and Susan sat idle for a few moments, happy to have reached their destination. They spotted a young couple on bicycles stop by a row of eastern hemlocks. Apparently they wanted to walk their bikes through the trees. Perhaps they'd saddle up again once they were on the small dirt road on the other side, maybe to see the Amish carriages up close. Both bikers wore t-shirts with the words Lancaster Care Staff printed on the back.

"By the way, that's a home for crazy people," Larry said to his wife. "Lancaster Care. I read about it when I was researching Intercourse. I thought you should know, just in case you decide to have me committed while we're here. Technically, it's not in Intercourse. But it's close. Did I tell you how Intercourse got its name?"

"Are you going to bore me all weekend with your knowledge of Pennsylvania Dutch country?" Susan inquired. "Because I gotta be honest with you, sweetie; I had something else in mind."

"So do I. Sorry"

"Is that how Lancaster Care is advertised, by the way? A Home for Crazy People? Or is that just you being you?"

"I think it's officially called 'A privately funded group home for the emotionally challenged,' or something like that," Larry explained. "But Home for Crazy People saves time, and we're only here for three days. If we're gonna do what we both have in mind, then saving time is a good thing. Are we agreed?"

"We're agreed. Now shut up and let's check in."

Larry turned off the ignition, and then he and Susan got out of the car. Larry opened the trunk and took out their suitcases.

"You know what?" he said. "I didn't see any kids since we got to Intercourse. Isn't that great?"

"Why is it great?"

"Because I'm not in the mood for kids."

"Well, don't get too used to it, Larry," Susan warned. "People in Intercourse have kids. Which makes perfect sense, when you think about it. And some bed-and-breakfasts allow kids, too. Remember Martha's Vineyard? Five or six kids in the place all weekend long? Just don't get upset if you see a kid or two."

"When do I ever get upset?"

"Lately? All the time."

"Well... so do you. Sometimes."

"Excellent comeback."

The Night Fever Inn did indeed allow children. Larry, pretending he really didn't care but was merely curious, had asked about it at the front desk. The proprietor, an elderly, corpulent woman who introduced herself as Martha, picked up on his concern and assured him there would be no children for the three days that he and Susan would stay at the inn. It embarrassed Susan that Martha had picked up on it.

"I *will* say, however," Martha added, "that some of the adults who stay here are not nearly as well behaved as some of the children."

The lobby of the Night Fever Inn was small and crowded with curios, though designed in such a way as to make a stroll through the room almost effortless. As Larry and Susan walked across, they heard the Bee Gees in the background singing *How Deep is Your Love*. Three walls had framed movie posters for *Rocky*, *All the President's Men* and *The Bad News Bears*. A life-size model of R2D2 stood in a corner, as if guarding the magazines that were stacked in three neat piles on the small round table next to it. At the top of one pile was *Life*, on top of another, *Newsweek*, and on the third, *The Saturday Evening Post*. All were from 1973, 1974 and 1975, respectively. One magazine had a photo of the orbiting Skylab spacecraft, another showed Gerald R. Ford being sworn in as President of the United States, and the third featured the image of a shark leaping out of the ocean, with a tagline above his head that warned "You'll never go in the water again!" On the shelf under the window was a large videotape recorder similar to the one Larry's parents had when he was a toddler.

Larry and Susan looked around for a minute or two, and then Martha led them down a hallway that ended by their bedroom. Because of her size, Martha waddled more than she walked. The hallway wasn't terribly long, and they arrived at the room just a few moments after they had exited the lobby. Martha opened the door; it had no lock on the handle. Larry put the suitcases on the floor by the foot of the tall, four-poster bed.

"Such a beautiful room," Susan smiled. She admired the white wicker chest by the side wall, the hand-sewn mosaic curtains on the windows, and the lace doilies on the pine-wood dresser. Also on the dresser were two small photos in frames, one of John Travolta as disco dancer Tony Manero from the movie *Saturday Night Fever*, and the other of Diane Keaton as the kooky love interest in *Annie Hall*.

While the room itself was large, the bathroom was small. Susan noticed this the moment she inspected it. "Oh!" she said instinctively. But she quickly decided not to care. To her way of thinking, as long as the bathroom served its purpose, everything would be fine. She realized Martha must have had heard her say "Oh!" when she first walked into the bathroom, so she rushed to tell the smiling proprietor everything was lovely. "Simply charming," Susan said.

"Thank you, ma'am," Martha responded. The 'ma'am' put Susan off a bit, but was said with such geniality that she let it go.

With years of experience behind her, Martha knew that the look on Larry's face meant he wanted to be alone with his wife.

"Good time to rest up, folks," she smiled. "Later on, whenever you want, my assistant, Lance, who's also my nephew, will tell you about breakfast, afternoon tea, the housekeeping schedule, the history of the house—if you're interested, that is—and things you can do nearby. There's no lock on the door, but there is absolutely no reason to worry about your privacy. Either Lance or I will always be at the front desk. Someone is here around the clock. You'll be left alone when you're here, and your things will be safe when you're not."

"Thank you," Susan said. "Thank you very much."

Martha nodded, smiled, and left the room. She closed the door behind her.

"Interesting woman," Larry commented. "Not exactly a barrel of laughs, though."

He took off his shoes and pants and tossed them on the floor, then stretched out on the firm mattress. It felt good. Perfect antidote for a seven-hour drive and a mountain of frustrations left behind. Susan took off her pants, straightened them out, and placed them at the foot of the bed. Then she stretched out next to her husband. Down by their waists, their hands touched. The touch was warm and prompted them to roll just slightly toward one another. Larry gently pulled off Susan's blouse and massaged her bare arms. Then he used his foot to push Susan's bloomers down to her ankles and kick them onto the floor. Susan did the same with Larry's underpants, which landed on top of her bloomers. They both moaned with anticipation.

The door opened. It startled Larry and Susan out of their rising passion the moment it had started to rise. Susan grabbed her pants and threw them over her legs and torso; Larry grabbed a pillow from behind him and placed it over his crotch. In the doorway was a slightly disheveled woman holding a short-handled broom and a rusted metal dustpan.

"Oh! I'm so sorry," the woman said as she glanced at the floor. "I should have knocked first. It was empty just a little while ago." The woman's face was pleasant, though it looked exceedingly tired. She had a kind though uneven smile, and gray-brown hair that apparently was pinned in the back earlier on, but by now had mostly escaped its chipped barrette.

"That's all right," Larry said. "No harm done."

"Sometimes I have less brains than a walnut," the woman giggled. "I hope I didn't embarrass you."

"Just a little," Larry admitted, "but we're okay. Don't worry about it."

"Good. I'm glad you're okay. I'm Tessandra. Tessandra Bellissa. That's my first name and my middle name. My friends call me Tessie Bell for short."

"That's quite a unique name," Larry said. "I like it! I'm Larry and this is Susan. Our friends call us... well... Larry and Susan."

"Pleasure to meet you, Larry and Susan."

"Nice to meet you, too, Tessie Bell," Susan smiled. "This is a beautiful place."

"Oh, yes it is, isn't it? That's sweet of you to say. Well... I'll come back later... Oh—before I go—" she said, using her little broom as a pointer, "if you need to know anything about the house, or the town, or anything else at all, please don't hesitate to ask."

"Thank you," Susan said. "Martha said we could ask her nephew, but we'd be happy to ask you, too."

"Have you lived in Intercourse your whole life?" Larry asked.

"Oh, no. I'm from Philadelphia," Tessie Bell replied. "But I've been here for a long time now. I know everyone in town, and everyone knows me."

"So you've become a real townie, huh?"

"A townie? Well, not really. Just a wanderer, I suppose. A questioner. An observer. I don't know, really..."

"An observer? A questioner?" Larry tried not to sound *too* inquisitive, lest it appear suspicious. "Let me guess: you're a writer! Because frankly, you talk like one. And if you are, maybe you and I will have something more to talk about than just why I happen to be wearing a pillow on my crotch."

"Me? A writer?" Tessie Bell responded with surprise—with several nervous giggles to go along with it. "Oh, no, not me. I'm not the writer. Just a spectator, I suppose. A spectator of life. Of people and things. It's all so interesting, don't you think? Life? So full of beauty and hope. And tragedy and misery. Right and wrong. Love and loss. Oh, dear me, listen to me. I can go on and on and on, like a babbling brook."

Susan grinned, for she knew that the ramblings of this odd, sweet little woman will one day in the future make for quite a memorable footnote to their vacation in Intercourse. Larry smiled, too, but his was labored, for lying there near-naked made him think of nothing but his near-nakedness, and the thought of his near-nakedness reminded him of how much he wanted his wife right now.

"Well, goodbye, my dearest lovebirds. I apologize," Tessie Bell finally said. "You have all afternoon and all night to make up for it. Life goes on. Don't forget the afternoon tea at four, and the library upstairs."

"Library?" Susan asked. "Larry would *love* to see that. Wouldn't you, Larry? Did you say it's upstairs? Maybe we'll check it out before we go out for dinner."

"Oh, it's marvelous," Tessie Bell acknowledged. "Hundreds of books. A book lover's paradise. I go up there every once in a while, in between my rounds. Just to look. Just to see."

"Larry's a book reviewer for *The Mountain Caller*. That's a newspaper in Massachusetts, where we live."

"Oh, how wonderful! There are some marvelous books up there in the library. Books I know, books I never heard of, books I've forgotten all about. Books, books, books. Some with beautiful covers, some with their covers torn off. So many. So, so many." Tessie looked at Larry. "Are you familiar with *The Ukulele Girls*?" she asked.

"Yes, as a matter of fact I am," Larry acknowledged, forgetting for a moment that his primary goal was to rid the room of Tessie Bell. "Written by that author who published her first bestseller when she was sixteen, damn her."

Susan gently elbowed Larry in the ribs. She disliked his intermittent self-pity parties.

"How about the book *Finding Philly*?" Tessie continued.

"Yes! *Finding Philly*. A very short book." Larry turned to Susan. "I reviewed that the day before we moved into the house."

"How I'd love to go back to Philadelphia one day," Tessie Bell said wistfully. "So many memories. But... well... who knows? Anyway, did you read *Clocks Without Hands* by any chance?"

"As a matter of fact I did! And just thinking about it makes me sad. *Clocks Without Hands* was the third book I reviewed for *The Mountain Caller*. By Bertram Logan, I think. Is that right?"

Tessie nodded. Larry turned once again to Susan.

"Bertram Logan was that poor guy who was with his young son and daughter at the top of the World Trade Center on 9/11. It was a popular book, and he was scheduled to be interviewed by a magazine later that morning."

Susan shook her head sadly. She recalled having heard that heartrending story and felt her body actually shiver when Larry repeated it just now.

"Awful," she whispered woefully. "Just awful."

"Maybe one day even *I* can write a book," Tessie offered, "with all my silly problems and memories and ideas... Oh dear, who am I kidding? Who would want to read a book by an old fuddy duddy like me?"

Larry took a deep breath, which merely encouraged the pillow, still on his crotch, to remind him what he had been wanting to accomplish with Susan. So, from his prone position and covered only by that pillow, he turned as much as he could to look out the window. It was a move he made expressly to shake Tessie Bell out of her bookish ramblings.

It seemed to work.

"Well, there I go again, gibber-jabbering like a flock of lost birds. Off with me!" She playfully smacked her own behind with the dustpan. "Goodbye, my little angels."

"Goodbye," Susan said as Tessie closed the door behind her.

"I can certainly see why Martha has her here," Susan commented.

"To clean rooms, I would think," Larry said dryly.

"No. To make people smile! Even when they're mostly naked!"

"I guess. But just to be safe, I'm gonna move the dresser to block the door. You never know about the Tessie Bells of this world. She might think of another book she wants to ask me about."

•   •   •

Larry and Susan spent the next hour dealing only with their passion. No other topics — neither books nor bosses, children, Tessie Bell, or houses for crazy people — were welcome in the room, and none made an appearance. Then they rested, showered, and went to the front desk to ask for an opinion on where to dine. Lance, who was as conspicuous in height as his Aunt Martha was in girth, stood behind the desk. The theme from *Welcome Back, Kotter* played softly in the background.

"Afternoon, folks," he said. "Off to dinner?"

"Yup," Larry said. "Any suggestions? Something quaint, preferably walkable, with outstanding food?"

"Just make a right outside the inn and keep walking. You'll come across five or six good choices within a few minutes."

"Excellent. Thanks."

Larry and Susan strolled down East Newport Road. There were many people on the sidewalks. Larry assumed at least half of them were tourists and the other half residents. A pub called Cappers caught Susan's eye. Larry said it was fine with him.

Cappers was dimly lit, quiet, and smelled delicious. They sat by the window that looked onto the sidewalk.

"Would you ever want to stay in a place like Intercourse longer than just a weekend?" Susan asked. A tall young woman placed a basket of freshly baked bread on the table, while a short young man poured water into two tall glasses.

"No, I wouldn't want to stay in a place like Intercourse for more than a weekend," Larry said when the tall woman and the short man departed. "Too many people around. In the summer, at least. I just want to be alone with you. No tourists. No Marthas. No Lances. No Cassandras. No tall bread ladies or short water boys. No one."

"It's *Tess*andra, not *Cass*andra."

"Whatever."

They sipped their waters and tore off chunks of the steaming bread, dipping them in the little dish of olive oil that was next to the basket. They chewed on the bread hypnotically, driven by the hunger that had begun several states ago.

"Promise me we're not gonna make too many specific plans while we're here," Susan asserted. "Just spur of the moment decisions. Like we agreed. Right?"

"Absolutely," Larry concurred. "But I *am* going to put aside some time to work on my novel. That's enjoyable for me. Maybe even outside in the gazebo at the inn."

"I have no problem with that. And I'd love to find some time to jot down some more ideas for my own agency."

"I have no problem with that."

The young lady returned to take their order, but they hadn't yet decided and asked her to please come back in a few minutes.

"Certainly," the server said. "Take your time." Larry saw her expression turn from sweet to sour and wondered why. He also noticed that she was glancing at the window, and so he, too, turned his head to look—and saw Tessie standing on the sidewalk, smiling and waving through the glass.

"Hi!" Tessie called out, giggling, her voice muffled by the glass but still audible. She held a shopping bag in her hand.

Larry, muttering through his teeth like a bad ventriloquist, said, "Please don't come in here, please don't come in here, please don't come in here."

Tessie walked into Cappers and came over to their table. The server had already departed.

"I was just passing by," she said. "Window shopping. I didn't realize this was a restaurant at first. I thought you two were mannequins and that this was a clothing store! Isn't that so silly? Mannequins eating bread and drinking water? How crazy is that?"

"Not as crazy as..." Larry stopped himself from saying more when he sensed his wife's angry eyes upon him.

"I won't keep you," Tessie vowed. "You're having dinner. I just wanted to say hello. I recognize you two from somewhere."

"Yes, of course—the Night Fever Inn," Susan smiled. "A little while ago, Tessie. You remember, don't you?"

"You know my name!" Tessie gushed to Susan. "It's really Tessandra Bellissa, but most people call me Tessie Bell."

"That's an interesting bag," Susan said to try to move the conversation along. "Such an unusual logo. J.J. Beamer. Is that a store here in town?"

"Oh no, no, no. It's in Philadelphia. This shopping bag is actually about twenty-five years old, my dear. Look how good it's held up. You see, I take very good care of it. Like a baby. I should write a book about it one day. It's a special bag because it comes from a place that I love and miss very much. It's where life began, and where life was good for so many years... Oh, listen to me blubbering on about writing a silly old book on happiness and sadness. I'm so silly. Silly, silly, silly. Aren't I silly?"

"Why do you take such good care of the bag?" asked Larry, mildly curious—though he also wanted to stop Tessie from saying the word silly again.

"It was from a very special time and a very special place in my life, and I just want to remember it. I'd love to go back to Philadelphia one day. It's really not that far at all. Well, for me it is. For me it's miles and miles away."

Tessie Bell looked around, first to the left side of the restaurant and then to the right. "Here I go again," she said, "carrying on. Please—enjoy. Ooo—that bread smells so good. Listen, you two, have a wonderful dinner, and maybe I'll see you again."

"There's plenty of bread, Tessie," Susan said. "Have a piece."

"Well, maybe just one piece. You're so sweet." She took it, ate it, and seemed to enjoy it immensely.

"Would you like another? Would you care to join us?"

Larry closed his eyes in mental pain. Susan saw him do it in her peripheral vision and kicked his leg under the table.

"No no no, absolutely not," Tessie said. "Not another piece. But thank you, dear. You're very kind."

"Do you get to eat at the Night Fever Inn? Will we see you there at breakfast?"

"The Night Fever Inn? Oh, I doubt that, dear. I'm a gourmet cook myself, you know."

"Really? Where do you cook? At the inn?"

"Oh, I don't cook. I don't even have a kitchen. No one lets me cook! Well, I'd better go. I've stayed long enough, my little lovebirds."

Tessie grabbed one more piece of bread and departed. Larry and Susan sat there for a few moments in confused silence.

•   •   •

After they had walked off dinner and dessert, Larry and Susan returned to the Night Fever Inn to sit in the gazebo at the side of the house. First, Susan took a few minutes to return to their room to retrieve her notepad and Larry's manuscript. Larry waited for her in the gazebo.

The room was just as they had left it, with the bed a mess and towels on the floor. Susan knew that was not unusual since B&B bedrooms were usually straightened up just once a day, usually after breakfast. She walked through the lobby on her way back to the gazebo. *You're the One That I Want* from the movie *Grease* played in the background. Susan saw Martha at the front desk. Martha asked if she and Larry were enjoying themselves, and Susan assured her they were.

Outside, Larry and Susan worked on their respective projects for about twenty minutes. Then Susan closed her notepad and Larry neatened up his handwritten manuscript pages, and together they sat quietly in the gazebo, listening to the birds and the occasional rhythmic beat of horses' feet ambling along the dirt road beyond the fence.

The next morning, after breakfast, Larry and Susan returned to their room to decide what to do that day. It had been made up by then. It was neat and smelled clean.

"Tessie Bell did a good job," Susan said

"Can you please stop saying Tessie Bell?" Larry begged.

Susan suggested they go outside. The gazebo, she said, was so beautiful and comfortable that it might inspire them in their respective projects. She went to the bathroom to fix her makeup. Larry, too, wanted to get his hairbrush, which was on the vanity above the sink. But he had forgotten how small the bathroom was and knocked into Susan when he entered. She dropped a small bottle of nail polish, and the bottle shattered on the tile floor.

"Oh no. I hope they don't hold it against us," she said.

"Why would they hold it against us? It's *your* nail polish," Larry said.

"The broken glass, I mean. The polish on the floor."

"I'm sure a lot worse happens here all the time. I wouldn't worry about it."

"Okay."

Moments later, they passed the front desk, manned this time by Lance.

"Gazebo time?" Lance inquired.

"Yes," Susan responded. Larry sensed she wanted to mention to Lance the broken bottle of nail polish, so he pushed her along to feign a burning desire to show her something outside. That way, she could not mention it.

"Well, *that* was rude, pushing me like that," Susan said to Larry once they arrived at the gazebo.

"Sorry. I had to. You promised you wouldn't worry about it."

They sat. Susan looked around and collected her thoughts.

"Oh my God," she blurted out.

"What?"

"Look! In that little patch of woods behind the house. Isn't that Tessie Bell? It looks like she's cleaning up in there? Do you think they make her do yard work, too? In addition to all the housekeeping? Is that fair? Is that even legal?"

"I don't know," Larry sighed. "But I hope to God that she doesn't come here so that you can ask her if it's fair and if it's legal."

But hoping to God didn't help, for the only way out of the small patch of trees was through the left side yard of the Night Fever Inn, next to the gazebo. And sure enough, Tessie came barreling out, trying to avoid as many branches as she could. She held a tattered baseball cap in her hands.

"Are you all right?" Susan asked. Her voice startled Tessie, who hadn't known that the two of them were sitting there.

"Oh, my! You frightened me. But that's all right. I've been frightened many times in my life—before, during and after. I'll be fine, my little darlings. I'm Tessandra Bellissa. Everyone calls me Tessie Bell."

"Yes, we know. What the heck were you doing in the woods?" Larry asked.

"Somebody in town told me they saw an old Philadelphia Phillies cap behind this house. Someone lost it. Probably blew away in a storm."

She turned the cap around to show them the Phillies logo.

"See? How lucky am I that I found it before another storm grabbed it and blew it across the ocean? Lucky me! A Philadelphia Phillies cap. How lucky."

"You must really love Philadelphia," Larry said.

"Oh, I do. I really really do. I'd give anything to go back there. Just to see it again. I grew up there, got married there, had my children there... But... oh well! I'm sure you know how it is. Things happen. And now I have so many responsibilities. It never ends..."

"That reminds me, Tessie," Susan said in a soft voice.

"Yes, dear?"

"I accidentally dropped a bottle of nail polish in our bathroom. I'd be perfectly happy to clean up as much of it as I can by myself before you get there."

"Oh, I'd be happy to help, dear. I always like to help. My middle name is help. What room now?"

"The last one in the hall. On the left. You did such a great job fixing it up this morning, by the way. I wanted to mention that."

"Did I? Well, it's no problem at all, my little butterfly. But first I have to go upstairs. Then I'll clean it up. Things do need to be cleaned up, you know!"

"You have to go upstairs?" Susan asked. "Are there are more bedrooms up there? I thought it was just the library."

"I really don't know, dear! I don't *think* there are more bedrooms up there. I do know the library is up there, of course, but... hmmm... oh well..." Her voice trailed off.

"I'm going back to our room now," Susan said, "so I guess I'll meet you there in a little while. Okay?"

"Fine, dear," Tessie said. "You go along. I use a special hidden door in the back whenever I want to get inside. Isn't that sneaky of me? So sneaky! Sneaky little Tessie Bell! That should be my real name."

"Okay," Susan said. "See you in a few. Come, Larry."

Susan and Larry went back to the lobby. Lance was there, checking in another couple.

"Back so soon?" he asked.

"We met Tessie Bell in the backyard. She's coming to our room in a little while to help me do something," Susan explained. She didn't want to mention the broken bottle of nail polish.

"Tessie Bell?" Lance asked.

"Yes. Your housekeeper."

"Oh. I see," Lance muttered.

Susan and Larry walked away quickly; they didn't want to interrupt the new arrivals any further than they already had. They knew what it was like to want to settle in at once.

In the room, Susan used a washcloth to pick up some of the broken pieces of glass and threw the shards into the bathroom's tiny garbage can. Larry, meanwhile, reached over to his suitcase and found a Lancaster County brochure that he had thrown in there just before they left their house in Massachusetts. He sat on the bed to look through it.

Ten minutes later, Susan sat down beside him. She sighed. He sighed. They sat there waiting for Tessie to arrive.

"If you're a good girl," Larry said, "I'll make friends with the new couple who just checked in so that *they* can bother us nonstop until we leave Intercourse."

"Don't be sarcastic. Nobody's bothering us right now."

"Not right *now*... Maybe we should warn them."

"Warn them? About what?"

Just then, Tessie Bell walked into the room.

"Oh! Hello there," she said. "I didn't realize the room was occupied yet."

Susan and Larry glanced at each another, but before they could exchange a word, three other people hurried through the door. One was Lance. The other two, a man and a woman, had white lab coats over their regular clothes, with the words Lancaster Care stitched under the left breast pocket of each coat. The two of them had very stern expressions.

"There she is," Lance said.

"Come with us, Tessie Bell," the woman said gingerly.

Tessie Bell became visibly agitated. She uttered a few sounds, but none of them were actual words. She bit her lip and shook her head, and the biting and the shaking seemed almost automatic, instinctive, uncontrollable, especially since it became more pronounced after a moment or two.

"What's going on?" Susan asked.

"But I'm on my way to Philadelphia," Tessie said to the woman in the white lab coat. Her voice trembled. There was much urgency to it. "Only for a few hours. I just came here to get another pillow. Please. I didn't do anything wrong. I didn't. I promise. Please…"

"You're not on your way to Philadelphia, Tessie, and you know it," said the man. "You say that all the time. And you *did* do something wrong. You know you did. You left again without permission. So come with us now and everything will be all right. I promise."

"No, it won't," Tessie cried out. "It *won't* be all right. Nothing will ever be all right. Something else will happen. Just like it did then."

"What are you talking about?" Lance asked, although his words reeked of disinterest.

"I don't understand," Susan said.

Larry stared at the floor for a silent moment.

"I think I do," he whispered to no one in particular. He looked up. "Can you give me just two minutes?" he asked the man and the woman in the lab coats. "Just two minutes before you do anything. Okay? Just stay here. Don't move. Lance, tell them to give me two minutes."

Lance looked perplexed and annoyed, but nodded to the man and the woman.

Larry bolted through the door, hopped several stairway steps at a time to get to the second floor, and ran to the room at the end of the hall. He could tell just by glancing through the open doorway that it was the library. He saw a wall of books. When he was inside, he saw two more walls of books, and read the book spines on the shelves as rapidly as he could. *Sayonara* by James Michener. *A Season in Purgatory* by Dominick Dunne. *Tuesdays With Morrie* by Mitch Albom. *Peony* by Pearl Buck. *Clocks Without Hands* by Bertram Logan. As Larry had recalled the day before, *Clocks Without Hands* was the third book he had reviewed for *The Mountain Call*. His editor had complimented him on the review. But Larry also remembered how that compliment was ineffective in raising his spirits because the day before he wrote that review, the book's author, Bertram Logan, had perished with his two young children when the World Trade Center was destroyed during the September 11th terrorist attack. Logan had been in the one of the towers to be interviewed by a journalist later that morning.

Larry grabbed the book off the shelf, opened the front cover, turned a few pages, and found the printed dedication:

"To my darling Tessie Bell. Thank you for your exquisite love, your eloquent inspiration, and our precious children. All my love, Bert. Philadelphia, PA."

Larry put the book back on the shelf and returned to the room. Everyone was in almost the same spot as he had left them, although Tessie Bell now sat on the rocking chair, a forlorn look on her face, almost completely devoid of spirit. Quite a change from someone who, despite everything, once seemed nothing *but* spirit. The white-coated man and woman had their arms folded, and Lance looked angrier than he was before. Only Susan's demeanor hadn't changed.

"Okay. Thanks, everyone. I just had to check on something. We can go now."

"Go?" asked Susan. "Go where?"

"*You* know! We're taking Aunt Tessie to Philadelphia for the day. Back home for a visit." He turned to Lance. "That's why we came down here. Your Aunt Martha knows all about it."

"You're her nephew?" the stern woman in the lab coat asked Larry. "I thought her nephew's name was Jonathan."

"It is. Jonathan Logan. But I use my pen name when I'm traveling."

The man and woman looked at Lance, and then at each other. No words were spoken. Only Tessie Bell's breath could be heard — with increasing gasps of anticipation and hope.

"We'll have her back by tonight," Larry said, breaking the awkward silence.

The man remained unconvinced.

"You'll have to sign all the appropriate papers," he said.

"We did all that by mail!" Larry wailed as if it had explained it a thousand times before. "Jesus Christ, people! And besides that, I've called *five times* in the last week alone just to confirm all this and to make sure there were no screw-ups. What's with your staff? Are you guys *still* having problems in the front office?"

"Well," the man uttered sheepishly, "yeah… a few."

"Please work on that," Larry demanded. "What are my donations being used for anyway? Office parties? Come on now."

At which point, he and Susan escorted a giddy Tessie Bell out of the Night Fever Inn and into their car for a visit to Philadelphia.

Weinerface

Unfortunately my name is Aaron Frank. Want to know the truth? It stinks.

It probably wouldn't be so bad if I didn't have red hair and freckles and suck at basketball and wear pants that are too short and write stories in my room instead of sometimes smoking cigarettes after school under the bleachers with other kids. But the thing is, I do have red hair and freckles, and I suck at basketball, and almost everyone knows that I write stories in my bedroom after school and that I never smoked a cigarette, not even once.

The first name I remember being called is Aaron Frankfurter with Ketchup on Top. That was around third grade, I guess. After that there was Aaron Weiner, obviously because some people call frankfurters weiners. (I don't, but other people do.) Then there was Aaron Freckleweiner, Weinerbrain, Weinerface, Dot Face Strawberry Head, Aaron Frankenstein, Freckle Freak, and a couple of others. I can't remember them all. There was even one kid last year who I hardly knew who always made fun of the black kids and the Chinese kids at our school and he decided to call me Alan Flank instead of Aaron Frank while he stretched his eyes with his fingers. Get it? Chinese stuff? Alan instead of Aaron and Flank instead of Frank? I guess he thought he was a real genius. But what he really was was an actual idiot.

Weinerface is the name I hear the most these days.

Kids can be really mean and stupid. That's one of the scary things about being a kid who isn't mean and stupid. And when your name is Aaron Frank and you have bright red hair and about a million freckles and you're not good at sports and your teacher asks you to read stories out loud that you wrote at home that wasn't even homework, they can be a whole lot meaner than almost anything on earth.

Which reminds me of this bully named Roy Getz. Something happened between him and me a few days ago that's kind of interesting. It's not really funny, if you think that's why I'm telling the story. If you want a funny story, this isn't it. It's just interesting. At least I think it is.

Roy is one of the kids that calls me all kinds of names, like Weinerface, mostly. So it's Sunday morning, and Roy is standing on the top step of Eddie Izzo's house, which is the house about four houses down from mine and on the other side of the street. I'm standing there, on the front steps of my own house, just kind of wasting time, trying to decide if I should stay outside to play or go inside to work on one of my stories, and when I see Roy standing there on Eddie Izzo's steps, I guess I kind of think to myself, Hey, here's a chance to show him that a dot face strawberry head freckle freak kid could shout the kind of stupid idiotic things that he's been shouting to kids like me for a million years. Besides, my own front door is right there, right behind me, which means that I could run into my house pretty quickly if I had to.

The thing is, Roy would never expect me to yell anything at all. It would be a total surprise. I was just one of those kids that never did things like that. But here was a chance to do it, to be a bully for a minute without having to punch anyone in the nose or in the stomach or anything like that. It was a chance to yell the kind of stupid stuff that I could never yell at school because if I did I would probably get beat up.

Actually, I guess I sort of asked for it—being made fun of, I mean. I know I can't do anything about my red hair and my stupid freckles, but I guess there are other things I could do, if I thought about it more. Like I could ask my mother to make my pants a little longer so that my socks aren't always showing. Or I could stop telling Mrs. Sheehan about the stories I write in my bedroom so that she wouldn't ask me to read them in class. And I guess my best friends are kind of weird, too, which doesn't help. Like Neil Eisen, who likes science a lot and understands molecules but wears turtlenecks to school. You just don't do that. And Michael Cabot, who can name all the greatest magicians in the world but can't name anyone in Black Sabbath. (Neither can I, though I can name all of the Beatles.) Want to know the truth? If you think about it, having friends like Neil Eisen and Michael Cabot is sometimes a little scary, too.

Anyway, having red hair and freckles and writing stories and being friends with people like Neil and Michael is why I get to be called Aaron Frankfurter with Ketchup on Top all the time, or Weinerface, or Strawberry Head, or any of the other stupid things that I get called. And it's why I get tripped in the hallway and slammed against lockers, and it's why my books always get grabbed out of my hands and thrown into the bushes by people like Roy Getz.

Actually, now that I think about it, Roy thought he made up Dot Face Strawberry Head, but I don't think it was him that made it up. Here's what I think happened. In gym one day he made this stupid plan with another bully named Vinny DeMartino to pick on me when we were doing warm-ups for a softball game. Roy was calling me Dot Face that day, and Vinny started calling me Strawberry Head. So Roy gets on his hands and knees behind me, and Vinny walks up to me and pats me on the shoulder likes he wants to wish me good luck in the game. (Like he would really want to do that, right?) But as soon as he pats me on the shoulder, he pushes me backwards and I fall over

Roy onto my back, with my legs sticking up in the air. So a few minutes later, Neil Eisen comes over and whispers to me that guys like Roy Getz and Vinny DeMartino usually do things like that two times in a row, for some stupid reason. So I'm looking out for them to do the pushing thing one more time, and when I know it's coming I sort of stiffen my legs real tight and instead of falling over, I kick Roy in the mouth without really meaning to. His mouth starts to bleed and he starts punching me and calling me a stupid Dot Face Strawberry Head. I can tell he thinks it's real clever, but it's actually just a pretty stupid combination of Dot Face and Strawberry Head.

Anyway, Mr. O'Neal, who's our gym teacher, doesn't help at all. I think he's afraid of Roy and Vinny too. Teachers are idiots sometimes, and that can be scary when you have to depend on them for stuff. Mr. O'Neal's stupidness made me hate Roy even more, because Roy loves it when he can get away with being a bully without getting in trouble. He eats it up like a piece of cake. My mother says that a lot. Eats it up like a piece of cake. I guess that's why I just said it. Anyway, that's sort of funny, now that I think about it, because Roy probably loves cake a lot because the thing is, he's chubby. For a bully, at least.

So when Roy stands on Eddie Izzo's top step and knocks on his door, I guess I'm kind of thinking about how chubby he is because I remember thinking how weird his clothes look, even all the way from my own house. He's really wearing just a plain blue tee shirt and plain jeans, but his belly stretches his shirt all the way out like there's a pillow inside, and his jeans sort of make his hips look like balloons. Roy actually looks dopey standing there. A fat blue dopey bully. It was scary to look at, even though it kind of gave me more courage to do what I wanted to do.

So Roy is standing on Eddie Izzo's top step waiting for Eddie to let him in, and the front door of my house is only a few inches away from me, so I'm feeling kind of safe, and I yell, "Hey,

Tubbo, what are you gonna do with Eddie Izzo? Watch cartoons?"

Roy turns his head, kind of slowly, like he isn't really sure what's going on.

"Guess what, Fatso," I yell, "they're buying new garbage bags at school so that you can have fresh underpants to wear next week." I'm sort of rocking back and forth on my feet, like I'm real confident or something.

Roy turns back to Eddie Izzo's front door but calls something out to me anyway. He says "I'd shut up if I was you, Weinerbrain."

So I yell back "I'd rather be a delicious weiner than a fat amoeba." (We had just learned about amoebas in school on Friday. Neil Eisen knows as much about amoebas as he does about molecules. I really don't remember anything at all about amoebas, except how to spell it.)

Then Roy knocks on Eddie's door again and I'm thinking that maybe he's ignoring me. But after he knocks, he looks my way again and says, "How would you like your stupid dot face to eat my fist for lunch."

So I say "No thanks. Already ate. Not as much as you, though."

I think he took a deep breath, because I saw his belly stretching the shirt, even though it could hardly stretch anymore.

He says "Dot face jerk. You think you're something, don't you?"

I say "No, but I know you're nothing but a fat garbage can." For some reason I thought that was very clever and I started to laugh.

Then he says "Weinerface strawberry jerk." He likes putting old names together to make new ones. I guess it's the only thing he's really good at. Anyway, he says "I'd shut up if I was you," in a sort of sing-songy way, like the way my father talks to me when he's warning me to do something that he's been warning me to do for a million years. You know—like when he puts almost real notes to something like "Aaron David Frank, this is the last time I will tell you to get your Matchbox cars out of the hallway!"

So then Eddie Izzo opens his door and Roy goes into his house.

There's really no reason for me to stay there on my steps, so I go inside to work on a story, and when I sit down by my desk I start to think that maybe I just made the biggest mistake of my life.

All of a sudden I wonder, What would stop Roy Getz from coming over to me at school in the morning, which is Monday, and beating the crap out of me? What would stop him from punching me and kicking me and spitting in my face and doing knee drops on my stomach and all the kinds of stuff that bullies do, right there in the schoolyard, in front of everyone, even Mr. O'Neal, who wouldn't do anything to help me anyway because he's such a scaredy cat. Probably Neil Eisen and Michael Cabot would say they tried to help me, but I bet they really wouldn't have the guts to help, and I guess I really wouldn't blame them. They wouldn't want to get in Roy's way, and I probably wouldn't, either, if it was one of them that was getting beat up.

So I'm thinking that I just gave Roy Getz a really good reason to absolutely kill me. It's almost like I put one of those bull's eye circle things over my face and was just waiting for him to punch me in the nose so hard that I get knocked out and that my nose gets broken. It's almost like he has the right to beat me up because he's the official bully and I'm the official kid that should get beat up.

Anyway, I'm sitting at my desk in my room, and I guess I'm thinking that I'll never write another story because I'll probably be killed tomorrow morning in school, and I know that it's my own fault, which I guess is sort of like suicide.

That night is a horrible, horrible night, which isn't a big surprise. I guess any night before you commit suicide or know you'll get killed would be a pretty horrible night. I'm sweating a lot, the way people sweat in the movies when they're really scared. I'm wondering exactly what will happen to me. I didn't tell my parents anything. I'm thinking about it over and over in my head and I finally fall asleep. But I wake up an hour before I'm supposed to with the stupid idea in my head that I should beat myself up in the morning so that when Roy does it at school it won't look too bad. I know that's pretty crazy, but that's what I thought.

When I walk to school that morning it sort of seems like everything is strange outside. Like everyone is staring at me. Like everyone's voice is sort of an echo or something like that. The books under my arm feel heavier than usual, if you can believe that. The crossing guard looks at me and her face is kind of sad.

When I get to school, I talk myself into not worrying about it too much. Maybe Roy won't be in. Maybe he forgot. Maybe his whole family moved to Florida or someplace like that overnight. Wouldn't that be funny?

But as I get to the side doors of the school, near the bike racks, Roy comes out of nowhere. One minute there's a big, green, stupid metal door in front of me, and the next minute there's fat, stupid Roy Getz instead. All of a sudden he looks bigger than I remembered. I think he was shaking his head slowly, and not smiling or even looking mean or anything, which is kind of freaky. It's like his face wasn't doing anything at all.

He says "You might want to never do that again, Weinerface. Got it?"

I remember trying to swallow, but not being able to. And then I just sort of nod my head yes.

Roy is actually almost smiling, and he says "I don't know if this is over or not. I'll decide later." He's still shaking his head.

"Where the fuck did you come from anyway, you orange weirdo?" And then he walks away, with a kind of nothing look on his face.

That's it. I told you it wasn't funny. I wouldn't believe it if someone else was telling it about themself. But what's what happened.

Anyway, I look at the stupid green door and grab my books a little tighter under my arm, and I sort of realized something. Which is that life is full of things you don't know about and also full of surprises that you don't always know will surprise you. I realized that life is full of happy things and not so happy things that can happen at any time. It's also full of lots of mistakes that you'll make. I realized that sometimes you can be lucky and other times you won't have any luck at all. I think I realized that day that life is like a real-life story that goes on and on and you never really know how things will change from one chapter to the next. Or from one stupid green door to the next.

Want to know the truth? That's really the scariest thing of all.

The Tale of the Magic Pause Button

Tara and her husband Todd walk through the county-owned woodland behind their home. Tara smiles. The land may belong to the county, but the joy belongs to Tara. She loves the woods. So does Todd. Woods are full of trees and wildflowers, pebbles and boulders, streams and lily pads, frogs and birds, clouds and sunshine, and these are all things Tara and Todd adore.

"I love it," Todd says.

"What do you love?" asks Tara lazily, as she and Todd walk side by side along the dirt path that meanders through the acreage.

"The smile on your face. I am smiling too. We deserve to smile. Do you agree?"

"I agree."

Todd is quite right, for he and Tara had spent many dark years in search of their smiles. They had weathered many personal storms, storms of sickness and money woes and family scars. Things had happened, as things do happen. But Tara and Todd always kept hope alive. They worked hard to bring light back into their lives. Their recent checkups at the doctor were exemplary, their bank account is once again solid, and everyone in the family is doing well. They even have plans to restore the in-ground pool that had come with the house but which for the last twenty years has been in such disrepair. Oh, how their little granddaughter Lucille — Lulu — would love to swim in that pool.

Yes, the old scars have healed nicely. There are now so many plans to make, so much hope and optimism to cherish. So bright does the present seem and such encouragement does the future hold that Tara and Todd feel even better and stronger than they had before the dark years even began.

"It is such a glorious day, and the woods are so beautiful," Tara says. "It feels wonderful. I wish there was a pause button we could press so that this wonderful feeling can last forever and ever. This feeling of calm. Of peace. The glorious day, the beautiful woods. Yes, we deserve our smiles, Todd. I wish we could hold on to our smiles hour after hour."

"We can," Todd says swiftly.

Tara glances at her husband. Her eyebrows arch in delighted surprise.

"We can? Oh, I see! You mean by our attitude. Is that right?"

"It is not only that," he explains. "Do you remember the man who sold us our house? He told us that there is a magic button deep in the woods. On a gigantic tree. On the side of the trunk of a big old elm, the side that cannot be seen from the dirt path. A magic pause button."

"Oh yes, yes — I do remember!" Tara recalls. "But he was such an odd little man. So very strange. I thought he was making it all up. He seemed to be the type to tell tall tales."

"I thought that as well," Todd admits. "At least at first I did. But I spoke to him longer than you, Tara, and it very well may be, dear, that he was telling the truth about the magic pause button."

"Well," says Tara, "shall we try to find it? Which tree do you suppose has the magic pause button?"

"The man said the elm tree with the magic button has two branches that cross each other, like someone making an X of their arms in front of them. Like this." Todd demonstrates.

"Oh! I saw an elm tree like that around the bend! Way down there. Let us see if we can find it!"

So Tara and Todd turn around and stroll back from where they came, a two-minute walk during which they pass a sparkling brook with shiny stones that reflect the sunlight peeking through the trees, and a little chipmunk that darts back and forth under a moss-covered trunk that had fallen down years ago after a storm. Tara loves seeing the brook and the stones and the chipmunk, and for a moment she forgets why they had turned back on the path. She is entranced.

"Here it is," Todd announces, bringing Tara out of her trance. "The tree. An elm. The branches look like two arms that are crossed. This must be it, Tara. I will go to the other side to see if the magic pause button is there."

"Be careful," Tara warns.

Todd makes his way cautiously to the backside of the tree while Tara waits on the path.

"Do you see it? The magic pause button? Is it there?" she asks excitedly.

"I see it," he acknowledges. "Yes. Here it is. It is sunk deeply into the trunk, and it is very small. But the button might still be able to be pressed. Shall I press it?"

"Do you think everything will be all right if you press it? Nothing bad will happen?"

"I can think of no reason why we should not press the button. It seems safe enough. I see nothing about it that looks threatening. Besides, that old man would never want to put us in harm's way. He was a very nice man. Do you agree?"

"I agree."

And with that, Todd lifts his right hand and presses the magic pause button on the giant elm tree.

Nothing seems to happen. Everything remains the same.

"Do you think it worked?" Tara asks, somewhat giddily. "Nothing has changed, although I suppose that if time is truly paused, what sign would there be of that?"

Todd makes his way back to the path to stand beside his wife. "I suppose that's true," he says. "I suppose it might also be true that time has paused for no one but us! Perhaps time pauses for us to enjoy, while everyone else lives their lives! It is a funny, intriguing, and I must admit confusing thing to think about. Is it not?"

"Oh, yes, it is," Tara says, still giddy with awe and curiosity. "I wonder if there will be any way to tell exactly what has happened."

"Maybe it is all about our point of view," Todd offers as a plausible explanation. "Perhaps that strange old man was a philosopher of some sort. Maybe he meant that pausing time is strictly an affair of the mind, that it is connected only to our outlook on life, that it is merely a suspension of all worry, of all bad memories, of all unanswerable questions. I really do not know, Tara. What do you think?"

Tara breathes in deeply and smells the sweetness of the air. She sees tiny blue wildflowers that she had not noticed before, then looks straight up through a break in the trees and sees puffy white clouds. One cloud looks like a bunny rabbit, and that makes her smile, for she adores bunny rabbits. She loves to see all the animals in the woods run freely, and she loves to see birds fly effortlessly in the sky. "Nothing should ever be caged," Tara says instinctively, for it is something she has said many times in the past to many people in her life.

"That is true," Todd says, knowing that the comment, repeated many times over many years, comes straight from her heart. "It is also true that I believe the pause button has worked, Tara, for I myself feel suddenly uncaged. Do you feel the same? Fully uncaged to enjoy all the beauty around us?"

"I do. I feel the same," Tara concurs. "Let us walk some more, Todd. Let us keep walking as far as we can go. Farther than we have ever gone before. If the pause button is real, then we are free to see all the beauty around us. We have all the time in the world. Our only obligation is to be home by dinnertime, for Ben and Sophie will be at our house at six o'clock for Lulu's birthday party."

"Can you believe that our little granddaughter is turning four?" Todd observes. But then his face takes on a puzzled countenance.

"What is wrong?" asks Tara.

"A silly thought just occurred to me. If we have all the time in the world to do as we please, what does that mean for all our other obligations? I do not expect you to be able to answer, my dear, for perhaps that is just one of the mysteries to learn about as we go along. Perhaps we will have the answer one day. Or perhaps never."

"It is only fair, Todd, for a magic pause button to have some mystery. Is it not?"

"I suppose it is. Well put, my little poet."

His comment reminds her of something pleasant.

"I have already taught our little Lulu some simple poems," Tara says to Todd. "Just four years old, and I have only just begun to teach her all the important things in life that a grandmother is obligated to teach a grandchild!"

Todd chuckles at her words, but remains silent. He wishes not to make light of the situation, for there is still a bit of sensitivity about the visits of their son Ben, their daughter-in-law Sophie, and their granddaughter Lulu, sensitivity stemming from the fact that Ben, Sophie, and Lulu live so far away and cannot visit as often as Tara and Todd would like them to. That they see Lulu so infrequently is now the only thing in their lives that makes them melancholy. It is all the more vexing because Ben cherishes his childhood home in which Todd and Tara still live. Ben had said during a recent visit, "Oh, how I would love to move back into this house one day." The memory of that remark makes Tara chuckle with simple, harmless pride. Ben further reflected, "How I would love as well for my own children to move into this house one day." Recalling her son's words makes Tara smile as she and Todd continue their walk in the woods.

"Anyway," Tara says, returning to the here and now and the thoughts of the coming birthday party, "all the food is prepared and the cake has been made, and Lulu's present is next to the piano. Everything is set. As long as the magic pause button does not interfere in ways we do not expect, there is nothing to worry about, Todd, and nothing more to do. So let us continue to take pleasure in this feeling of—what did you call it before?—this feeling of suspension while we can."

They continue to walk along the path to relish in the sights, sounds and scents of the woods, and they comment on what they see and hear and smell, and both of them are happy.

When finally they come to the edge of the woods, close to where their own backyard begins, they stop and stare because they notice that the built-in pool, the one that had been in such disrepair, is no longer there. Ancient bricks, chipped and faded, still surround the oval where the pool was supposed to have been. But rocky dirt and grubby patches of lawn now fill the oval itself, and within that rocky, patchy oval are three tall poles that stick straight up into the air. At the top of each pole are wire cages, and in the cages are birds that can fly only the length and width of each small cage. The birds in those cages sing songs that sound far too abrupt to be true birdsongs.

"What is all this?" Tara asks, a look of serious unease on her face. Tara glances at Todd and he returns the stare. Both know that the sole question to be asked and somehow answered is at once simple and bizarre, and that question is, How can a built-in pool disappear and dreadful bird cages on tall poles appear in its place all in the time it takes to walk a mile in the woods behind their house?

Todd looks at the back of the house. What had once been a beautiful glass slider is now a chipped wooden door.

"The house..." Todd says—but he leaves the rest of the sentence unfinished.

On the patio is a lounge chair, and on the lounge chair reclines an old woman, with her chubby legs stretched out in front of her. Will she know what happened? Should they ask? This is what Tara and Todd both wonder silently, each aware of what the other is thinking. Then, out of the chipped wooden door exit two people, a man and a child. The man holds the child's hand.

"Could that little child be our little Lulu?" Tara asks. She forgets for the moment about the pool and the poles and the cages and the door and all else that had been muddling through her mind. "Can that be our son Ben holding her hand, and his wife Sophie on the lounge chair? They all look so very different. Maybe my eyes are just very tired. After all, it has been a long day, and my eyes do get weary." For a moment, Tara has a wisp of hope.

The toddler lets go of the man's hand and runs over to the old woman on the lounge chair. As she runs, the toddler shouts happily, "Grandma Lulu, Grandma Lulu, can I sit on your lap?"

"Grandma Lulu?" Todd says softly.

There is a long moment of silence.

"I think we have our answer," Tara responds. She looks once again at Todd and he returns the glare. Both understand, instantly and explicitly. Despite their good health and what had been unlimited optimism for the future, their smiles disappear.

The Shifting Winds of Imagination

Ms. Raina Noonan   November 15, 2083
Simon & Schuster
1230 Sixth Avenue
New York, NY 10020

Dear Ms. Noonan:

As a scientist, my father's enduring importance is subjective, given the results of his last two inventions. However, that he was a genius is irrefutable, even if a cursory review of his life and career does not make that abundantly clear. Regardless, one cannot dispute that his life and career, particularly the last few years, could be the basis for a captivating biography.

I would like to write that biography, Ms. Noonan. I would call it *The Shifting Winds of Imagination*.

My father, Carl Amsterdam, who created two of the most remarkable (and curious) inventions known to humankind, died a brokenhearted man who had to endure the gloomy, irreversible tainting of a legacy that, under different circumstances, would have been, and would have remained, positively stunning.

Ms. Noonan, my proposed book will be not just a biography of one of the late 21st Century's most intriguing and unappreciated inventors, but also a first-hand account of my culpability in his fall from grace — or more precisely the grace that almost was; a grace that was nearly within his grasp. Taken together, this double theme will make *The Shifting Winds of Imagination* a mesmerizing literary account, and perhaps one of the most thought-provoking and highly marketable additions to Simon & Schuster's list in a long time. I hope you agree.

Many people remember that at two separate junctures in his life, my father became the laughingstock of our nation, and perhaps of the world. But what they do not know is exactly how and why that happened, and very few realize it led to a deep depression that preceded his death at the relatively young age of seventy-five.

My father went into science very late in life, at age fifty-eight, mostly because of my urging. I knew how smart he was, and that he had more knowledge of physics, mechanics, biology, chemistry, and astronomy than anyone I had ever known or studied. I constantly badgered him with 'what-if' questions as I got older simply because I firmly believed that he should not spend his entire career building miniature golf courses, as he did for years in Rehoboth Beach, Bethany Beach, and other resort areas of the Delaware coastline. Sure, his miniature golf courses were the most popular in the region, with holographic pirates that chased after golfers, and golf balls that talked back to you with personalized comments — but Carl Amsterdam was made for far greater things. What might surprise most people is that my father's demise can be attributed to all those 'what-if' challenges I presented to him once he finally made the switch from miniature golf courses to scientific discovery. I will explore all of that in my book.

I must be clear: I still believe that a man with my father's intellect, inquisitiveness and skill deserved to leave miniature golf courses behind and flex the scientific muscles that were built into his DNA. I do not regret having been the force that compelled him to switch careers. What I *do* regret is having planted the specific seeds for two big scientific projects, seeds that eventually grew into a sort of wisteria vine that, in the end, professionally speaking, choked him to death.

Ms. Noonan, when I was a child, I used to have the most vivid and unusual dreams. They riveted me and kept me spellbound. They were more enticing than movies and more mysterious than life. I knew that if anyone could combine neurosurgery with opto-mechanics to come up with a device to record dreams and play them back, it would be my father, Carl Amsterdam. The idea consumed me. (Not him, at first.) I kept after him. I begged and pleaded. And finally, about fifteen years ago, he created what came to be called, simply enough, the Dream Machine.

CNN, as you may recall, asked Dad to debut the Dream Machine on their network. The weekend anchor, Natasha Post, hoping for phenomenal ratings, asked him to come to the studio early, go to sleep backstage, use the machine to record whatever dream he had while sleeping there, and play it back on the air during the live broadcast. Dad complied. (He was always very amenable where media requests were concerned.)

While he slept backstage, Dad was certain he had a dream in which he flew like a bird, and he had no qualms about showing it on the air, even before watching it himself.

But as we all know now, the dream that the Dream Machine played back on CNN was not about flying like a bird; instead, it showed my father and Natasha Post orally pleasuring each other's private parts, naked on a plush light-blue carpet that had images of clouds on it. The story that has filtered down confirms that the control room personnel were too mesmerized to stop the broadcast, and as a result, for seventy seconds the entire world got to see what the Dream Machine recorded.

Dad became a bit of a hermit after that, though he continued to tinker around in his workshop.

Hoping to get him back on track and to forget the recent past, I persuaded my father to work on another childhood obsession of mine. I had always been fascinated by the fact that all the communications devices that are in our pockets, in our homes, in our vehicles, businesses, schools, everywhere really, emit electromagnetic waves of one kind or another that carry the sights, sounds and data for which all these devices are used. I believed that being able to actually *see* those waves would be an astounding experience. What do those invisible waves look like? How do they travel? Do they have colors? Do they dance? Do they have personalities of their own?

After six years of research, Dad developed what he called the Transvisor, which makes almost anything that is invisible visible—from radio waves to wind to gravity.

As you may recall, seven years ago, the President of the United States launched a national effort to help the country regain its technological edge. He invited my father to the White House to demonstrate the Transvisor at a press conference in the West Wing to help kick off the administration's new science initiative. First, Dad had a private meeting with the President and several Cabinet members, concluding with a sumptuous meal. Then the group entered the press briefing room for the conference.

The Transvisor was hooked up to a large monitor so that people in the conference room, as well as a worldwide television audience, could see the visual component of whatever the device detected—while also showing the device itself and everything around it. Dad suggested he stand ten feet away so that the Transvisor can detect the waves not just as they came out of the cellphone, but as they fanned out around the president. The trajectory of the waves, and the expression on the face of the captivated President, would have value of their own, Dad insisted.

Dad turned on the Transvisor, and a West Wing assistant turned on the monitor. People in the room and around the globe saw the smiling President, head to foot, as he held up the cellphone. But instead of just cellphone waves, what the Transvisor revealed, and what the monitor showed, and what the planet witnessed, was the President of the United States having a colossal attack of flatulence. The flatulence appeared on the large monitor as green oblong patterns, not unlike the sails on a boat in the middle of a windy day, fanning out in three directions from behind the President. Even respected science journals like *Discover* later joked about it, calling the West Wing the West Wind.

Carl Amsterdam worked on no more inventions after that, Ms. Noonan. He did no more research and made no more experiments. Reporters and critics were relentless. My father went into a deep depression. He stopped working, withered away, and died four years later.

Did a genius like my father deserve the fate with which he was saddled? *The Shifting Winds of Imagination* will explore his life and career, his rise and fall, my respect for him, and my struggle to move on. After all, I still wrestle with my accountability in the matter. There have indeed been personal repercussions with which I must deal, including a fairly lackluster romantic resume, which I attribute to my own preoccupations, such as telling my father's story to anyone who will listen. While the women I meet are lovely people—very nice and usually quite pretty—I suppose they sense in me this strange obsession which I am now sharing with you, and perhaps it is that character trait of mine that drives them away. (As a brief whimsical aside, while that certainly is not why I want to write *The Shifting Winds of Imagination*, having a bestselling book would undoubtedly be good for my social life!)

Thank you very much for your time and consideration, Ms. Noonan. I look forward to hearing from you at your earliest convenience. This would be a project on which I would be happy to work nearly full time. In fact, that would more or less be a given, as I am currently unemployed and have only the Dream Machine to occupy my time. In short, I assert I will be able to deliver a finished manuscript to Simon & Schuster fairly quickly. Some friends of mine allege that I spend far too many hours watching my own dreams, but to tell you the truth, right now that's all that keeps me going.

Best regards,
Ron Amsterdam
6876 Cider Lane
New Castle, DE 08742

A Story with No Ending

Allen is feeling good. The day started well and a good ending is in sight.

For one thing, despite still having to work as a crewman on the Port Jefferson-Bridgeport Ferry, his latest rejected short story solicited a personal note from the fiction editor at *The New Yorker* telling him to keep developing his unique style and to submit more work in the future. The note had arrived this morning. It is one of the nicest rejection letters he has ever received.

For another, after fifteen months of dating, he is certain that Dina is the one. This morning he had a purchased a beautiful ring and planned to ask her to marry him tonight. His idea is to ask her on the beach after having dinner at a chic bistro in the village.

Allen wants to be a writer. Short stories, mostly, but also novels, plays and movies. He has yet to have anything published, but he's eager and resilient. Also, his job earns him enough money to pay the rent on his comfy Port Jefferson apartment while affording time to work on his writing projects. Even when he's aboard the ferry, once all the cars are secure and the ferry pushes away from the dock, Allen has about twenty minutes to look out onto the Long Island Sound, between Port Jefferson, Long Island and Bridgeport, Connecticut, and think of more stories, more characters, and more interesting approaches to take with his writing.

He has one idea in particular he is eager to try. He wants to create an entirely new genre in which short stories have no endings. Nothing decisive. Nothing definitive. Open to creative interpretation and open-minded speculation.. He hasn't actually written one in that style yet because he is waiting for an inspiration from real life to provide the literary spark. He is confident it will come soon. Considering how well he's been feeling today, he entertains the notion that it might come sooner rather than later.

Dina arrives at four-thirty. The two of them sit in the living room of his apartment and talk about Allen's latest short story — the one he is most proud of, the one that *The New Yorker* had sent back with a lovely personal note from the fiction editor.

"Maybe you should try writing a different ending for that story and submit it somewhere else," Dina gently suggests.

"Actually, what I'd really like to do is write something entirely new and avoid having any ending at all," Allen explains. "Every writer uses an ending. Maybe I can be the groundbreaking scribe who doesn't! Besides, don't you like the fact that I don't want to be just another sheep? That I don't just want to follow the crowd and play by all the rules? That I want to go my own way?"

Those are, in fact, among the traits that Dina likes most about Allen.

"You're right," she says. "Forget I said anything. Just keep on being you, and that will make me happy."

Allen kisses her.

Together they snuggle on a chaise lounge on the fire escape patio which, three stories up, looks out over a portion of the retail district of Port Jefferson. Couples and families saunter down below on the street, enjoying the summer afternoon near the water. Allen pours two glasses of wine. After a few sips, Dina leaves the fire escape to go to the bathroom to freshen up. Allen goes into the living room. Their plan is to leave the apartment at seven to dine in the village.

Dina calls out from the bathroom to ask if she had left her pocketbook on the coffee table. Allen confirms that it's there and says he'll bring it to her. On the way to the bathroom, Dina's cellphone rings. It's in her pocketbook, so Allen reaches in to grab it and sees the name Lori on the screen.

"It's your friend Lori," he says as he hands her both the phone and the pocketbook by the bathroom door.

"Thanks. I'll try to be quick. I know she likes to talk a lot," Dina says.

Dina takes the cellphone and the pocketbook. She leaves the bathroom door open about six inches. Allen goes back into the living room to relax and think about his next short story — the one he wants to be devoid of an ending. But his train of thought is interrupted because Dina's end of the cellphone conversation, which he can hear clearly through the partially open bathroom door, is quite disconcerting:

"..... What? That's terrible, Lori ..... That's what Dick wanted to do for your second anniversary? Well, did you tell him how you felt about it?..... Wow, Dick's really not thinking of you at all. He only thinks of himself..... Oh my God! That's awful, Lori. He *knows* that you don't like heights, and he *knows* that you don't like raw fish. What did you say to him?..... What did he say when you said that?..... Dick obviously cares a lot more about what his stupid friends think than about what you think, Lori. You should've just stayed home..... Really? That's what he said he would've done if you stayed home? What is he — in third grade? Listen, Lori, the more you stay quiet about this, the harder it's gonna be later on..... Are you kidding me? That's not even funny. Did you ever say anything like 'Why did you marry me' or something like that?..... And what did he say?..... That's just wrong. A husband doesn't talk like that to his wife..... No, I don't think Dick can hear you.... Well, then just go outside to be sure.... Me? Why would he ever want to talk to me?..... The sensible friend? Well, maybe I'm sensible, but if he thinks I'd ever side with him..... Okay. Go. I have to get off, anyway. Call me tomorrow to let me know what happens..... Bye."

With Dina's end of the conversation ringing in his ears, Allen is livid as he sits in the living room. He wonders, fleetingly, if some kind of story about Lori's dreadful situation might provide the basis for the story he has in mind. He remains on the easy chair, silently and almost motionlessly seething. Allen prides himself on the exemplary way he has treated the women in his life, always with the utmost respect. His father's marriage to his mother was still going strong thirty years later, which is why Allen willingly abides by those admirable traits.

Dina comes out of the bathroom, puts her cellphone and pocketbook on the coffee table, then returns to the bathroom.

"Just two more minutes. I promise," she assures him. This time, she closes the bathroom door behind her and locks it.

"Don't rush," Allen calls out in what he hopes is an unruffled tone. He doesn't want Dina to know anything about the anger he feels from having heard what he overheard moments before.

The cellphone rings again. The screen displays the name Lori. Allen picks it up and immediately speaks—but quietly so that Dina can't hear.

"Lori, it's me, Allen. Listen carefully. People don't change. As a writer, I consider myself an observer of people, and one thing I'm sure of is that people don't change. Drop Dick now, like the boiling piece of shit he is. In fact, right after I hang up, I'm going to start a new short story about a guy like Dick. He'll be the most immature, idiotic bastard you'd ever want to meet. Just like the real Dick. He'll say things and do things and think things that prove he's a dimwitted, narcissistic, juvenile, scared little man-child. He'll never change, and Dina agrees with me. You probably know this already, but she never liked the guy in the first place. We've both said many times how we wish you'd get divorced and get your life back. You're still young, there are no kids in the picture, and you're able to stand on your own. You don't need that blowhard jerk. So will you? Will you leave that asshole?"

"Hey, Allen," Dick says on the other end, "can I please speak to Dina?"

Serendipity Doo Dah

Marcus started his career as an artist at Walt Disney World in Florida. For twelve years he drew thousands of versions of Mickey, Minnie, Goofy, Pinocchio, Snow White, Tinker Bell, Ariel and countless other characters in various poses for posters, walls, mugs, hats, tee-shirts and napkins. But Marcus liked neither the company policies nor the way employees were treated. So he quit and moved to New York City, where he joined CKD Media as an art director. For the next twelve years, he sketched advertisements, logos, letterheads and business cards for dozens of clients. Ironically, the Walt Disney organization purchased the agency shortly after he began working there, and while Disney had little to do with the day-to-day operation of the shop, in effect, Marcus worked for Disney all over again.

He didn't like CKD Media, either. Too many narcissists, too many braggarts, too many toxic people.

After twenty-four years in art and advertising, Marcus was ready to walk away from the field entirely. It was not that he despised art and advertising; he despised having to work for other people.

The first thing he did after he quit was withdraw all of his savings. Because his salary was pitiful in Orlando and living in Manhattan was so expensive, his savings account wasn't as healthy as it should have been after gainful employment for so many years. He could have had a lot more, but a few years ago he gave $175,000 to a friend who had planned to write, produce and direct an independent film. He was an old college friend who had also once worked for Disney, in California, at the movie division. Besides investing the capital, Marcus was asked to round up dozens of props for the movie, which was to have taken place in 1929. Marcus enjoyed that part of the project very much because he had always been a collector of things anyway — trinkets, gadgets, gizmos, souvenirs, knickknacks, novelty items, even (despite his aversion to the name) Disney memorabilia. Also, the prospect of earning hundreds of thousands of dollars from the movie's success in return for his investment was a thrilling incentive.

But the project fizzled. The movie was never made. His friend spent all the money flying to different countries to attract foreign financiers — to no avail, as it turned out. Marcus lost his entire investment. But he kept all the props. He had to rent a storage unit in Manhattan in order to keep them all.

After Marcus withdrew his savings, he gave up his apartment and left all of his furniture behind. He had to use a portion of his new storage unit for his personal belongings, for even at home he had hundreds of trinkets, gadgets, gizmos, souvenirs, knickknacks and novelty items. Now he had twice as many. The storage locker, without an inch of space to spare, came in handy. It was also expensive.

Marcus really had no one with whom to commiserate about his uncertain future. He had dated a handful of times, but established no lasting relationships. The few friends he had were work friends, and now that he was without work, they were no longer friends. Other than collecting, which for him was a solitary pursuit, he had no particular hobbies or activities that he enjoyed. And since people often meet other people while engaged in hobbies and activities, Marcus met no one. The only physical activity in which he was involved was running. He ran fast—so fast, in fact, that no one ever wanted to run with him. It may have kept him in shape, but it made him no new friends.

Without a place to live, Marcus hopped into his Ford and drove around. Sometimes he slept in the car, sometimes he checked into motels. He drove out to Long Island, up to the Adirondack Mountains of New York State, down the Jersey Shore, and across Connecticut. He had no definite plan. As he got higher into the mountains he smiled for the first time in a long time because he realized while gazing into the rearview mirror that no bosses stared at him, that clocks didn't tick incessantly, and that elevators no longer waited for him to go up for insipid client meetings or down for boring corporate lunches.

Marcus stayed in a motel in a town called Saranac Lake, in the heart of the Adirondack Mountains. The quiet and stillness were appealing. Marcus drove around town and discovered that also in Saranac Lake were a library, a diner, a small movie house, and a new two-room town hall that doubled as the local historical society and museum. He heard from a librarian that the town was one of the most sparsely populated in the state, but popular with hikers and campers. And even then, it was easy to walk in the woods for hours without bumping into a soul.

Marcus liked Saranac Lake very much. He thought he might stay.

But he also knew that soon he would have to earn money and create a life for himself. He would need something to do each day—a sense of engagement, accomplishment, reality—a sense of *something*. After a few weeks in the Saranac motel, Marcus purchased a tiny, ramshackle, one-room cabin on a spit of land at the side of a dirt road called Allie Lane that cut through the woods. He decided to turn it into a curio shop. After all, he had more than enough curios in storage back in New York to fill up the cabin from wall to wall, from floor to rafter. There was no use and no financial sense in keeping all those knickknacks in the Manhattan facility. Besides, that was his old life; this was his new one. He could sell the trinkets, gadgets, gizmos, souvenirs, novelty items, and antiques in his very own shop! He loved the idea. The cost of the cabin was low. It had an outhouse in the back with a decent-enough toilet and sink, and there was a shower inside the cabin cordoned off by a translucent plastic curtain. The annual property tax was just over half of what he used to spend for rent in a single month in Manhattan. He could open up his new shop just as soon as he transported all the stuff to Saranac Lake from the city storage locker.

Because he felt so lucky to have come up with such a wonderful idea for a business, and because he felt so lucky to have found such a pretty town and inexpensive cabin, Marcus chose Serendipity as the name of his shop.

Over the course of nine days, Marcus drove back and forth to Manhattan to retrieve all of his possessions from the storage unit. He had to spend a few hundred dollars on gas and to replace the car's alternator, but he knew that all worthwhile ventures require an outlay of capital up front.

Whenever he saw something that someone had discarded on the side of the road, or if something stuck out of a dumpster in a parking lot, Marcus would pull over to inspect it to see if it should be added to Serendipity's inventory. Somehow, he always made extra room in his car. He found many things and felt lucky—again—that whenever he took an alternative route, it was lined with intriguing road-side junk that he could throw into the back.

Yes, Marcus said to himself—Serendipity was an excellent name for the shop. He painted a sign and nailed it above the front door of the cabin. The front door was dilapidated, but to his mind, it was full of character.

•   •   •

Marcus may have had luck on his side, but what he didn't have was a business plan.

Even though he had spent his entire career in advertising and promotion, at Serendipity he concentrated only on his inventory, as opposed to creating ways for people to know about the shop.

Nor did he consider the need for business insurance, the proper way to collect sales tax, or what to do with the tax after it was collected. Those essentials he ignored. Those were things he knew he'd learn little by little by talking to people he met in town, at the diner, at the library, and elsewhere in Saranac Lake.

Allie Lane forked off of Route 3, and Serendipity was two miles in. Route 3 itself stretched for eighteen miles, and most travelers who passed through Saranac Lake had to be on it for at least part of the trip. Marcus made three signs out of scrap wood that he found on the grounds of an abandoned furniture factory. Onto the wood he hand-painted *Serendipity. Allie Lane. Two Miles Down.* One sign he put on Route 3 a mile to the south of Allie Lane; another he put a mile to the north. He added little arrows to each sign. The third sign he put on Allie Lane just a few yards past the exit off Route 3. To that sign he added the words *Serendipity. Antiques. Curios. Collectibles. You Name It, I Got It. Straight Ahead.* Instead of driving his Ford, Marcus ran to put up those three signs. He ran eight miles all together that day; that helped him save gas, avoid wear and tear on his car, and stay in shape. He hadn't run in many weeks and felt that he had lost some momentum. He was slower than usual. But he felt good about Serendipity and believed that once he settled into a routine, he'd go back to regular running and his stamina would return in full.

Marcus purchased space for a small display ad in the local newspaper. He had heard that the weekly paper was available at every motel, restaurant, and retail shop in Saranac Lake. He designed the ad himself.

Serendipity opened in the middle of April. For a sales desk, Marcus used an old blackboard that he placed on four milk crates. His cash register was a small tin Disney lunchbox. Nine people showed up the first day. A man bought a fish tank. A woman bought a clock. Another man asked about the cot he saw in an alcove off to the side; Marcus had to tell him it was his own bed. Everyone seemed to enjoy the shop, even though most people just looked but did not buy. Marcus chatted with all comers and told stories of how Serendipity came to be. Even when they walked out empty-handed, visitors still had a good time. So did Marcus.

He allowed the ad to run in the newspaper a few more times, and he made more signs and nailed them to more trees in both directions on Route 3. Once again, he ran to put those up the new signs. He felt his running was still below par, but improving. Over the next few days, two dozen stoppers-by stopped by, and Marcus sold seven items. That was less than he would have preferred, but more than nothing, nothing being a prospect he tried not to think about but knew was a possibility.

He took a break one morning in May to go to the library. He read some magazine articles and skimmed a few books about new businesses and learned that it can take up to a year-and-a-half for a new venture to turn a profit. He was glad to read that because the next day he had to pay his electricity and telephone bills, sign on for business insurance, and open a separate bank account to store away funds for local, state and federal taxes. When he paid the bills and calculated the insurance premiums and the tax bills, he realized he could be broke in six months.

Over the next few days, a handful of customers stopped by, and Marcus made a few more sales. Then one night, a bear who reminded Marcus of Baloo in the Disney movie *The Jungle Book* (a character he had drawn dozens of times) broke into the outhouse and hauled both the sink and the toilet off their pedestals. Marcus had to buy a new sink and a new toilet and hire a plumber to install them. When a townsman in the diner asked him why he didn't opt for a junk toilet and a junk sink and install them himself to save money, Marcus said it was because a decent bathroom, even though it was in an outhouse, was important for customer satisfaction. Besides, he added, he had no plumbing skills.

June, July, and August brought several parents on their way to drop off and pick up their children at two nearby sleep-away camps. There were also a few dozen college kids who came to the area for summer hikes, to skinny dip, or to camp out for a week in the woods. Many tourists on vacation, going either north to Canada or south to New York City, also stopped by. On five separate occasions, youngsters with their families saw Serendipity's extensive Disney collection and begged their parents to let them purchase a few items. Several preteens enjoyed an old, colorfully decorated *Song of the South* music box that continually repeated the line "Zip-a-dee-doo-dah, zip-a-dee-ay." But each time a child begged to buy something, their short-tempered parents were in a rush. They refused and told their whiney children that they could purchase Disney items on Amazon and that they didn't want to have to schlep anything else in the car. That frustrated Marcus, but he held his tongue. After all, as the saying goes, the customer is always right.

In late August there was a break-in at Serendipity. Marcus had been at the diner that night. The three most expensive items at the shop were the three items stolen: six-foot-tall delicately carved wooden deer created by a local sculptor. The sculptor had let his work reside at Serendipity for free and agreed to be paid only when they were sold. Marcus had to pay him for the three deer that were stolen. That was difficult to do since the thief also took all the cash that Marcus had in the Disney lunchbox. Marcus gave the sculptor what he had in his wallet and went to the bank to withdraw some more. He gave it all to the sculptor who, out of sympathy, forgave Marcus the final forty-five dollars he owed.

In September, on a morning that Marcus set aside to calculate how much longer Serendipity could last, he received a notice from Saranac Lake Town Hall informing him he had never applied for the proper commercial license to operate a business out of what officially was residential property. He also received a notice from the Saranac Lake Police Department informing him of the illegality of posting commercial signs on the highway without authorization and a permit. Combined, the application, the license and the permit would cost two-thirds of what Marcus had left in his bank account. He had no choice but to pay.

He sold twelve items in October. In November there was a torrential downpour which created a leak in Serendipity's roof and ceiling. Fortunately, the damage was relegated to just one corner of the cabin where Marcus had stored his beloved record collection, which nobody seemed to want to buy. The records were ruined, but the Disney items, which were next to the records, were untouched. Repair costs for the roof and ceiling reduced his account to less than $50, as the friendly teller at the bank gently informed him.

At the diner in December, Marcus overheard two men at the next table talk about health insurance and life insurance, for which Marcus still had not arranged. Disney World and CKD Media had provided both his health insurance and life insurance when he was employed at one and then the other. When one man at the next table told the other man what his monthly premium was for the life insurance, Marcus breathed a sigh of relief, for it didn't seem excessive. But when the other man followed up with the cost of his monthly health insurance premium, Marcus nearly spit out his coffee. It was exorbitantly high. Although he was healthy, Marcus knew everyone needed health insurance. And with the headache he had just developed, along with the queasy feeling in the pit of his stomach, who knew how long it would be until he was no longer a healthy man?

For the first time since Serendipity opened, Marcus did not feel serendipitous. He decided to close up the shop.

•　　•　　•

The next day, as Marcus was about to remove the Serendipity sign from the door, a woman from town stopped by to look for an old-fashioned egg beater, which she recalled having seen at Serendipity a few weeks earlier. She said she saw someone on an old television show using an egg beater and suddenly longed to have one for herself. As she paid for the item, a black car with Maryland license plates pulled up in front. Marcus saw it was a rental from Avis, so the driver could have been from anywhere. As she left the shop, the egg beater customer smiled at the black car's driver as he walked into Serendipity. He was tall, had on a spotless dark gray winter coat, and wore sunglasses. He carried a small leather briefcase. Marcus had a bad feeling. He thought to himself: no one needs sunglasses or a briefcase in Saranac Lake, especially at a place like Serendipity, and especially on a cloudy December morning—unless, of course, that person had bad intentions. After all, the thief from last summer had never been apprehended, and the one and only report the police had on the matter was from a local resident who said he saw a car drive back and forth in town throughout the day and that the driver wore sunglasses. With that thought in mind, Marcus, who could not help but display a miserable scowl on his face, told the man that he had to close Serendipity early that day. Something had come up, he said.

The man continued to look around even as Marcus prepared to close the door, but then he returned to his rented car without incident and drove off. Marcus remained suspicious long after the black car was gone.

Marcus took the sign off the door and painted the words *Out of Business* on the other side. He nailed the wooden sign back to the door and then put a few Serendipity trinkets in five boxes. Then he took a break and handwrote a letter to town hall in which he asked them to expunge the name Serendipity from the town's business rolls. He put the letter in an envelope, along with a copy of the permit, sealed it, and planned to run it over to town hall the next day, even though he hadn't run in several weeks. In fact, he had grown tired of running. It was something that no longer empowered him or gave him any pleasure. He was slower than ever and knew it all too well.

That night Marcus slept uneasily — three, maybe three-and-a-half hours tops. When he awoke the next morning, he noticed the rented Avis out front. Certain the man wanted to rob him and hurt him, he glanced around to see if there was anything he could use as a weapon, something solid or sharp. But he found no weapon and decided to hide instead. He went to the back of the cabin, crouched behind a massive tree trunk, and stayed there, silent and still. After a minute, he heard the man's car drive off, so Marcus returned to the shop. Nothing was missing, but there was a handwritten note on the counter:

Hi. My name is Bryce Carter. I work for the Walt Disney Company in California. I drive around the country searching for props for our live-action movies. There's so much in your shop that would be perfect for eight of our upcoming feature productions. (Everything except the Disney items. We have plenty of those!) I had hoped to purchase your entire inventory for $1.8 million dollars. That, of course, would mean that you'd have to go out of business. But I see by the sign on your door that you are already out of business anyway. It must have been sudden, since yesterday you were still in business. Sorry it didn't work out. I wish you well.

Marcus ran down Allie Lane faster than he had ever run before.

Bitten by a Badger in Blauvelt

"Why? I'll tell you why. Because my wife left me, my boss hates me, I have no guts to do anything about it, and if I explode into seven million disgusting pieces right here in the middle of the hallway, no one would give a shit. That's why. Other than that, everything's peachy. Okay? Happy now?"

That would be my friend Mark, responding to a simple question I had asked about why he looked so depressed.

We were in the hallway just outside the door of my third-floor office. Lunchtime was twenty-five minutes away, and I had hoped to get a lot of work done before then because I had a lot of work to do after — in fact, enough work to last until breakfast the following morning. But Mark was depressed, and he's my best friend, so I wanted to give him a few moments to vent, regardless of my own anxiety. Work would just have to wait.

What I *really* wanted was for my friend Mark to pull himself together before Mr. Boss-Man heard him whining like a dying warthog right there in the middle of the hallway. Mark didn't need more problems than he already had.

The fact of the matter was that his wife *did* leave him and his boss *did* hate him. Well, okay — maybe his boss didn't actually Hate him with a capital H. But neither was Mark on the guy's employee-of-the-month roster. His name was Rudolf Reiner (he was my boss, too), and for what it's worth, no one is *ever* on his employee-of-the-month roster.

You might not have known it by his hallway warthog whining, but Mark is actually one hell of a likable guy. He's smart, full of wry humor, and on top of everything else, the son of a bitch is damn handsome. His thick, black hair and his warm, blue eyes give him a jump on the competition. The bastard seems to have it all, which is why I simply refused to believe that no one would give a shit if he exploded into seven million disgusting pieces right there in the middle of the hallway.

That's what I told him as we stood in the hallway together.

"Well, one day I'll try it in your office," he replied. "I'll explode into seven million pieces just to prove it to you."

"Terrific," I said, trying to match him quip for quip. "Then I'll be the one who has to clean up all your disgusting guts."

"No you won't," he replied.

"Why not?" I asked.

"I ain't got no guts."

•　　•　　•

Let me tell you a little about the troubles Mark used to have at work.

We were employed by Wanderlach Optical Products Corporation of Blauvelt, New York, the American subsidiary of a large German company that manufactures glass lenses. Mark was a product manager for one of the product lines. I was the public relations manager. Our boss, the aforementioned Rudolf Reiner, was the vice president of marketing. Reiner resembled a sort of psychotic eagle, with a large, round, hairless head, predatory eyes, and curled, claw-like fingers. We called him the Bald Ego because there was only one way to do things in Wanderlach's marketing department: Rudolf Reiner's way. The man was incredibly arrogant. Mark had always treated the Bald

Ego with respect, just to play it safe. Smart move, if you ask me. You never know about bosses. They can turn on you.

But like most of us at the company, Mark didn't like Reiner at all. Once Reiner made up his mind about something, he expected you to carry out his orders like a soldier, no questions asked. That's one reason Mark always found himself in hot water with the guy. As respectful as he tried to be, Mark also wanted to remain true to himself. He liked to weigh every side of an issue before he took action, which Reiner always interpreted as indecisiveness. Mark was constantly on the lookout for advancement opportunities inside the company, which Reiner equated with disloyalty.

It took little for Reiner to find an excuse to criticize Mark. "Mark, you don't stay late enough," he would say on a Monday; "Mark, you're too tired in the morning," he'd say on a Tuesday; "Mark, you spend too much time away from the office on business lunches," would be a Wednesday comment. Things like that.

Case in point: Reiner had called him on an interoffice line one day last week while I was in Mark's office. Mark pressed the speakerphone button so that we both could hear. "I want you to proof the new marketing report a hundred times," Reiner demanded. "A hundred times! Do you hear? There was an incorrect figure in the last report. I know you received the figures from Accounting and were told to use exactly what you were given, but don't you think you should assume mistakes on their part? Maybe you are just not cut out for product management, Mark. Yes?" Reiner hung up. I heard the loud click over the speaker. Mark looked at the phone, punched his left shoulder with his right fist and barked, "Jawohl, commandant!" I laughed. But I didn't know whether to feel sorry for Mark because of how he was treated by the Bald Ego, or jealous because of how easily he bounced back from such criticism with the simple turn of a phrase and a sparkle in his eye.

Anyway, that was Mark's situation at work.

• • •

Now let me share a few details about his home life at that time.

Mark's easygoing style and satiric wit contributed to the breakup of his marriage to Debbi.

Debbi was a beautiful, intelligent and serious young woman who was very handy with a ruler, hammer and ratchet set. She was the accounting manager for an architectural and construction firm owned by her father and two older brothers in Nyack. When Debbi came home from work every evening, she'd continue the never-ending quest to upgrade the townhouse in which she and Mark had lived until recently. Debbi took little time out for fun and relaxation; she was always working — until seven-thirty or eight o'clock at night at the firm, and then until eleven-thirty or midnight at home. My then-girlfriend Cindy and I tried to double date with Mark and Debbi, but it was always so difficult for Debbi to find a night she'd be willing to give up. Altogether, the four of us went out three times since I met Mark three years ago.

I have to pause here in the story to admit that I, too, may inadvertently have contributed to Mark and Debbi's breakup because of something I said the last time I was at their place. We were all sitting in the living room. I heard a noise next door. I asked Debbi if sometimes she could hear people talking in the attached townhouse. But instead of Debbi, it was Mark who answered.

"Can we hear people next door? You mean Brenda and John?" he teased. "Well, let's put it this way. They had sex last night and Brenda was on top, which they both like a whole lot.

Other than that, no, we really don't hear what goes on in there. Although," Mark added, "they do complain about Mario barking all the time." (Mario is Mark's miniature collie.)

Debbi didn't find her husband's comment amusing at all. "If you would help me a little bit more around here," she snapped, "I'd have time to put up the stone accent wall I've wanted to put up for the past six months so that there'd be no sound leakage at all between the townhouses."

"*Sound leakage*," Mark repeated—not as a question or exclamation, but as a comment on his wife's stuffy character. Debbi knew that's how he meant it and didn't appreciate it. Not one bit.

"Why don't you just move in with Brenda and John if you don't like the way I talk," she hissed, and went straight for the doorway.

"At least I'd have sex for a change!" Mark called out as his soon-to-be ex-wife left the living room. "Top, bottom, middle—wouldn't matter!"

A few nights later, Mark phoned me and said, "Well, it's just me and Mario now."

"Debbi left you, huh?" I wasn't surprised. "I'm sorry I asked about the neighbors. I feel like it's all my fault."

"It's not your fault."

"What did she say?"

"Debbi? Well, she gave me twenty-four hours to vacate the premises. But at least I got the TV and the dog." His matter-of-factness about the gloomy situation rendered me speechless. "Hey," he said, "are you there? Hello? Why aren't you saying anything? *You're* the big public relations pro, not me. You're supposed to say something pithy and witty, full of meaningless euphemisms. That's P.R., isn't it?"

"That's B.S., not P.R. Besides," I said, "I want to be truthful with you, Mark. No B.S. You're my friend, and I know this thing with Debbi must be painful, even though you two weren't getting along."

Apparently it *was* painful, because it was just about that time that Mark's biggest depression set in. It's when his self-imposed social exile began. He moved to a small apartment on the west side of Blauvelt. Cindy and I saw him only twice during that time. The first time was when we passed by his apartment and saw him and Mario sitting on the curb. The second time was when he invited us over to watch a movie with him and a 'date,' who was his five-year-old niece. We watched *Toy Story 3*, but halfway through, his niece had him switch to *Frozen*. Mark did whatever his little niece wanted. Smart move. You never know about five-year-olds. They can turn on you, too.

Anyway, that was his situation at home.

●　　●　　●

Now it's time to bring you up to date.

Fritz Stolt, chairman of the board of management of our German parent company, was due in from Cologne for a big U.S. marketing meeting. The Bald Ego told Mark that he could skip the meeting because, in Reiner's words, "You really never add anything significant to marketing meetings that I myself can't convey more effectively. Yes?"

That's when Mark's pitiful face appeared in my office doorway. That's when he made the crack about exploding into seven million disgusting pieces right there in the hallway.

"Wanna take a stroll through the park with me?" he asked moments later. Blauvelt State Park is only two blocks from the Wanderlach building. It has several walking trails. I had been there with Mark many times.

"A walk through the park? Why? You need to clear your head?"

"If I needed to clear my head, I'd get a lobotomy," Mark said. "I just want to take a walk. That's all."

"How come?" I asked.

"I don't know. Maybe there will be nobody there and we can run around naked like two little prehistoric kids with no responsibilities and nothing but time on our hands."

"No thanks, Mark," I said. "I don't like to be naked on my lunch hour."

"Why not? We can strip away all the pressure."

I refused to smile.

"Oh, come on, pal," he continued. "I'm the one with no guts, remember? — but I'm still willing to do it. Why not you? Come on, let's go."

"I can't, Mark. It's not even twelve o'clock yet."

"So?"

"So if Reiner sees that you're not in your office, *I'm* the one who's gonna have to explain to him where the hell you are. He knows we talk about everything. What am I supposed to say — 'Sorry, Mr. Reiner, he's outside stripping away all the pressure'?"

"Sounds good to me."

"Can't you at least wait until twelve? I'll go with you then."

"No. I can't wait. Like you said, I need to clear my head. Things are rough. Haven't you heard?"

"Things are rough all over."

"All I need are a few stray minutes. Who knows — maybe something extraordinary will happen. All I know is that I've got to go *now!*"

"Why now?" I repeated desperately, hoping he'd reconsider. "Just wait twenty-seven minutes. Just twenty-seven lousy minutes."

"No!"

Mark paced in straight lines across my office floor, back and forth, like a caged tiger. "I come to work, I do my job, I go home,

I go to sleep, and nobody knows and nobody cares about any of it. Then it starts all over the next day. Wake up, come to work, go home, go to sleep—*alone*, I might add—over and over again. When I'm here, Reiner treats me like an intrusion, and when I'm home, nobody treats me like *anything* because nobody even knows I'm there and nobody is ever there with me, except for Mario, who would much rather smell some other dog's ass than listen to me complain all night. The damn dog gets more action than *I* do, for crying out loud."

"Mark," I cut in sharply, "this thing you're going through is largely self-imposed. You know that, don't you? I hate to sound like some anal-retentive psychology major, but—"

"It's not self-imposed, pal. It's just imposed. I'm not one of the lucky ones. That's all there is to it. Look at you."

"Me?"

"Yes, you. You chose public relations for your career, you're good at it, your job is secure, you have a beautiful girlfriend, and you have nothing to complain about. So are you gonna come to the park with me, or am I gonna have to shoot you in the groin?"

"Can't you wait just twenty-six more minutes?"

"To shoot you in the groin?"

"To go to the park with you."

"Sorry," he said—and like a shot, he was out of my office and on his way to Blauvelt State Park to run around naked like a prehistoric kid with nothing but time on his hands.

•　　•　　•

Twenty-five minutes later, as I walked from my office to the water fountain, I heard a commotion around the corner. I went to see what was going on. There were people gathered in another hallway that has a window facing the parking lot at the front of the building. I joined them by the window and looked out, and below, three floors down, in the lane that separates the parking lot from the front entrance, was one police car and one naked man holding a few crinkled-together pages from *The Journal News* around his waist.

The naked man was Mark.

As two police officers got out of their car and approached him, Mark looked up to the third floor, where I was standing with a dozen other employees, most of whom were giggling with embarrassment. I assumed by the look on Mark's face that he hoped I'd be watching at that very moment and would rush down to the street to be with him. He knew I was one co-worker—one genuine friend—who would at least try to help him get out of this unusual and unprecedented situation. So I ran to the stairwell, jumped several steps at a time on my way down, and when I finally got to the lobby, I saw through the big glass doors that a circle of people now surrounded Mark.

An ambulance pulled up just then, and right behind the ambulance was another police car, and further down the block was a TV news van. I ran toward the automatic doors so fast that they didn't have a chance to open all the way by the time I was ready to pass through and I nearly crashed through the glass.

The TV van, from WNBC News in New York City, pulled up beside the ambulance just as I got to the street, and a man in a blue suit jumped out, followed closely by two other men, one small and portly who held a large video camera, and the other tall and skinny with earphones on his head and a small control box in his hands.

"What happened?" the man in the blue suit asked Mark as he stuck a microphone in his face. The man looked down at Mark's bare legs, one of which had several puncture wounds. A path of dried blood meandered from there down to his ankle.

"I got nipped by something in the woods," Mark said. He pointed toward the road that led into the park, and as he did, one sheet of newspaper fell to the ground, the one that covered his rear end. There was a murmur from the crowd. He left the paper on the ground instead of bending down to pick it up; bending down probably would have made the situation worse.

"You were bitten?" the man asked. "What bit you?"

"I don't know. A groundhog, maybe. Or a badger or something." He tried to stretch the single sheet of newspaper around his entire middle, but it ripped, and that left Mark completely exposed. There was another gasp from the onlookers, louder this time, almost in perfect unison. One of the police officers handed a thick brown blanket to Mark, and he wrapped it around himself. The blanket looked itchy. Another police officer tried to move the TV guys out of the way.

"After whatever it was bit you," the newsman said, "then what happened? It didn't rip off your clothes, did it?"

"No. I lost my clothes," Mark said. "I was sunbathing."

"In the nude?"

"Yes."

"What do you think happened to your clothes?" the newsman continued. "Were they stolen? Do you think someone is playing a practical joke on you?"

One of the police officers put his arm around Mark's shoulders and tried to turn him toward the ambulance.

"I don't know," Mark said. "I just couldn't find them. After I got bit, I sort of lost my way."

"Why were you sunbathing in the nude?"

Mark looked at me. I shrugged my shoulders. I didn't know what sort of advice was appropriate at the moment; it was a public relations crisis the likes of which I never had to address in my career.

"Why were you sunbathing in the nude?" the newsman repeated.

"I don't know," Mark finally said. "To strip away all the pressure, I guess."

I didn't think it was an especially funny line, but the newsman and the police officer laughed, and so did many others in the crowd.

"Where do you work?"

"Wanderlach Optical. Right over there."

"Are things so rough that you have to strip away the pressure?"

"Things are rough all over."

Again, laughter all around.

"Looks like they're taking you to the hospital," the newsman said.

Mark looked down at his leg. "I guess that's a good idea," he acknowledged.

Two paramedics took him from the police officer and walked him to the rear of the ambulance. "Can my friend come with me?" Mark asked a paramedic. I stepped in closer.

"I suppose so," the earnest young man replied.

Mark and I slid into the back of the ambulance. One paramedic came in with us and swabbed the bottom of Mark's leg with some clear ointment and bandaged it. Then he went to join his colleague up front, leaving me alone with my friend. Within moments, the ambulance was driving away amid cheers and applause. The siren was off, though the engine was very loud.

I crouched next to Mark as he sat on a long, cushioned bench under the window that looked into the driver's compartment.

"So," I sighed, "you really *did* run around naked like a prehistoric kid. I don't know if I should pat you on the back for doing what you wanted to do or smack you on the ass for being so damn stupid, Mark."

He smiled.

"But God punished you for going nuts out there," I said. "He made you get bit *and* he made you lose your clothes. You see? That's your payback for being a lunatic."

Mark leaned in closer to me. "I didn't lose them," he said. "They were stolen. And I wasn't sunbathing. I just said that because... well, I just felt it was better to say that, considering that a microphone was being shoved down my throat at the time."

"Stolen? Your clothes were stolen? Who stole them? The badger?"

"Listen. I was on the trail. When I was all the way in the middle of nowhere, I saw these two naked women on a blanket in a little clearing in the woods. They were drinking wine and insisted that I join them. Before I knew what was happening, they had my clothes off and we were doing it right there in the woods."

"Doing what?"

"*It*, dummy. Do I have to draw you a picture? I was doing it with them. First with one and then the other."

"You mean...?"

"Yes. The *wild thing*. The *act*. The *deed*. As Shakespeare put it, the beast with two backs. Or in my case, the beast with *three* backs."

"That's unbelievably stupid and dangerous these days, Mark."

"They had condoms with them."

"How do you know they were real condoms? Or good ones? That takes a lot of guts, what you did, and you're always saying that you don't have any guts."

"Well, I guess that's one thing I have guts for — especially the way I was feeling. Anyway, when we were all done, they told me to close my eyes and rest with them a while, and when I opened my eyes the two of them were gone, and so were my clothes. Fortunately, I had left my wallet in my desk drawer and my cellphone in my briefcase. *Un*fortunately, it was a brand-new shirt and a very expensive pair of pants and I'll never find shoes as comfortable as the ones they stole!"

"So what you're saying is that you decided to do whatever these two anonymous women told you to do as easily as you decide where to park in the morning—is that an accurate assessment of the situation, Mark?"

"They wanted to make me happy. Don't you see? These girls seemed to really care. A lot more than Reiner, and obviously a lot more than Debbi. I liked that because nobody cares anymore. I felt like my luck was finally changing. At least until I found out that they took my clothes and my shoes. I guess they weren't the angels I thought they were. You never really know about naked women in the woods. They can turn on you."

"*I* care, Mark. You know that, don't you?"

"Yes, I know that. But they were prettier than you. Both of them. *Both* of them," he said. He emphasized the word *both* just to make sure that part sunk in. "Anyway, when they were gone, I started back toward the entrance of the park, but the rocks were killing my feet. So I walked along the edge of the path because I thought there would be fewer rocks there. I sort of drifted into the woods, and a few seconds later I felt this painful stab in my leg, and when I looked down, I saw this brown furry thing attached to me. I freaked out. I shook my leg really hard, and whatever it was finally dropped off and ran into the woods. Then I saw two old pages from the *Journal News* on the path and I covered myself up with them and walked back to the building. Police cars and an ambulance were parked out front by the time I got there. I guess someone in the parking lot must've seen me walking to the building and called the police. Pretty amazing, huh?"

I was speechless, but it didn't matter because we had arrived at Nyack Hospital and Mark was wheeled to the emergency room, where several eager nurses attended to him as if he were the second coming of Christ.

The nurses were as taken with Mark's looks and personality as they were with the excitement of having a swarm of reporters and cameramen in the hospital. I spoke to one nurse, a stunning brunette named Donna, and learned that Mark would receive a series of shots and would have to return to the hospital in a few days for a checkup, but that otherwise everything seemed fine. Donna stayed with Mark in the emergency room and asked him if he needed anything else before being discharged. Mark said, "Sure. How about some clothes, a Coke—and your telephone number."

Several hours later, Mark and I took an Uber back to Wanderlach so that he could retrieve his wallet and briefcase and drive his own car back to his apartment. When he arrived home, his cellphone rang constantly. *The Journal News*, *The New York Daily News*, WCBS-AM from New York, and even *Good Morning, America* all called that first night and sent people over to his apartment early the following morning. He knew he'd be late for work and had to decide what to do about that. I told Mark to call Reiner and explain, but he said he didn't have the guts. He was a little late for work in the morning, but it hardly mattered; Wanderlach Optical was mentioned dozens of times in the newspapers and on the television programs and never in a negative way—and Reiner loved that. I knew it must have taken all of Mark's self-restraint to avoid crucifying Reiner in public. But it was the smart thing to do, and Mark's no dummy.

A segment aired on *Good Day, New York* in which Mark talked about "how an ordinary day can suddenly turn extraordinary in the course of a few stray minutes—extraordinary being a subjective word, of course." Later, in his office, I tried to give him a few tips about not using so many "uhhhs" and "you knows" in his interviews, but his phone kept ringing and people continued to pop into his office, so I had little chance to dispense my professional advice.

The next day, *USA Today* ran a story called "The Naked Lunch Hour: Young Marketing Exec in Blauvelt, NY Finds the Answer to Corporate Burnout." In it, Mark talked about how dead ends can sometimes seem like infinite possibilities, if you know how to approach them. He said that finding a secluded spot to strip down outside in the middle of a busy day was an idea that just came to him on a whim when he was feeling claustrophobic at work. The writer called Reiner for a quote, and Reiner said nice things about Mark. I wanted to congratulate Reiner on how he handled the interview, but he had no time to see me.

That night, Mark received a call from a *Today Show* producer asking him to appear on the show in New York City the following morning. Mark invited Cindy and me to go with him to the studio. I had a lot of important work to do at the office, so I told Mark I'd watch a recording of the show another day. Cindy was very disappointed and decided to go without me.

"Bitten by a badger in Blauvelt. Tomorrow on *Today*," teased a TV promo that evening. Even though it had not been confirmed it was a badger that had bitten Mark (one of the emergency room doctors said a badger would have done much more physical damage), the alliteration was just too good for *The Today Show* to pass up. I learned later that day that prior to going on the air, the show's production crew had a problem with one of its cameras, and Mark talked to the technicians about Wanderlach lenses and which ones they might like to try. During the on-air segment, Mark was asked about Wanderlach Optical and its product portfolio.

The human resources director at Wanderlach told Reiner that she was inundated with resumes from people who heard about the company on *The Today Show*. Word also came down that the Wanderlach receptionist received more than two dozen requests from trade reporters who asked to speak with Mark. The Bald Ego was promptly made aware of that. (Previously, trade reporters called to speak to me.)

• • •

A few days later, Debbi called Mark simply to congratulate him on his brief celebrity. She emphasized she had no desire to rekindle the flame. But that was fine with Mark, because he was now dating Donna, the stunning nurse from Nyack Hospital. I suggested to Cindy that we double date with Mark and Donna, like we had done with Mark and Debbi, but Cindy said she wanted to break off our relationship and see other people.

I called Mark on Friday, but the call went to voicemail. I tried a few more times but never reached him, so I drove over to his place to surprise him; I thought perhaps with some media hoopla having finally died down that he wouldn't be too busy to go out for a beer.

Just as I was about to leave my apartment, my cellphone rang. It was the Bald Ego. He was still at the office.

Reiner told me he had decided to appoint Mark as Wanderlach's new public relations manager and was letting me go. He said he would give me whatever help I needed to line up interviews, to prepare my resume—anything I wanted. He'd even look elsewhere in the company for me, if that's something I'd want to consider.

"Does Mark know?" I asked.

"No. I'll tell him on Monday," Reiner said. "I'll do everything I can to make sure there is no animosity between the two of you. I know you are good friends and I don't want to be responsible for ruining that. Yes?"

I drove to Mark's place and knocked on the door. Mark answered promptly and pulled me in. He was buckling the belt on his pants. Donna, even more radiant than she was at the hospital, stood by the bedroom door, tucking in her shirt. No wonder Mark didn't answer his phone; he had probably turned it off completely because he had obviously been otherwise engaged. Donna smiled at me.

"I can't believe you're here," Mark said. "You're psychic! I was just gonna call you. Donna and I decided to go away for the weekend. A little B&B in Newport. We found it online and called. Believe it or not, they have a vacancy. We're leaving now and I wanted to know if you could watch Mario. You don't have to stay here. Just come by twice a day over the weekend to feed him and walk him so that he can poop."

Mario ran out of the kitchen to greet me. His tail was wagging vigorously.

"We'll be back late Sunday night," Mark continued. "Just in time to get ready for work on Monday morning! The pooper-scooper and bags are under the kitchen sink, the leash is on the front door handle, and the keys are on the living room table. Think you can do it, pal? For me?"

"Do I have to play with him, too?" I asked.

"Well, he does have a few new toys in the bedroom that the two of you can play with. But only if you have the time."

"He poops at that little park at the end of the block, right? I'll take him now. He has that look in his eyes."

"You don't mind?"

"I don't mind. What the hell. Maybe my ordinary day will somehow become extraordinary in the course of a few stray minutes. Maybe all my pressure will be magically stripped away. I mean, things are rough all over. Right?"

Mark barely heard any of what I had said. He was too busy closing up a small suitcase. Then he took Donna by the hand and led her to the door. She was beaming with anticipation.

"Thanks again, pal," he said. "You're the best. I owe you one."

Mark and Donna left the apartment and closed the door behind them. Mario stood by my feet and looked up at me affectionately. I unwrapped the leash from the door handle, attached it to Mario's collar, then went into the kitchen to grab a plastic bag and the pooper-scooper from under the sink. Outside on the front steps of the apartment building, I looked left and then right, trying to remember which direction to go in order to find that little neighborhood park. But before I could decide, Mario pooped right there on the top step. He sniffed his handiwork, then begged to begin his walk down the block. I really didn't see the point, since he had just accomplished what he was supposed to accomplish in the park. I would have preferred to scoop it up, then go back inside to sit and stare into space like the zombie I was. But Mario's puppy-dog eyes beseeched me, so I relented and let him lead the way. You never know about dogs. They can turn on you.

Ho Ho Ho

Dear Doug:

Thought I'd drop you a line to see if I could put a bug up your ass to jump-start the old friendship after all this time. That's right, a note on a piece of paper. An actual letter. One that comes in an envelope, upon which is stuck a stamp with my actual saliva on it. I'm sick of emails and texts. Time to get back to basics. Saliva is as basic as it gets.

It's been 15 years, Doug. Time—a real piece of work, huh? One day I'm taking my SATs and applying to NYU and the next day I'm using my 401k to open an IRA. Sucks, if you ask me. (Time, that is, not the 401k. My 401k is gonna make me very comfortable when I'm as old as that thousand-year-old math teacher we once had, Mr. Ross. Remember?)

Listen, pal, it's almost Christmas, and you're only 2 hours from the Big Apple. So hows about coming in to spend the weekend? We'll go to a comedy club, catch a B'way musical, maybe check out the Christmas show at Radio City, look at the fancy department store windows. (I hated doing all that shit with my family when I was a kid, but with you it will be different.) Anything you want to do, we'll do. I'll take you to the best damn restaurants in Manhattan. We'll drink a little. Or a lot. (You still have some brain cells left to kill, don't you? After all, it was only a decade and a half ago that we chugged obscene amounts of beer in the Canyon Avenue playground at midnight! Remember???) You can crash at my place. I've got plenty of space—even a spare bedroom that has its own bathroom fully loaded with a fancy brass-and-smoked-glass magazine rack stuffed with The New Yorker, Vanity Fair, Penthouse, Entertainment Weekly, Time and the latest catalog from Victoria's Secret. Have I piqued your interest, buddy boy?

Most of all, we can talk. About our old teachers. Like idiotic bald-as-a-billiard-ball Mr. Healy, whose chin looked like it was connected directly to his chest without the benefit of a neck. Or we can talk about the old crowd. Like all the girls we vicariously screwed (one of whom I bumped into the other day, but I'll get to that in a minute). We can talk about our jobs. About life, liberty and the pursuit of happiness. About anything, really.

Only 2 hours away, Doug! I know, I know, it's not just 2 hours, it's also been 15 years—which I guess is maybe why it's as hard for you to make an appearance in Manhattan as it was for Mr. Healy's neck to make an appearance in social studies. But that shouldn't stop you, kiddo. Not only are the 2 hours easy to tackle by train, car or bus, but I'll bet you my JBL LX600 3-way speakers with the 10" woofers and titanium dome tweeters that even the 15 years will be easy to sweep under the rug. (Speaking of which, there's also a beautiful plush green rug in the guest bathroom which feels really nice on your tootsies when you step out of the shower, even when you're alone, which I try not to be, but usually am anyway.)

15 years, Doug. 15 goddamn years. Jesus. Remember in high school how we used to talk about how we couldn't wait to leave our one-horse town and live in NYC when we got older, and about what we wanted to be? Me, a network news anchorman living on the entire top floor of the Dakota, and you, a pilot for Delta or United, screwing two stewardesses at once in your Central Park West duplex during stopovers at Kennedy or La

Guardia. Well, Christ Almighty, kiddo—other than the fact that I'm in NYC, I guess we can still dream our elusive dreams. I ain't no network news anchor (yet) and you ain't no pilot. But at least we're both happy, right? Right right RIGHT?!?!?! AbsofuckinglutelyRIGHT???

Sorry.

Actually, if you want to know the truth, I envy the hell out of you, Doug. I really do. As far as I can tell from my spies in the old neighborhood (and how is my mother, by the way?) you have such a—what's the word I'm looking for? Unpressured? You lead such an unpressured life up there in Woonsocket, you bastard—driving those cute little kids to school who idolize the hell out of you, and flirting with all their cute young mothers. 50 bucks says you score at least 4 times a month with a lovely lonely horny Rhode Island divorcee. 50 bucks! You can pay me when you get here. Just slip it under the brass-and-smoked-glass magazine rack in the bathroom on top of the plush green rug. And I bet that after you screw a lovely lonely horny Rhode Island divorcee, you go back to your cozy little apartment and do whatever the hell you want to do. Am I right? Do you still listen to Coldplay? Do you still go to all those air shows and hot-air balloon festivals? That's why I envy you. When you want to do something like that, you just do it. I'm too busy hosting "The National Beat" to have much of a social life. It's only a 90-minute program, as you probably know, but it takes up so much of my damn time. I suppose that wouldn't be so bad if "The National Beat" wasn't such a smarmy TV show.

So don't send me back some stupid letter (or worse, email) telling me some crap like you don't want to visit because you don't feel you're on the same level with me anymore just because I host a popular TV program and live in a pretty damn nice place across from Lincoln Center. Sure, Doug, it's a TV show—but it's "The National Beat," for Christ's sake, a show that makes "Access Hollywood" look like "60 Minutes." The only good thing about it is that everyone knows who I am. (One reason for that is because the show is always getting sued by one celebrity or another, and my name is always mentioned in the goddamn news reports about the lawsuits. But they usually sue the producers, not me personally.)

There was a show last week, by the way, that was a real pain in the ass. We did a segment that makes me feel like whatever success I've had by becoming a TV host has been crapped on by the things I have to say on air. Want to hear about it? Well, you're going to anyway. Maybe it'll make you think that driving a bus in Woonsocket ain't so bad after all.

Okay, here's what happened. Ever hear of Marissa Carlin? That tall, stacked, slightly bow-legged girl who stars in "One Life to Live" on TV? Well, someone sent my boss a 15-year-old playbill from a community theater production of "Hair" in Millerville — you know, that old show that has one scene where everyone stands around naked for a few seconds? Stan, my boss, the executive producer of the show, had the segment all worked out in his head before anyone on our staff even did any research or conducted any interviews. He wanted the segment to be all about this young TV star who began her career doing nudity on stage. Cute, huh? That's Stan. Major dope. (At least he has a neck.)

Anyway, I had a tremendous argument with him. I said to him, Stan, there is absolutely nothing wrong with an actor or actress having been in "Hair." If you're looking for some kind of scoop, or to cast some sort of bullshit shadow on Marissa Carlin, you might be disappointed when our reporters come back with the research and the interviews. That's what I told him. And Stan said to me, Just make sure they don't disappoint me, Matt. That's all he said, and then he walked away.

So our staff interviewed Marissa Carlin and we prepared the segment and we milked the sucker for all it was worth (because, frankly, that's what keeps the ratings up and the big paychecks coming in, and I've always been a sucker for big paychecks). We played up the nudity thing and tricked some spicy quotes out of some old geezers who live near the theater, even though they never even saw the damn play. Stan loved the segment. Loved it to pieces. I felt like a scumbag for doing it on the air, but hey, I host a TV show for a living, and I always wanted to work in TV, right? And I make a pretty good salary, right? And I have an unbelievable expense account, right? And everyone knows my name, right? So I must be one happy fella, right? Right, right, right, right, RIGHT???!!! Am I AbsoFuckingLutely RRiGGghhTTT?

Sorry. Again.

Anyway, did you see that episode of my show? This is how I started it out (FYI, I write my own intro copy): "Fifteen years ago, just before I turned eighteen, my best friend Doug and I tried to sneak into the local adult theatre in Woonsocket to see a few naked women on screen. Little did we know that just a few miles away, in Millerville, beautiful nineteen-year-old Marissa Carlin, currently seen on the soap opera 'One Life to Live,' was standing on a stage without a stitch of clothing on her blossoming young body."

I made you famous, Doug! Your name came out of every TV set from Manhattan to Monterey. I've given you your 15 minutes of fame! My sister Maureen called from Virginia to ask me if you were the Doug I was talking about in the segment, and I told her you were, and I'll bet you my entire collection of iPhones, iPads, iPods, and everything else that starts with an i that nearly everyone in Woonsocket made the quite logical assumption that you were the Doug I was talking about.

So, Famous Doug, will you come for a visit? You don't have to worry about it being an all-Matt weekend, because you never know who you'll meet on this gigantic island. Like two days ago, for instance, I ran into Michelle Sheerlink. That's who I was referring to at the beginning of this letter. You'll never guess what happened. Go ahead, try. It's a free country. (Well, actually, nothing's free anymore.)

Remember how you talked me out of a dozen depressions in 10th grade when I was hopelessly in love with Michelle but she was stupidly in love with Arnie Rumford or Dale Feldman or some other asshole? Remember how I used to stare at her from my 2nd clarinet chair while she sat so sweetly in 1st flute? Remember her short messy haircut that was really more adorable than messy? Remember that goofy smile that was actually more seductive than goofy? Remember how I used to ask her out at least twice a year and how she used to say that she loved the way I had the guts to do that even though I must have known that she was more interested in being my friend than wrecking our friendship by dating? Remember remember remember REMEMBER? Do you AbSoFuCkInGlUtElY goddamn RreeMMmeemBErrrRRrr?

I'm tired of saying sorry. But sorry.

Anyway, I'm sure you also remember how I stopped being interested in Michelle when she began to change toward the end of high school. When she fell in with THAT crowd. Began to smoke and drink. Drugs. The whole damn thing.

So I'm walking home from my office last Wednesday night. The city's already in Christmas mode. Windows lit, bells jingling, all that. First I stop at an ATM to collect 20 crisp 20s to last out the week, as far as quick cash is concerned. Then, as I'm walking down Broadway, I fall in step behind a guy who's as bald as Mr. Healy, and his head is reflecting all the Sony, Nikon and Toshiba neon signs. (Poor guy had only Japanese companies bouncing off his scalp. I wonder if that means anything. Probably not.) Anyway, the whole thing reminds me of when we came into the city on a school band trip one year, I think it was 11th grade, and we made fun of all the bald executives, and while I'm thinking about the old days, and about you and me and the old gang and all that, all of a sudden I see someone who looks almost exactly like Michelle Sheerlink standing in front of the Pierre Hotel. It floors me. But I know it can't be her because this girl is standing under the brightly-lit canopy wearing a silky white halter-top and very short white cut-offs, and she's casually glancing around as if she's looking for a john. If you don't comprende yet, amigo, let me spell it out for you: this particular girl is a hooker. A plain old, garden variety, run-of-the-mill, honest-to-God prostitute. But the resemblance is so striking, and she's so damn beautiful no matter WHO she is, that I stop in front of her just to stare for a moment. I can't help it. That's how strong the vision is — it makes me stop and stare at her. Anyway, she looks me up and down and says, "Merry Christmas. Wanna have a good time?"

And that's when I realize it really is Michelle Sheerlink. I'm not sure exactly how much time goes by — 10 seconds, 15 maybe — but I finally say, "Is that you?" She stares at me. Again, I'm not sure if it's 5 or 10 seconds, but she finally says, "Hi there."

I say "Oh my God" — and then I regret saying it because I don't want her to think that I'm judging her in any way. You know what I mean? In fact, her eyes open wide as if she's in the earliest stage of shock, which is what I didn't want to happen. So I put one hand on her shoulder, and I put one finger over my mouth as if to say Shhhh, sort of to let her know that she doesn't have to say anything, that no explanation is needed, that I know as well as anyone that life takes us on interesting and sometimes bizarre little side roads and into strange and sometimes ominous little alleys. (I used that line in a segment last month. I don't want you to think I always talk like this.)

Anyway, I want to tell Michelle that the times I remember being her friend were among the happiest of my life. I want to remind her that I really didn't know what problems she may have been having that last year in high school when we hardly knew each other anymore. I want to tell her it's because of all my cluelessness that I can't hold her in any sort of contempt for the things she's done since then. I want to tell her that I can't be disappointed or judgmental about her life since I don't know what happened. I want to tell her that I'm willing to pick up where we left off. I want her to know all this, and I think the hand on her shoulder and the finger over my lips saying Shhhh did the trick, because her face loosened up and she smiled and let me put my arm around her waist as we began to walk down the block. Yup, that's what I did—I put my arm around Michelle's waist and walked down the block with her. What the hell do you think I'm gonna do—lecture her right there on the sidewalk? Arrest her? It's a free country, isn't it? (I know, I know...) But you see—it's Michelle Sheerlink, for Christ's sake. Michelle, who I used to have unbelievably sweet fantasies about all during 10th and 11th grade. THAT Michelle!

As we stroll along the sidewalk, she asks me what I do for a living, but I really don't want to talk about "The National Beat," or anything else. So I just say I'm still exploring my options, and then I beg her to tell me about herself and what she's done since high school. She sort of laughs (nervously, I guess) and tells me how she studied theater at the University of Rhode Island, became the top actress there, won student awards and all that, but how she left halfway through to do commercials and Off-Off Broadway, and how she did a favor for a friend by performing in what her friend said was a low-budget soft-core porn video, and how that led to other videos, and how her parents found out and disowned her, and how her manager took advantage of her, and on and on and on... Jesus, Doug, it was sadder and more intense than any story I've ever covered in my whole stinking career.

We get to my apartment, and she's genuinely awed by the size of it. I try to act cool, suave, sophisticated, and I think she really enjoys that. Doug, I swear to God, I feel like George Clooney as I pour two drinks, dim the lights, and put on soft music. I half expect Steven Spielberg or Martin Scorsese to step out of the shadows any minute and say "Cut and Print!" I'm sure she feels like a beautiful ingenue in the same make-believe movie because she does her part as if some award-winning romance screenwriter wrote it for her. She smiles, we toast each other, and she sort of extends every moment with a dramatic stare or sigh or short saunter around the room. (That's another line I used last month.) And then... well, read on, pal.

We undress each other and throw our clothes on the floor. She rubs my arms, and then my legs, and then my back, and then my neck, all very slowly and softly. I do the same to her. I feel and kiss and enjoy every part of the woman I had worshipped when she was a girl just a few years ago. And she responds. She RESPONDS. With pleasure. Obvious pleasure. Vocally and physically. Are you following this? HELLO—get the picture? We use up every square inch of my double-queen-sized bed with the hand-carved, four-poster canopy. Sexy and sweet and wonderful Michelle Sheerlink. She in my bed. Me in her. Jesus H. Friggin Christ. We do it thrice. (Do you like that word? I don't think I ever used it before.) First with me on top, then with her on top, then side by side. It was exceptional, pal. EXCEPTIONAL! (That's the complete opposite of average, if you were wondering, especially when it's all in caps.)

Afterward, we fall asleep in each other's arms. I wake up about an hour later when I hear her rummaging by the foot of the bed. The lights are still dim and the music is still playing softly. Michelle is picking up my pants from the floor and putting them neatly on the edge of the bed, and I'm about to tell her not to bother, that I'll straighten up in the morning, but she says, "It's okay, I'll get it."

She takes 20 crisp 20s out of my wallet, drops the wallet on the bed, and walks over to the door.

She says "Thanks. It was really good." And then she leaves.

I drafted a segment about her this morning and handed it to Stan just a little while ago. He said he'll put it together and run it on "The National Beat" next week. New Year's Day, I think. It's gonna start off like this: "Up next, the sad but true story of an actress who started out on top as a promising college student in Rhode Island but ended up at the bottom as a common prostitute in Manhattan."

Like I said, I write all my own intros.

So there you have it, Doug. Got enough brain cells left from the old days to fathom the whole damn thing?

Call me. Let's get together. Maybe next weekend? Hey—I could really use a merry Christmas.

Your pal,
Matt

The Naked Gambler

The *New Jersey Monthly* Interview: Peter Airmont

Peter Airmont is stuck down the shore.

For most of us in New Jersey, that sounds like a vacation, for 'down the shore' is a common phrase used to describe all the popular beach communities in the central and southern parts of the state. But for Airmont, the phrase means something quite different, for he happens to be incarcerated for the third time in three days, in three different New Jersey counties. His first detention was in Cape May County, the second in Ocean County, and as this interview was conducted, he was being held in a jail cell in Atlantic County.

The 49-year-old trade magazine editor says that after a lifetime of abiding by all laws, rules and standards of personal and professional conduct, "Fate intervened. Maybe now that I have a criminal record I'll finally find the kind of success as a writer and photographer that seems to be reserved only for people who are addicts, who commit crimes, or who have been in the nuthouse or the slammer once or twice. I've got them beat. I've been in the slammer three times!"

Until last month, Airmont was the long-time editor of the Wall Treatment Journal, an Edison-base monthly newsletter devoted to highway sound barrier design and construction. He was let go from that job after his second incarceration.

For years, Airmont has tried to sell his essays, short stories, and nature photographs to magazines and newspapers across the country on a freelance basis, but with very limited success.

"I told my ex-girlfriend Kaylee — before she was my ex-girlfriend — that if I could get arrested three times in a row, I'd probably finally find the success that I've been dreaming of," Airmont told New Jersey Monthly. *"She barely listened to what I said. Maybe now she'll come crawling back to me."*

We spoke to Peter Airmont in his cell at the Atlantic County Detention Center.

New Jersey Monthly: You grew up in South Orange, Peter, and worked for 24 years in Edison, but you spent a lot of time over the years on New Jersey's southern peninsula — which was also the location of your three arrests. Your first was in Cape May. Can you explain?

Peter Airmont. Sure. I've always liked the atmosphere in Cape May. It makes me feel like I could be a writer. It has a creative aura. Plus, there's a beach there called Higbee that I used to go to a lot, until about fifteen years ago. That's when I found a bed-and-breakfast in Sea Isle City that I liked a little better than the one where I used to stay in Cape May. So I stopped going to Cape May. But I did miss Higbee Beach. It used to be clothing-optional, and what I liked about it was that it gave me a sense of freedom, literally and metaphorically. I liked being unencumbered by a bathing suit. There was something almost spiritual about it. When everyone's naked, there's no judgment. No one can be singled out when everyone is naked. We're all the same in the eyes of God.

NJM. That's a notable sentiment, Peter — but it doesn't explain your incarceration. You said you stopped going to Cape May fifteen years ago. Yet that's where you were jailed the first time. What's the story behind that?

PA. Like I said, I stumbled onto a bed-and-breakfast in Sea Isle City that had a huge upstairs studio with an unobstructed view of the ocean. The owner keeps that studio reserved for me four times a year, for a week at a time. They cater to me like I'm a celebrity writer or photographer. My creative juices just flow better there, even though I haven't sold anything yet. Anyway, that B&B was closed this summer for a big paint job. So I went back to Cape May. It's like an old friend. And I stopped at Higbee Beach. I was there early in the morning. No one was there. I took off my clothes, stretched out on a blanket, and let my mind wander, just like in the old days.

NJM. Higbee hasn't been clothing-optional for several years now.

PA: I found that out when a policewoman woke me up. I never read about the clothing-optional suspension in the papers. They don't report that stuff up in Edison. Plus, I didn't see any signs that said No Nudity Allowed. When the cop woke me up there were thirty or forty people on the beach, a couple of families, some with kids, and I guess I was having a certain kind of dream that made my nakedness more apparent, if you know what I mean. Anyway, I was arrested and spent half a day in the Cape May County Correctional Center.

NJM. Couldn't they have just given you a warning and a fine and skipped the prison sentence?

PA. You'd think so, right? But the policewoman said I was belligerent. Plus, I had a fancy 35mm camera with me, with a telephoto lens. I guess they didn't like that. But I don't remember being belligerent.

NJM. What happened next?

PA. When I was released, the desk sergeant asked me about my camera, and I mentioned all the work I do with landscapes, beachscapes, gardens, that kind of stuff. He didn't seem particularly interested. Then he asked me why I liked clothing-optional beaches, so I told him exactly what I told you. He said that he and his wife are members of the New Jersey Garden Society, and that there was going to be a meeting later that afternoon in Ocean City. He said the group has its own house where they meet to discuss gardening and then they go outside to the back of the house where they have lots of gardens to take pictures of. He said most of their members are into photography.

NJM. So we assume you went to that meeting, Peter.

PA. I did. The first thing I noticed when I turned into the driveway was this gorgeous amaryllis in the living room window. It was framed so perfectly, and the curtains on either side had complimentary colors and were sort of billowed around the amaryllis, almost like it was planned that way. Very unusual. So I set up a tripod and put a close-up lens on my camera. I stood on the lawn a few inches in front of the living room window and snapped twenty or thirty shots. Then I decided to peek at the gardens in the backyard. But on my way there I saw a smaller window on the side of the house with a single peony in a vase. The sun was shining on the vase, which turned it into a prism. The vase threw colored rays and dots of light onto the peony and onto the window. It looked amazing. So I went right up to the window and fired off another two dozen shots. Then, almost out of nowhere, a cop approached me and put me in handcuffs.

NJM. We're presuming that it wasn't the home of the New Jersey Garden Society.

PA. I swear that's what I thought the desk sergeant said in Cape May. But what he really said was the *Nude* Jersey Garden Society. I guess someone saw me taking all these photos through the widows and thought I was a peeping

Tom trying to make a buck. The cop didn't even bother to find out what was going on, and I was too shocked to figure it out on my own.

NJM. So that began your second stint in jail.

PA. Yeah. In just two days. We finally got to the bottom of it, but not before I spent the night there. They reduced the fine from $750 to $25. I thought that was really nice. I called my office in Edison to tell them what happened, and that's when they fired me.

NJM. That's a tough break, Peter. Our condolences. If we were to guess that the third incarceration had something to do with nudity, would we be far off?

PA. You'd be right on the money! As soon as I was released, I drove back home to Edison. Kaylee was at my apartment, taking back the last of her stuff that she didn't take with her when she first moved out. God, she's gorgeous. But she was just so sick and tired of my lousy income all these years, and all my boasting about selling stories and photographs for a lot of money. I can't really blame her, I guess. Anyway, I told her that I had been arrested twice in the last two days, and I reminded her that if I got arrested just one more time that I'd probably end up getting famous, and that if I made a ton of money writing and shooting, I could buy her anything in the world she wanted.

NJM. What was her response to that?

PA. She said to call her when that happens.

NJM. What did you do after you spoke with Kaylee?

PA. I went to an ATM and then drove to Atlantic City. The casino at the Golden Nugget. I took off all my clothes, started to play the slot machines, then just waited for the police to arrive. People were calling me the Naked Gambler, and a bunch of people took my picture. The Atlantic City cops weren't very nice. They roughed me up and threw me in here. They say that in the morning they're going to take me to a psychiatric hospital for an exam. But right after I get out of there, I plan on calling Kaylee to tell her the good news.

NJM. The good news being that you were arrested a third time, for being the Naked Gambler in the casino at the Golden Nugget. Correct?

PA. Yup. And now that I've fulfilled the need to get arrested three times, I'll be able to sell my stories and photos. I'm sure there'll be a lot of money involved. Maybe a lot of interviews, too. Coast to coast. Can you imagine the look on Kaylee's face when that happens?

NJM. No, Peter, we can't. Thank you very much for taking the time to speak with us.

The High Line

The Mehr sisters, Annie and Kim, met on the West Side of Manhattan once again to walk the High Line. They love the High Line—an old elevated freight train trestle transformed into a beautiful pedestrian-friendly garden that spans almost three dozen blocks from Greenwich Village to the Garment District. Annie, forty-two, lives in Newton, a suburb of Boston, and Kim, thirty-nine, lives in Franklin Park, a suburb of Pittsburgh. Their homes are six hundred miles apart and it takes over nine hours to drive from one to the other. Between the distance and the demands of their domestic and professional lives, the sisters don't get to see each other very often. They're both so busy. But when the High Line was completed, Annie and Kim said the hell with all those demands and decided to meet once a year on a weekday on the West Side of Manhattan. New York City was not exactly a halfway point, but the High Line was something they both enjoyed immensely. After all, they grew up in the New Jersey suburb of Verona, where there were plenty of trees and flowers and interesting landscape architecture. That's why the two of them still loved flora and ingeniously designed natural surroundings, which is what the High Line is known for. So as a meeting place, it makes perfect sense.

As children, Annie and Kim had always gotten along very well, even though they suffered a devastating psychological blow that could have torn them apart, the way devastating events have torn other families apart. When Annie was fourteen and Kim eleven, their father, David Mehr, vanished. The case has never been solved.

David Mehr was a brilliant financial whiz. His aptitude was confirmed time after time when the girls were young, as David helped the companies for which he worked earn millions of dollars, even when their CEOs, COOs and CFOs thought such fiscal growth was all but impossible. As the girls grew, so did David's reputation throughout corporate America, although on his own he pursued no publicity at all. In fact, he actively avoided it. David was painfully shy, emotionally weak and — as many insisted — completely devoid of ambition. But Annie and Kim knew almost nothing of all that. As far as they were concerned, their father was simply a funny guy who was loving and patient, a kind man who knew how to explain things well, a gentle soul who made them feel safe no matter where they were. When surrounded by his own family, David was fine; in social situations, however, he was terribly uncomfortable. As the girls came to realize later on, perhaps that's why social situations were few while they were growing up, and perhaps that's why the two of them didn't know that other David Mehr at all — the one people called strange.

Eventually, they learned a bit more about their father, but not from their mother; they learned from several of David's former coworkers who had contacted the girls after a newspaper reporter wrote a story about the cold case. The headline was "After a Decade, Financial Executive's Disappearance Still a Mystery." Many people in various ways explained to the young women that although their father had been thoroughly convinced of his own financial aptitude, he was extraordinarily worried about what was in store for his family in the future. There was something inside of David Mehr that simply made him distrustful of his own ability to plan well for the coming years. He was afraid of growing old, of *being* old, of the mistakes he might make as a parent as the girls grew into young women, of the errors in judgment he knew he might make in countless domestic matters that could jeopardize the future of his family. Also, as much as he was socially uncomfortable, he was equally unnerved in business situations (other than when he was behind a desk, alone, in a small office, with the door closed); that, too, made him dreadfully fearful of his future as a reliable source of income for his wife and daughters. He feared having to speak at corporate meetings and had what are best described as panic attacks whenever he was required to participate in small-group meetings with his superiors. David was terrified of job interviews. As the girls had learned from one of his oldest coworkers, he never pursued a job on his own, but let that task fall to other people who recognized his talent and procured positions for him on his behalf. He was too timid to plan his own career. As several former acquaintances had speculated, he had the brains to be a CEO, COO or CFO, but neither the temperament nor confidence to be anything more than an ingenious though isolated financial planner and a brilliant though solitary numbers-cruncher. Because of his internal demons, David Mehr had never been executive material.

The five-month police investigation into his disappearance turned up nothing. They did not find a body. Ideas, conjectures and rumors were all that existed. One theory is that he suffered a severe mental breakdown one day at work near the docks in Brooklyn, wandered off, stowed away on a cargo ship and now lives incognito somewhere in Europe. Another theory is that the Mafia was so impressed with his financial wizardry that they kidnapped him and forced him to work for them exclusively in exchange for their promise to make sure that the Mehr family was well provided for in perpetuity. That rumor emerged from several fronts, such as the fact that shortly after David's disappearance, his wife Sarah, who wanted to scale down to an apartment, was made an anonymous offer on the house for three times the asking price, and also that Annie and Kim were accepted into an expensive private school, all expenses paid, even though they had never applied. Things like that. Maybe it was true. That's what Annie and Kim had to admit to themselves — that maybe the Mafia, or some other group, nefarious or otherwise, had their father holed up in a tiny office somewhere out of state, or even out of the country, where he worked his financial magic to help them make millions of dollars while they kept him safe and well fed; and in return for his clandestine devotion, a promise was made to him that his family, whom he doubted he could take care of as he got older, would be safeguarded forever.

"This is so beautiful," Annie exclaimed as she stared at a cluster of viburnums that popped up robustly between the railroad ties. Even though it was crowded up on the High Line, she and Kim did not feel crammed at all, as they had felt earlier in the day as they walked along Seventh Avenue. Up there on the cultivated freight track the throngs of people were not throngs at all, but a smooth-flowing sea of happy natives and international tourists who looked relaxed, minded their own business, and went out of their way to be out of everyone else's way.

"I wonder if we'll see anyone we know," Kim commented.

It wasn't a far-fetched notion, for Verona was only forty-five minutes away, and both Annie and Kim had worked in Manhattan at the start of their careers. And though neither said it aloud, the fleeting thought that maybe they'd see their father during one of their High Line journeys also crossed their minds. It was the kind of city attraction he'd love. That notion, in fact, crossed their minds no matter where they were, no matter what they did, and no matter who they were with. It was just one of those things. Highly unlikely — but possible.

Annie and Kim glanced at each other and smirked, fully aware of the transitory notion that had just passed through their minds. Smirks and fleeting thoughts like that often preceded happy memories. That day on the High Line was no exception. The memories came swiftly.

"Remember when we were on line at Nathan's?" Kim said. "I was about six, and this guy tried to cross the line and said, 'Excuse me,' and Dad looked at us and said, 'Why should I excuse him? Did he belch? He didn't even eat his hot dog yet!'"

"I do! I remember! The guy heard him and had the weirdest expression," Annie said as she laughed freely, and for a long time. "And we looked at each other and started laughing at the same exact time. And remember the time just before he... well... you know... right before that, when we went to Washington by train and got so lost trying to find the station on the way home? We finally found it and ran to the train. We were out of breath, and the conductor said to us, 'How are you all doing today?' and Dad said quietly, 'Well, at least we're on the right track.' And the conductor had a delayed reaction and then he couldn't stop laughing."

"And you and I looked at each other and also started laughing," Kim added. "We couldn't stop, either!"

The two women walked a little more while their laughs slowly subsided.

"Remember the Christmas party at that job he had in Queens?" Kim said. "His friend Mike asked him where he bought his suit, and Dad said, 'I bought it at a very fancy store called Annie and Kim's—"

"And then," Annie said, picking up the story, "Mike asked what our names were, and Dad said our names were Lord and Taylor."

"Mom still talks about how we started laughing at the same exact time," Kim recalled.

They were about a half mile from where they had started, closer to midtown now, with the Empire State Building in view. The immediate scenery had changed a bit; there were different kinds of plants and flowers, the railroad tracks and ties had moved from one side of the trestle to the other, and more people were now snacking on ice cream and pretzels. But the vibe of the pedestrians, the loveliness of the weather, and the overall charm of the High Line remained exactly as before.

Annie and Kim were proud of themselves — proud that they could talk about their father without becoming overly sad. They talked about him many times throughout the year, on the phone, mostly, about what he was like, about his silliness and his kindness, about what may have happened, even about what he might be doing today, if only — Yes, they were proud of themselves that the tears they shed these days were tears only of laughter, not despair. Maybe they had inherited their father's bright mind, but spared his fragile and unstable psychological profile.

They missed him very much.

"If only his greatest gift of all was the one he needed to get along in this stupid world," Annie said as she watched a handsome young father walk hand-in-hand with two adorable little girls on the High Line.

"His greatest gift of all?" Kim asked. "What do you mean — his ability to make us laugh, no matter what?"

"Exactly. If that's all he needed to get along in the world — to make us laugh — then he'd probably still be here."

They thought about that as they sauntered.

"Wanna get frozen yogurt?" Annie asked. "I think we just passed a place."

Kim's smile said yes, and she pivoted around. Her pivot ended in a hard stop and a motionless head because of a man she saw standing by the yogurt stand.

"Oh my God!" she whispered loudly. "Oh my God!" she said a little louder. "Oh my God!" She shook her hands, as if to dry them, even though they weren't wet. "Oh my God!"

"What's the matter, Kim?" Annie looked to where Kim was staring to see what was making her sister tremble. And then she saw it, too.

"Oh my God. That looks like..."

They saw mostly the back of his head but also a little of his right-side profile. Kim grabbed Annie's upper arm—a nearly involuntary movement that had a mind of its own—with such force that Annie winced, but didn't complain. The sisters moved as a nearly single entity, making slow, measured steps in the man's direction. They stared at him as they got closer, subconsciously ignoring the people in front of them while instinctively avoiding them at the same time. The man was the same height and build as David Mehr, had the same salt-and-pepper hair, and seemed old enough to be a thirty-year-older version of the father they had known. These thoughts were not uttered aloud, but memory, spirit, and emotion connected Annie and Kim enough—despite the distance between their homes and the divergent lifestyles they led—for them to know what each was thinking. Both hoped it was true—and also nervous as hell at the prospect that it really was. Kim still had her hand on Annie's upper arm as they got closer to the man by the yogurt stand, and Annie bit her lip so hard that she forgot about the pain in her upper arm from her sister's iron grip.

When they were just two feet behind him, the man sensed their presence and turned around.

"Can I help you?" he asked in an affable tone.

David Mehr had light blue eyes. This man's eyes were dark brown. David Mehr's nose was small and round. This man's nose was longer. David Mehr had a small mole on the lobe of his right ear. This man had none.

"Oh... I'm sorry," said Annie, apologetically. "We thought you were someone else." She looked down, not yet sure how to feel, and certainly clueless of anything else to say.

The man's polite smile did not wane, nor did the twinkle in his eye disappear.

"You thought I was someone else? I assure you I'm not, young lady," he said. "I'm me, and I have *always* been me. I've never been someone else."

Almost as if choreographed, Annie and Kim looked at one another and laughed in unison. They couldn't stop. The laughter turned to tears. Happy tears. Annie and Kim said a million things to each other in those few moments, though they didn't utter a single word.

"Thank you," Annie said to the man. "Thank you so much. Thank you so very much."

The Mehr sisters continued along to enjoy the rest of the High Line.

The Ilks

Jimmy Ruskin belongs in Señora Rosario's Spanish class like Archie Bunker belongs at an NAACP fundraiser. For that matter, Jimmy belongs in high school like Edith Bunker belongs at a Mensa meeting. That's because Jimmy is a musician who lives, breaths and sleeps rock, jazz and blues but has no interest in history, physics and Spanish.

Two days ago, I sat next to Jimmy in Spanish class, at the back of the classroom and one row away from the side wall. Jimmy was also at the back, against the wall. He always chooses an out-of-the-way desk so that instead of conjugating *habla* and *tener* in his notebook, he can conjugate *Aqualung* and *Born to be Wild* into arrangements for the guys in Chance. Because of my angle, and because Señora Rosario was otherwise engaged at the moment with a broken overhead projector, I could see that Jimmy was writing a bass guitar line for *Sunshine of Your Love*, and a fairly easy one, from what I could tell. That was probably because his new bass player wasn't as good as his old one. Chance had lost its original bass player to the Bridgeport Juvenile Correctional Facility thanks to bad timing during a drug buy in South Norwalk last month. Jimmy, the founder, keyboard player and lead vocalist of Chance, needed a bass player quickly because the band has a paid gig next weekend in Stamford, and the guy

Jimmy found is okay, but not great. That's why the bass line had to be incredibly simple.

I leaned to my right, as if I had an itch on my left side that needed to be scratched, and whispered *Sunshine of My Love* just loud enough for Jimmy to hear. He had not yet written the title on the makeshift sheet music he had created out of notebook paper, so it surprised him when I said the name of the song.

"You knew that just from this one line?" he whispered back. I nodded my head. "Pretty good, Feingold," he said.

I was certain that would be the extent of our conversation. After all, to use a word my mother seems to enjoy, I am not of Jimmy's ilk. There is simply no basis for a bond of any kind. Jimmy Ruskin smokes, drinks, refuses to wear anything that isn't ripped, destroys vending machines when he's thirsty, and skips at least five classes a week. By comparison, I'm... well... I'm Bruce Feingold. Case closed.

But what I have to confess to myself, and what I will probably never admit to my mother, is that although not of his ilk, I admire Jimmy's talent, dedication to music, and devotion to his band. For all his bad boy swagger, his main thing is music, which I find admirable. Also, almost daily I must face the reality that Jimmy's ilk is the ilk that has the most fun in high school. I see Chance whenever they play, not just because of the music, but also because there are always plenty of beautiful girls that hang out around the band. I may not be of Jimmy's ilk, but it sure as hell is an ilk that can make a guy like me very jealous.

"You play a couple of instruments, don't you?" Jimmy asked quietly after I whispered the name of the song. Señora Rosario was still busy with the cord of the broken projector to notice we were chatting.

I was stunned that Jimmy knew anything about me at all. That was a pleasant surprise. He was right—I played a few instruments, but mostly in the school concert band and marching band. To musicians like Jimmy Ruskin and his ilk, that doesn't count for much.

"Trumpet and French horn at school, a little piano and guitar at home," I explained.

He continued to work on his bass line.

"How about I do one for you?" I suggested.

"What do you mean?" he asked. "Do what for me?"

"I'll write the notes to a lead vocal and you guess what song it is."

Jimmy smiled. He liked the idea. We both glanced up to see that Señora Rosario was now by the bookshelf under the windows, probably searching for a reasonable facsimile of whatever it was she had originally intended to show on the projector. There was still time to play around. So I quickly drew five staff lines on a piece of notebook paper and jotted down a dozen notes and rests. I showed it to Jimmy.

"No Time," he said just three seconds later.

I smiled and nodded. He was right—and he knew it. Then he went to work on another lead vocal line of his own, which he showed to me.

"Stairway to Heaven," I said. Jimmy grinned. "Let me do one more before Señora Clueless regains consciousness."

I sensed a companionship I had never felt before with someone of Jimmy Ruskin's ilk. So I put a twist on the musical game. Instead of a line from a classic rock song, I wrote the lead line to the theme song from *All in the Family*, which I had watched on TV the night before with my mother and father. I showed it to Jimmy. He looked stumped—but only for about ten seconds.

"'Boy, the way Glenn Miller played,'" he smiled as he sang the lyrics to a sitcom theme, "'songs that made the Hit Parade...' From that show on TV, right?"

Now *I* was the one who was stumped; was I to believe that Jimmy Ruskin actually took time out of his life—the life of someone of his ilk—to watch a family show on TV? At home? With his mom and dad? Was that even possible?

In her Spanish accent, Señora Rosario said, "Would you like to sing for the class, Señor Ruskin?" She had finally turned around and saw Jimmy talking to me. There was a book in her hand.

"Sing for the class? Instead of taking a test?" asked Jimmy. "You bet!"

The classroom erupted into laughter. Señora Rosario was not pleased.

"I would like you to come to the front of the class and read a story from this book," she demanded, determined not to let Jimmy get away with his impertinence. "You too, Señor Feingold. And class, when they finish reading the story, I want you to write a paragraph that summarizes what the story is about. In Español, of course. Sí? Bueno. Llegado a la parte delantera de la sala de clases, Señor Ruskin y Señor Feingold."

Jimmy and I went to the front of the classroom. He struggled valiantly—and indifferently at the same time—to read the first few pages of a short story called "La Lección de Pepé" in Spanish. Pepé was a mischievous boy in Ecuador who made his own rules, but learned a few valuable lessons along the way. Jimmy read the part where Pepé's father forces him to choose between two chores on the family farm. I read the part where Pepé can't decide which chore to select, so he flips a coin. "Cara o cruz?" Pepé says to himself as he walks to the barn—heads or tails. But only *after* he flips the coin, once it is back in the palm of his hand, does Pepé decide which chore represented heads and which one represented tails. "Es lo único lógicoes lo único lógico," he says, meaning 'It is the only logical thing to do.' It was classic Pepé behavior that the character flaunted throughout the book.

When Jimmy and I were allowed to return to our desks, I was certain he no longer had any interest in being on friendly terms, since I was partially responsible for the two of us being singled out like that by Señora Rosario. But I was in for another surprise. Jimmy smiled and said, "Smart kid, that Pepé. I can learn a lot from him! Thanks, Bruce."

I would like to believe that it was clear to both of us that I was no longer the same Bruce Feingold I was before: Bruce Feingold, president of the debating club; Bruce Feingold, senator in the Model Congress; Bruce Feingold, trumpet and French horn player in the Bridgeport High School Wind Ensemble and the Bridgeport Marching Rangers... No—now I was Bruce Feingold, friend of Jimmy Ruskin. I remember thinking at that moment that one day I could even be Bruce Feingold, member of Chance. That alone would be worth a dangerous walk on the other side of the tracks. Tracks of a different ilk.

•   •   •

Chance debuted last year at our high school's annual Spring Charity Carnival. They covered songs by Yes, Steppenwolf, Jethro Tull and a few other groups. They were an instant smash. I had formed my own band at about the same time, with a few of my friends, though I doubt a comparison is even necessary. We call ourselves Halcyon to try to appear hip. (My idea was that a lot of clueless kids would think that halcyon is some sort of illicit drug.) We play covers of songs heard mostly on AM radio. I thought that by sticking with a middle-of-the-road repertoire, and playing at a volume not known to burst eardrums, we might be hired by all the adults who would prefer *not* to hire Chance, and we could make some real money at the same time. Of course, I also knew that meant that the hot high school girls would never show up to watch us play.

I regretted Halcyon just a few weeks after I formed the group—the name, the songs, the arrangements, the guys—just about everything about it. It lacks something. Passion, maybe. I really love the way Chance puts so much emotion into its music. I suppose it's a combination of interesting arrangements, good playing, and a sort of this-is-what-it's-all-about attitude on stage that does it for them—and for me. Plus, I'd be lying if I didn't say I was eager to get to know the kind of gorgeous girls who seem to gravitate toward Chance.

But did I really want to go down a path that could very well tempt me with the life of a Chance member? Smoking pot, staying up all night and missing classes the next day, getting suspended for weeks at a time. Did I have the strength to upset my parents like that, or to alienate the few genuine friends I have?

But why does it have to be one or the other? Why can't opposing ilks have a peaceful coexistence? Where are all these rules written down, and who writes them in the first place?

I debated these complex questions in my head for the rest of the day in school and throughout the following day. I fantasized about starting another group of my own, less like Halcyon and more like Chance. I doodled band names on the inside back covers of all my notebooks. Bunker Hill, Crossroads, Fate, Peaceful Coexistence, and a bunch of others. It could be a band that performed the kinds of songs that *I* wanted to perform, and we'd play them the way *I* wanted them to be played. I knew I could do all that and still study for tests, remain on the debating team, stay in the marching band, and routinely overdose on nothing more dangerous than Lifesavers. Even someone like Stacey Baer, a beautiful, personable and intelligent girl who I had a crush on and who loves Chance as much as I do—even a dazzling girl like her might want to talk to a guy like that, a guy who could wail lyrics and tickle ivories like Jimmy Ruskin while essentially being Bruce Feingold.

I thought it was possible. I wanted to believe it. I also considered the fact that I was merely deluding myself. It wouldn't be the first time.

Jimmy and I were back in Señora Rosario's class Friday morning.

"Mind if I give you an opinion?" Jimmy asked as we sat down in our usual seats.

"Go ahead."

"You should leave that little bubble gum band of yours and do something else."

At least I was confident enough to joke around with him now.

"How can you skip five classes each week and still have such clever ideas?" I smiled.

Jimmy laughed. Señora Rosario handed out quiz sheets, uttering an *hola* or a *buenos dias* each time she set a piece of paper down on a desk.

"I heard you play once. With Halcyon. Not bad, Bruce."

"What? Me? You heard me play? Are you kidding? Are you friggin' kidding me? Where did you hear us play?"

"Roger Solomon's sister's sweet sixteen party. I was up in the attic with Roger smoking weed and feeling up Nancy Green."

"How was it?"

"The weed or Nancy Green?"

"My band. Halcyon."

"Like I said, Bruce, you should do something else with what you've got. You're talented."

Señora Rosario was at the front of the classroom now and told us to read the sheets carefully. She said she'd be back in a moment, and then she left the room. I felt like calling out 'Gracias, señora!' simply because she was giving me more of a chance to talk with Jimmy.

"You arrange too, don't you?" he asked.

"Yes," I said. "You wouldn't happen to be looking for a second keyboard guy, would you? Someone who could double on brass when needed? And arrange. And sing backup?"

The courage it took to say all that was entirely new to me; I hadn't had that kind of nerve just three days ago. This newfound intimacy with Jimmy Ruskin, this ilk-bridging bond, this hurdle that I seemed to have crossed, made it all second nature to me. Thoughts of marijuana, pills, liquor, all-nighters, skipping classes, getting suspended—those thoughts were missing in action at the moment. That's all there was to it. An entirely new ilk was being forged.

Jimmy seemed to consider what I had said about letting me join Chance.

"Tell you what," he finally said. "We're rehearsing Sunday night at John DeCarlo's. I'll tell the guys that I asked you to stop by just so that we can hear what a trumpet would sound like on a couple of numbers. They were all against it when I suggested it a while back. I'll suggest it again. I mean, I started the damn group, right? Don't forget to bring your trumpet. And while you're there—"

Señora Rosario stepped back into the classroom. She had a habit of taking time to gather her English thoughts before speaking, and that allowed Jimmy a few extra seconds to finish his thought.

"And while you're there," he continued, "maybe I'll drop a few hints to the guys about you possibly joining the band—if I think it's working out, that is. Of course, that's only if you end up wanting to come to the rehearsal."

"Why wouldn't I want to come?"

"Well," he said, "we'll be doing a lot of stuff, if you know what I mean. Stuff we usually do. Anyway, we start at eight, and after that we go out to talk about it, and that lasts to about… well… who knows? Probably all night. School might not be an option on Monday."

Jimmy must have detected a note of indecision on my face.

"Think about it, Bruce," he said. "If you want to show up, show up. If not… not."

•   •   •

After class, Jimmy met me in the hallway outside of Señora Rosario's room.

"Take it easy, Bruce," he smiled. "Maybe I'll see you at John's house Sunday night."

He walked down the hall and disappeared. I stood there for a moment and didn't move. Then I felt someone tap my shoulder. I turned around. It was Stacey Baer.

"You and Jimmy Ruskin are friends?" she asked.

By her expression, I could not tell if Stacey was astounded, impressed, or skeptical. I think it was a little of all three combined. I had never stood as close to Stacey as I did in the hallway that morning. She was a Cover Girl advertisement come to life. Purely intoxicating.

"Well," I said, trying to sound as unruffled as possible, "we talk about music a lot. I give him advice, he gives me advice, we test each other's musical knowledge, that kind of thing. Jimmy's a good guy."

"Cool! I had no idea. How many instruments do you play, anyway?" Stacey asked.

"Five."

"Do you still have your band?"

"Yeah—but I might join someone else's band soon. I'm thinking about it."

"Are you busy Sunday night?"

"Sunday night? Well, there's something I probably should do that night."

"Oh, that's too bad," Stacey said. She closed her pretty lips together tightly—which only made her adorable dimples more pronounced.

"Why is it too bad?" I asked.

"Because I'm having a little party Sunday night at my house. Just like four or five people. Mostly friends from the drama club. Records and snacks and talking—that kind of thing. I would've loved to hang out with you. Get to know you a little bit. But if you're busy..."

"Oh! Well… Maybe I won't do that other thing and do your thing instead."

"Oh yeah? Well," she smiled as she touched my arm, "if you really want to, that would be great. If not, well… It's totally up to you. Eight-o'clockish. The last house on Cirrus Lane, on the right. Okay? Maybe I'll see you there. Bye, Bruce."

Stacey gave my arm the tiniest squeeze, then let go and walked down the hall. I stared after her until she disappeared around the corner.

Cirrus Lane. Good name for a band—Cirrus. Like the cloud. The cloud on which I sailed that afternoon. Can you blame me?

Stacey Baer.

On the other hand, Jimmy Ruskin had asked me to play with Chance and maybe join the band.

Talk about a crossroads. A turning point. A moment of truth.

I needed a good way to decide. So I flipped a coin. It was the only logical thing to do.

Bingo!

Two young women in a white, slightly battered Cadillac convertible passed by on Brick's right, a bit faster than Brick was traveling at the moment. The driver of the Cadillac had long blonde hair that danced wildly in the wind. Her friend's hair danced too, though it was darker and shorter. Brick pumped his new 1968 silver Jaguar with more gas to take the lead once again, just as the blonde had done moments before. After all, he reasoned, the two women seemed to want him to do that, what with the way they smiled and raised their chins ever so slightly when they had momentarily pulled ahead. It was a signal, Brick decided, a mating call. Two Cinderellas in pursuit of one Prince Charming. It was his duty to use his silver machine in that manner so that they could taste its worth and commit to memory the vision of its handsome driver. Yes, they wanted it. That's what Brick believed.

Jesse, in the passenger seat, wasn't so sure.

Brick was John Brickley, president of Brickley & Burke, one of the top wholesale distributors of photographic products in the United States. Jesse was Jesse Wirth, Brickley & Burke's advertising and promotions manager, twenty-five years Brick's senior, but a handful of notches lower on the corporate totem pole. As he urged his boss to slow down, Jesse had to decide how authoritative he should sound. Jesse knew that playing cat-and-mouse on a twisty section of a heavily patrolled two-lane highway in rural Ohio, a few miles east of Youngstown, was not a wise thing to do. As everyone at Brickley & Burke knew, Jesse Wirth was not only older, but infinitely wiser—though they also knew that of the two, John Brickley was the assertive one, the aggressive one, the callous and stubborn one. At that moment, with the Jaguar in hot pursuit of the Cadillac, all Jesse could think about was how much he wanted to arrive at the photography convention in Baltimore in one piece, and he searched for the right words to use in order to make sure that would be the outcome.

"John, I don't think we should speed up so much," Jesse said over the wind that hissed through his slightly open window. "I saw a few police cars a couple of miles back."

"Loosen up, Jesse," Brick smirked. His own window was closed because he didn't want the wind to mess with his black, impeccably groomed hair. But neither did he want to sweat. So he insisted Jesse keep *his* window open a crack. It was May, and unseasonably warm, and the new Jaguar's air conditioning system had not been installed at the factory as promised; Brick would have to bring it back to the dealership in Oak Park the day after they returned to Chicago from Maryland. But Brick couldn't bear the thought of *not* showing off his gleaming automobile at the convention, which is why he used it for this trip despite the missing accessory. Besides, the long-range forecast had called for relatively mild temperatures for the next few days.

Jesse didn't mind his open window, even though conversation was more difficult because of it. He decided not to mind such trivial things for one important reason: Brickley & Burke was an enormously successful company, and Jesse was pleased to be along for the ride in the twilight of his career.

Amateur photography was on the rise, and Brick's Chicago-based firm was the first to provide to camera stores and department stores a wide variety of high-quality, easy-to-use, affordable alternatives to all the professional photographic products that were on the market. Jesse Wirth, after having dealt with unethical clients at three advertising agencies and a touch of anti-Semitism at two others over the course of his thirty-five-year career, settled down in a corporate surrounding where, at the very least, he knew he was respected. Brick did indeed respect the 'old man,' as he often referred to Jesse both in public and private. But rarely did he make a public display of that respect. He preferred to let people think it was the other way around, that it was Jesse who respected Brick. (There was a bit of irony in the fact that Jesse was the sole Brickley & Burke employee who got away with calling Brick by his real name, John, a name that Brick didn't particularly like.)

Once more, Brick pulled closer to the left of the white car with the blonde and the brunette.

"Lean back, kiddo," he said to Jesse, "I want to get a good look before I pass them for good."

As the Jaguar lined up with the Cadillac, Brick slowed down and saw that the blonde had a beautiful face and perfect white teeth, and that her friend had smooth, beautifully tanned shoulders, fully exposed.

"Bingo!" Brick decreed.

Jesse wondered: What is this little boy thinking now — that the blonde and the brunette will follow him to the next rest stop? Invite him to dinner?

Brick and Jesse were on their way to a photography industry convention at the Lord Baltimore Hotel which, in Jesse's opinion, was a very important event for the continued momentum of Brickley & Burke's marketing and promotion. The convention was to begin the following afternoon, and Jesse hoped they would arrive early. From a promotional and advertising point of view, it was important to mingle with trade press people and potential clients before the convention officially started. Jesse knew that parking could be a problem and that registration could be a red tape nightmare, and he shared these concerns with his boss many times. But Brick was Brick. In one ear and out the other.

·   ·   ·

It was their first trip together out of state since Jesse had joined the firm. As a team, Brick and Jesse routinely visited many dealers in the Chicago area, and so too had they gone to many industry dinners, although always within an hour of their Michigan Avenue office. Brick was easy to take in small doses. Jesse was nervous about this longer trip. Even on those shorter business excursions in Chicago, Brick sometimes disappeared, usually to a secluded alcove to 'talk business' with one pretty administrative assistant or another. Jesse was often embarrassed for him. But as Jesse's wife Rose once told him, why be embarrassed for him if he's not embarrassed for himself? So Jesse tried not to care.

They spent the night at a motel an hour west of Pittsburgh and hit the road again at eight o'clock in the morning. At noon, they pulled off at a truck stop diner for a quick bite to eat. They were in a town called Cumberland, just inside the Maryland border. After they ordered sandwiches and iced tea, Brick explained to Jesse his plan to build a nationwide network of salesmen and to have one large annual Brickley & Burke national sales meeting at an exclusive country club of his choice.

"In a year or two," Brick said confidently, "when a country club hears that Brickley & Burke is coming to town — Bingo! The red carpet goes out and the gorgeous masseuses in their satin robes come over to give each of our guys a well-deserved rubdown. It'll be great."

Brick's comment reminded Jesse of a meeting the two of them had in Chicago with a new photo dealer. They met him at the

Chicago Hilton. While they were there, Brick paid for a massage for Jesse, the dealer, and for himself. Jesse wasn't interested in the massage, but Brick had insisted. He even made fun of Jesse later that day in front of the new dealer, calling him a boy scout and a man so faithful to his wife that he breaks into hives by simply looking at another woman.

John Brickley, at that Hilton meeting, dropped another fifteen or twenty notches on the respect scale, as far as Jesse Wirth was concerned. Jesse thought to himself: I'll still work for the guy, I'll do a good job for him, I'll be amicable—but I won't respect him. He can probably live without my respect, anyway, so he won't get any. Not now, not ever.

And that was the way it had been ever since.

•   •   •

"What are you thinking about, Jesse?"

They were in a booth at another truck stop diner, this one in Frederick, an hour from Baltimore, and remarkably similar to all the others. It was the middle of the afternoon. Brick had just returned from the counter, where he had bought a newspaper. When he returned, he found Jesse staring trance-like through the dirty booth window.

"Jesse, what are you thinking about?"

"Sorry, John. Just daydreaming, I guess."

"Look at this headline," Brick said. He held up the newspaper. The headline read *Israel Raids Lebanon in Response to Attack on El Al Airliner.* "That's one hell of a tough little country, that Israel. Huh?"

Jesse wondered what Brick was up to now. Did he wish to pursue a serious line of conversation? That was unlikely because it had nothing to do with women, photography, or Brickley & Burke. Or, as an attempt to hold on to Jesse's loyalty, was he trying to convince Jesse that he truly was interested in his opinion on the matter?

Regardless of the true motive, Jesse was determined to cut the conversation short, having resolved long ago never to discuss politics or religion with business associates. And since that headline could easily bring up both politics *and* religion, it was to be avoided like the ten plagues. To change the subject, Jesse looked at his watch.

"Forgive me for changing the subject," he said, "but you did agree to try to get to Baltimore as early as possible, John. That's a good idea." Brick stayed silent. "That way we can get into the convention as soon as it opens without worrying about forms and all the other things we'll have to do. It'll be good for business."

"Okay, Jesse," Brick relented. "Maybe you have a point. But let me just take one look around to see if I can spot anyone going to the convention. That could be good for business too, you know — to get in a little industry chat beforehand."

"Only truckers are here, John. I don't think there's anyone here who's — "

"You're wrong," Brick interrupted firmly, like a father to a child. "When I was buying the newspaper, I overheard that Chinese guy over there talking to that well-built redhead about suggested retail prices. Sounded like convention talk to me. I'll be right back."

Brick stood up, brushed himself off, planted a smile on his face, and walked toward the redhead. Jesse surmised that John Brickley must have stood similarly tall with as expansive a smile when he worked as a radio advertising salesman after college. Heaping on the charm was how he made sales and got ahead. That was before his wealthy father, John Brickley, Sr., died and left John Jr. a large sum of money with which he and his college chum James Burke started Brickley & Burke.

As Brick passed the shapely redhead, he did a well-rehearsed double-take and then leaned over to say something to her privately. The Chinese man sat idly by. Brick and the woman chatted for a while. He gave her a business card. They smiled at each other. Then Brick returned to the booth.

"Bingo!" Brick said triumphantly.

"Don't tell me she's going to the convention!" Jesse stated, quite surprised at the coincidence.

"No," Brick replied. "But she said that her father owns a small department store in Washington, and he's thinking of stocking some photo equipment. She works at the store." Brick did not let his confident grin disappear. "She said we should stop by one day and she'll make us feel at home." He tapped his wedding ring on his water glass as if to toast himself. Then Brick and Jesse left the diner.

•　　•　　•

When they were thirty-five miles from Baltimore, Brick filled up his Jaguar one last time. The tank was already half full, but he didn't want to take time out during the convention to fill up, especially if he and some guests wanted to take a drive along the Maryland coastline. He wanted his tank full.

At the gas station, Jesse went to the bathroom at the side of the building and Brick went inside to buy a Coke. It was hotter than it had been the day before. When Jesse came out of the bathroom, he saw Brick just outside the door, holding his Coke as he talked to a tall, slender woman with jet-black hair. (Brick hadn't bought a Coke for Jesse.)

Jesse went back to the car and waited. He even ended up paying the two dollars for Brick's half tank of gas.

Five minutes later, Brick joined him. He was beaming.

"Bingo!" Brick said as he started the ignition.

Brick obviously wanted Jesse to ask what had transpired with the black-haired woman—but Jesse didn't bite. He was tired, hot, and wanted to get to the convention. He looked forward to it being over so that he could go home to be with Rose. He wished Brick would want to be with his own wife, but that was probably asking too much; people can't be changed— they have to want to change themselves. John Brickley, Jesse thought despondently, would never change.

"Is she gorgeous, or what?" Brick said. It startled Jesse out of his inner thoughts.

"What? Who?"

"That woman. No bust, but legs that don't quit. Nice ass, too. And that short black hair just turns me on. I can't explain it."

Half an hour later, Brick merged the Jaguar onto a one-lane highway that took them away from the thoroughfare on which they had been traveling.

"John," Jesse said, "you're on the wrong road. There's a more direct route into Baltimore."

"We've got plenty of time, old man," Brick said. "Listen, kiddo. I need strength for the convention and long-legged ladies give me strength. Face it, Jesse, there are a lot of middle-aged beauties in boring marriages looking for a guy like me to give them a boost from time to time. It makes them feel better and then they go out and buy things. That's good for business. Now listen to this. Back at the gas station, that tall, short-haired doll told me to meet her at a motel in Towson, just outside of Baltimore. Something called the Charlemagne Inn. And she has a friend for you, if you're interested."

Not much surprised Jesse Wirth anymore. This was the exception.

"What?" he bellowed.

"She said we can meet the two of them in a private little room called The Sunset Suite at the back of the motel," Brick explained. "At four-thirty. She repeated it three times, Jesse. The

Sunset Suite at four-thirty. She said they'll be waiting for us there. And she winked and said to make sure we're alone."

"John, you know I can't."

"Of course you can." Brick glanced over at Jesse and saw a look of serious distraction on his face. In the office, Jesse was always calm and in control; now, suddenly, he looked frightened and lost. "Listen, kiddo," Brick continued, "it's probably only five or six miles from the convention, and we really don't know what she has in mind for you and her friend."

"John—"

"I told her I had a colleague with me and she said it was no problem. But for all we know, her friend might just want to have a drink with you at the bar. I bet that's all it is. Nothing to worry about. You and her friend will have a drink and chat while mama long legs and I... well... while we get to know each other. We'll be at the Lord Baltimore for the convention an hour later. I promise." Brick smiled and slapped Jesse's knee. "Betcha the convention won't even start until you show your face. There's no photography industry without Jesse Wirth."

Good try, Jesse thought to himself—but it won't work. He knew his own breaking point still loomed somewhere out in the distance, but exactly where, he wasn't sure. Baltimore? On the ride back to Chicago? When would it happen? During which business meeting? At which convention? When would he tell John Brickley what he really thought of him? Maybe never, Jesse admitted to himself. Maybe it just wasn't in him.

He looked out at the white pine trees that lined both sides of the road because that was better than thinking too much about John Brickley. The trees were a pleasant diversion for a weak mind. Someone or something stronger than Jesse Wirth would have to give John Brickley the wake-up call he deserved.

•   •   •

The Charlemagne Inn looked like three old bungalows pushed together and held in place with clusters of mimosa trees. The parking lot was covered from one end to the other with a mixture of gravel and pebbles.

Brick parked the car, and he and Jesse walked to the lobby. It was four-thirty-seven, seven minutes later than they were supposed to arrive. Brick planned it that way; he liked it when people waited for him (although had no patience to wait for anyone himself). That, Jesse realized, was why Brick had gotten off the main highway and wasted time on a secondary road. He wanted to begin the convention with a victory, and keeping this long-legged, short-haired beauty waiting might increase his chance for a victory because the woman would be *oh so ready* for him. Brick wanted this one badly. Jesse could sense it.

Once at the inn, Brick and Jesse followed the signs that led them to The Sunset Suite. In the last hallway they entered, they saw little printed signs on all the doors: The Garden Suite, The Galaxy Suite, The Ocean Suite, and The Sunset Suite.

Brick patted back his hair, cleared his throat, and gave two solid knocks on the door.

"Don't worry," he reassured Jesse one last time. "You won't have to do anything you don't want to do."

The door opened almost immediately. Someone had been right there, inside, next to the doorframe. It was an old man on a metal folding chair. Jesse noticed him right away, but Brick did not. What Brick noticed as he looked into the room made his face turn ashen: two dozen elderly people sat on metal folding chairs around four large round tables.

A small, thin-haired woman at one table called out "Bingo!" At the far end of the room, behind a long bridge table, another old man looked up and said, "You're sure, Libby? You have B-11?"

"I'm sure, I'm sure," Libby said indignantly. "What am I, blind?"

Brick backed up to look once more at the sign on the door. As much as he hoped to have made a mistake, he had to acknowledge that he did not. The sign said The Sunset Suite. Brick's mouth hung open, speechless, and his body quivered ever so slightly as Libby stood up to collect her winnings. Jesse watched as his young boss's eyebrows furrowed at deep angles in a mixture of emotions that could have been confusion, or anger, or pain. Probably all three.

Jesse instantly realized that the leggy, short-haired woman at the gas station knew exactly what she was doing when she told the brash young executive to meet her in The Sunset Suite at the Charlemagne Inn at four-thirty. As he stood at the door of the suite, Brick had no clue what to do, none, probably for the first time in his life. And for the first time since having joined the firm, Jesse Wirth laughed at his young boss. It was a laugh that built slowly and then exploded, the sort of laugh he would never have released at a Brickley & Burke meeting or even in the car with Brick. But Jesse feared no reprisal because by the time the laugh actually came out of his mouth, Brick was on his way back to the parking lot. No doubt he'd lay a heavy foot on the gas pedal of the Jaguar to get back onto the highway as fast as possible.

Jesse knew beyond a doubt that they would get to the convention on time.

Tabernacle Tom and His Absolutely True, Really Weird Story

The weirdest story I ever heard? You mean that someone else told me? Let me think... True or not true?... True? You wanna hear a true, weird story that someone else told me?... Hmmm... Okay. Here's one. It happened this summer. There was this guy at Camp Gemini, a handyman named Tom... No, not Jeremy. *Gemini*. Camp Gemini. It's in Tabernacle, which is a little town here in New Jersey, in the south part, sort of, in the middle of nowhere. Somewhere in the Pine Barrens, I think. Actually, Tom called himself Tabernacle Tom, and so did a lot of us campers... Why? Because he used to live in New York City and was driving down to Wildwood for a vacation one day and there was a fire in the Pine Barrens near the Garden State Parkway and the highway patrol guys made all the cars get off and he ended up having lunch in Tabernacle and he liked it there so much that he never left. At least that's what he told us. Anyway, one night during the third session at camp, we asked Tabernacle Tom to tell us a true story about something weird or strange or magical or supernatural that once happened to him. So he did, and it was the weirdest story I ever heard. So that's the one I'll tell you. Okay? Ready? So, there were five of us in our group who absolutely love that kind of stuff—you know, magic and supernatural things and junk like that—and Tom seemed to be the kind of guy who would have all kinds of stories, which I guess is why we asked him in the first place... How did we know that about Tom? Well, we didn't really know it, we just thought it. Here's why. A couple of us in the group use nicknames for ourselves, like Major Nelson and Darrin Stevens—you know, from *I Dream of Jeannie* and *Bewitched* on TV?—and Tabernacle Tom knew about our nicknames but never made fun of us, so I guess that was a clue that he was a neat guy who would have some pretty weird stories. I mean, he thought it was cool for us kids to have nicknames from TV shows, so we thought that he had to be cool, too. You know? That's why we asked him if he had any weird stories. Anyway, those TV shows I mentioned? *I Dream of Jeannie* and *Bewitched*? Well, in case you don't know, in *I Dream of Jeannie*, Major Nelson is an astronaut who finds a genie bottle when he lands on some island somewhere, and Barbara Eden pops out and calls him Master and can do all kinds of magical things, like make things appear, or take both of them to another country in two seconds, or turn pain-in-the-neck people into donkeys and stuff like that. And in *Bewitched*, Elizabeth Montgomery is a beautiful witch named Samantha Stevens who's married to a regular guy named Darrin, and she can do the same things that Barbara Eden can do, except that Barbara Eden crosses her arms and blinks her eyes and Elizabeth Montgomery just twitches her nose... Don't worry—I'm getting to it. Just hold on a sec. This stuff is important to know first. So Tom always hung around our cabin at Camp Gemini, even when he didn't have anything to fix or clean up. I guess he just liked the stuff we talked about. Also, he loved Twinkies—I mean he really, really loved them, even though he was skinny—and this fat kid in our group named Jay always had dozens of Twinkies in the bunk, even though we're not supposed to have candy. Jay snuck it in from home and Tabernacle Tom had about five of them a day. He never got caught eating a Twinkie, but he actually got yelled at a few times by the camp director for other things, like hanging out with us kids. I don't think staff members are supposed to hang out with kids. Except counselors, of course. But Tom always did. He also spent a lot of time in the dining hall playing the jukebox, which he wasn't supposed to do either, and the camp director caught him there a few times. I don't think the camp director likes him too much. There was a rumor during the last session that he won't be back at camp next year. Oh — and he also told us that he might get drafted and have to go to Vietnam. I hope not. A lot of guys his age have to go. You know that, right? Anyway, there was this one night when we had no activities or anything like that, and our counselors were at some kind of staff meeting. So when we saw Tabernacle Tom walk by our cabin we asked him to come inside and tell us a story about something weird or strange or magical or supernatural that happened to him once. So he came in. But then he surprised us when he said that there is no such thing as magic. He looked really disappointed when he said it. He said, Boys, I hate to tell you this, but there is no magic in the world. There is nothing mystical or paranormal or psychic that ever happens. That's what he said. Isn't it funny how I remember it word for word? I guess it just stuck in my head because it was only a few weeks ago. Anyway, one of us said to him — maybe it was me — one of us asked him why he believed there was no magic in the world or anything like that, and why he was so sad about it. So he took a really deep breath and then he said, Well, boys, let me tell you a story about something that happened to me a few months ago, and then you'll see why. So this is the story he told us. He told us that before he got the job at Camp Gemini he had an apartment in New York City. He lived there all alone because his new wife had just walked out on him. He didn't have a job either. He didn't even have any food in his apartment, not even a Twinkie. He was really depressed. So one day he takes a walk around his block and sees an old man with a bushy moustache that covers almost his whole face and a big gold earring in one ear. Tabernacle Tom goes over to the old man because he looks like a really interesting guy, and the guy looks at Tom and says, May I help you? And Tom asks him who he is, and the guy says he's a mystic who travels through time to make wishes come true for people. Tom says, Yeah, right, and I'm John Lennon. But the guy just stares at Tom, and Tom stares back and gets this really weird feeling that something is up with this old guy — that there's something really unusual about him. So he asks the old man if he can make one of his wishes come true, and the guy says Yes, of course, my good man, I can do that — but just one wish. The old man asks Tabernacle Tom what his one wish will be, and Tom says that the thing that drives him crazier than anything else in the whole world is the fact that Major Nelson in *I Dream of Jeannie* never wants Barbara Eden to do the magical things that a genie can do and that Darrin Stevens in *Bewitched* never wants Elizabeth Montgomery to do the magical things that a witch can do. Tabernacle Tom says to the old man, There's something completely nuts about someone not wanting a beautiful genie or a beautiful witch to do magical things for you. Tom says to the guy, If I was Major Nelson or Darrin Stevens, I'd let my genie or my witch use their powers all the time to get things done or to make things happen that I want to happen. He says that Major Nelson and Darrin Stevens must have been complete idiots not to use Barbara Eden and Elizabeth Montgomery and all their powers to do all kinds of neat stuff. But the old guy just repeats himself and says, What is your one wish, sir? So Tabernacle Tom says, My one wish is for Barbara Eden and Elizabeth Montgomery to appear in my apartment so that I can ask each of them to do just one favor for me, because I'm not as stupid as Major Nelson and Darrin Stevens. So the old man asks Tabernacle Tom to take him to his apartment. When they're in Tom's living room, the old man rubs his hands together, closes his eyes, opens them, snaps his fingers, and suddenly Barbara Eden and Elizabeth Montgomery are sitting right there on Tom's couch. He can't believe it. He gets really excited. Tabernacle Tom says to Barbara Eden, Make a Twinkie appear on the coffee table. And Barbara Eden says, Go get one yourself, buddy. So Tom asks, Why should I do that? And Barbara Eden says, Because I'm not your maid, that's why. So Tom turns to Elizabeth Montgomery and says, Make my ex-wife fall in love with me again. Elizabeth Montgomery looks at Tom and says, What do I look like, a matchmaker? So Tom says, Can't you just twitch your nose and make it happen? And Elizabeth Montgomery says, I can twitch my nose, but your ex-wife won't like you any more than I do right now. So Tabernacle Tom turns to the old man and says, What's going on? What about my wish? And the old man says, You got your wish. And Tom says, How the hell did I get my wish? And the old man says, You did not wish for Jeannie the genie and Samantha the witch to come to your apartment. You wished for Barbara Eden and Elizabeth Montgomery. They are both here, but they are just actresses who have no powers. Then the old man tells Tabernacle Tom that since his wish has been granted, Barbara Eden and Elizabeth Montgomery would have to leave now. He rubs his hands together, closes his eyes, opens his eyes, snaps his fingers, and Barbara Eden and Elizabeth Montgomery disappear. The old man leaves the apartment, and Tabernacle Tom is really mad about the whole thing. And that's weirdest absolutely true story I ever heard.

The Rise and Fall of a COO

'Wunderkind' Peterson Ousted from Hemisphere Digital

**COO's Off-the-Cuff Cafeteria
Comment Said to Cause Dismissal**

Industry Reaction Still Being Measured

Special to the New York Times

Stamford, CT—Gary Peterson, the 36-year-old chief operating officer at Hemisphere Digital, a Stamford-based company that is one of the fastest-growing telecommunications firms in the country, was relieved of his position on Tuesday in a move that sent tremors through the industry. Hemisphere's president and vice president of human resources did not return calls for comments.

Mr. Peterson, who rose quickly through the corporate ranks at AT&T and Verizon for the last five years before being tapped by Hemisphere as a senior vice president last February, was known for his supportive management style and his innovative ideas. Named COO this past July, Mr. Peterson became the youngest senior executive in Hemisphere's history and reportedly earned an annual salary in excess of $1.8 million.

Despite the rising tide of anger nationwide against exorbitant executive salaries, several company employees interviewed by the *Times* indicate that Mr. Peterson was held in high esteem by the workforce because of how assertively he looked after their needs and interests. His biggest priorities at the company included employee recognition, employee engagement, and employee satisfaction. It was rumored last month that Mr. Peterson declined to take his scheduled vacation when he learned other employees had to work overtime to complete a special project. He stayed in the building with them for moral support.

Three of Mr. Peterson's former colleagues at AT&T and Verizon were quoted in trade magazines saying they knew that his specific career goal was eventually to become Hemisphere's COO, and that he worked carefully and prudently to make that happen.

According to several sources at Hemisphere, all of whom requested anonymity for fear of reprisal by current senior management, Mr. Peterson began the week last Monday visiting the company cafeteria to have breakfast with lower- and mid-level employees, as was his daily routine. Before ordering his food, Mr. Peterson looked through *Men's Health*, a magazine typically available on a table next to the coffee machine. He apparently turned to an advertisement in the magazine for the male enhancement drug Viagra. Mr. Peterson, it was reported, smirked, shook his head, and put the magazine back down on the table. He then ordered his breakfast and sat with a group of employees from the finance department. A copy of the magazine obtained by the *Times* shows that the advertisement headline and subhead said, "Smile again! Most men over 50 have some form of erectile dysfunction. So do something about it. Make your best-laid plan!" A series of accompanying photographs showed a woman sticking a ballpoint pen into its cap, suggestively, slowly and repeatedly.

Mr. Peterson returned to the cafeteria at 10:30 for a mid-morning coffee break (which, sources say, is an initiative he promoted for all employees as a way for them to get away from their desks and to meet other colleagues). As Mr. Peterson entered the room, on the cafeteria's wall-mounted television set was a commercial on CNN for Viagra. According to a video transcript obtained by the *Times*, the ad said, "Men, take charge of your passion. Don't let your energy level sag. Get it up! Ask your doctor if Viagra is right for you." The video showed an actor holding a large banana, and smiling. The cafeteria's cashier told the *Times* that Mr. Peterson's reaction was similar to the one he had had that morning after reading *Men's Health* magazine. Mr. Peterson then took his coffee to a table at the back of the cafeteria, where he sat with employees from the maintenance department.

When Mr. Peterson returned for lunch at approximately 12:30, John Elcott, president and CEO of Hemisphere Digital, and Cheryl Tunny, senior vice president of human resources, were in the cafeteria and asked Mr. Peterson to sit with them. Mr. Peterson opted, however, to sit with members of the corporate communications department. On the way to their table, Mr. Peterson overheard a radio that was playing in the kitchen, on which a Viagra commercial was being aired. One of the food service workers told the *Times* that what Mr. Peterson reacted to most stridently was a particular line in the commercial: "Viagra gives a stiff salute to men who want to live life as long and as hard as they can." Mr. Peterson, the food service worker said, shook his head, ordered his food, and sat down with the corporate communications employees to wait for his meal.

The corporate communications employees collectively seemed to be in a foul mood, according to a visiting coffee service representative with whom the *Times* also spoke. This is most likely due to the fact that a series of webinar-related issues were having a negative impact on a departmental project. The corporate communications team seemed inconsolable, so Mr. Peterson stood up, pushed his chair back, and addressed the group by saying, "Come on, people. Take charge of your passion!" Caught off guard, no one on the corporate communications team responded. So Mr. Peterson stood on top of the table, took a pen out of his shirt pocket, and shouted, "Let's give confidence a big, stiff salute." He took the cap off the pen and proceeded to replace and then remove it several times in a very suggestive manner. "Let's make our best-laid plans, and let's make them as long and as hard as we can." He bent down, grabbed a banana from an employee's plate, held it in front of him and said, "Remember, as long and hard as we can."

Mr. Peterson was terminated within the hour.

Men with Yellow Balls

My husband, Sam, urged me to forget about what happened after I told him I felt partially responsible for it. What happened was he nearly soiled his pants at the offices of *The Metro Sun*, a daily newspaper in New York City. I asked him why I should forget about it. He said number one, it wasn't my fault, number two, the operative word was *nearly*, and number three, the incident doesn't bother him at all. He insists it shouldn't bother me, either.

It doesn't really bother me, but it's such an unusual tale that it deserves to be shared. I'd like to be the one to share it. Despite Sam's assertion that it doesn't bother him, I bet if you dug below the surface you'd find he's just a little embarrassed by the whole thing, and he might never want to tell the story himself. So I must.

To begin with, it's important to know that Sam has wanted to have an article of his own published in a New York City publication since before we were married. (Anything other than the *New York Post*; he feels that the *Post*'s spoofy headlines show a lack of respect for professional journalism.) Sam and I married nine years ago. He has submitted articles to Manhattan-based magazines and newspapers every month since then. We live in Oyster Bay, on Long Island, and he has written about our town for local weeklies three or four times in the past. One article was about how all the monuments to President Theodore Roosevelt, who lived in Oyster Bay for much of his adult life, were in terrible disrepair. Another article was about all the songs that feature Long Island locales. (Billy Joel is mentioned several times. No big surprise there.) But it is the validation that a New York City byline would lend to his reputation that really drives Sam's ambition. He's an excellent writer, but the competition in New York is fierce, as you might expect, and as he's explained to me many times, publishers and editors rarely respond to submissions of completed pieces or even to proposals. Nor do publishers or editors offer much advice anymore on what a writer can do to increase his or her chances of getting published in the first place. The rejections, if they come at all, are impersonal emails or form letters. That makes Sam angry. I can't blame him.

Whenever Sam receives a rejection letter, or worse, when he receives nothing at all after weeks or months of waiting, my heart breaks a little more for him. His spirits invariably sink a notch or two each time.

Sam commutes by train to New York City, where he works at the Department of Transportation. As ironic as it may sound, Sam is in charge of writing, editing, and mailing denial letters to people who try to get reimbursed for dents and dings that their cars suffer when towed by the city from illegal parking spots. He hates the job. Despises it. That only breaks my heart even more every time I think about it.

Sometimes I accompany him on the train because I may go back to school one day to study to become an architect, and I like to seek out some of the more unusual designs in the city and study them up close. Plus, it's nice just to spend more time with Sam; I'm not sure, but perhaps that helps him a little. Someone to talk to. Moral support. Two weeks ago, I joined him for the hour-long commute. We parted at Penn Station. He went one way, I went the other. I stopped at a newsstand on Seventh

Avenue and noticed a daily newspaper called *The Metro Sun*. The story on front page was about how Westchester County, just north of the city, was currently hosting two motion picture production companies that were shooting movies there. It occurred to me that the *Metro Sun* might be interested in an article that explores how Long Island tries to attract television production companies to shoot sitcoms and dramas in several towns. I thought Sam could do the research and write an article about it. So I bought a copy of *The Metro Sun* and gave it to Sam that night when he got home. I mentioned my idea. He liked it and immediately sent a proposal to the editor.

Sam received a phone call a few days later from the assistant to Grant Jarvey, editor-in-chief of *The Metro Sun*. The assistant said that Mr. Jarvey would like to meet with him in person and talk about the article idea "prior to the strong possibility of having it officially assigned."

The Metro Sun has its headquarters downtown, in a tall office building near Greenwich Village. The building may have been one of Manhattan's smaller skyscrapers, but at twelve or fifteen stories, it was still impressive enough to make Sam feel as if he had slipped one toe in the door of professional New York City journalism. That's exactly what I wanted for him. He worked hard for it and deserved it so much.

Several architectural elements blended to give an austere, successful, old-money ambiance to the place, such as the marble facade of the building, the intricate design of the brickwork that surrounds the entrance, and the tall lobby windows. (Sam didn't share these thoughts with me; I studied this building a few months ago on my own, which is how I know all about it. Besides, Sam would never describe buildings that way.) As Sam walked in, he was confident that at last, after a decade of trying, he had a golden opportunity to get published in a New York City daily newspaper. The impressive lobby alone — all murals and echoes—made it seem worthwhile, regardless of the outcome. A byline and a paycheck would be the icing on the cake.

Holding his old leather briefcase, Sam walked further into the lobby and heard melodic voices sail out in harmony from some unknown point high in the cathedral ceiling. He said it was a peaceful and uplifting sound that made him think to himself, What a compassionate touch in the middle of such a heartless city.

There was a semicircle reception desk with a young woman seated behind it. The woman asked for Sam's name and checked it against a list on her desk. Then she gave him a clipboard with a form to sign. Sam put his briefcase on the reception desk and signed the form. The young woman told him to take the elevator to the ninth floor. He thanked her, grabbed his briefcase, went to the elevator, and pressed the 'Up' button.

The melodic voices followed him into the elevator. Each elevator wall had reflective gold panels. Sam looked at himself in a gold reflection and made a mental note to buy himself a new suit once *The Metro Sun* payment came through. The one he had on looked worn and ratty, like the three others in his closet at home. (For months I had been urging him to buy a new suit, but his stock answer was that a heartless job requires a wretched suit.) He also saw in the reflection that there was a sticker on the side of his old briefcase that hadn't been there before. It was a drawing of two hands clutching a ray of sun, and under that image, in Asian-style lettering, were the words *Peace Through Friendship*. He thought that perhaps someone on the street had slapped it on his briefcase when he wasn't paying attention. Sam told me he muttered 'Damn city' under his breath in the empty elevator when he saw the unsolicited sticker. But he was quick to add that he wasn't overly upset, for the reflection in the elevator panel also reiterated to him just how old his briefcase really was; a healthy payment from the newspaper would mean that soon he'd be able to buy not just a new suit but also a new briefcase.

When he arrived on the ninth floor, the elevator doors opened and Sam stepped out into a smaller lobby. He noticed that the image that was on his briefcase — two hands clutching a sunray, with *Peace Through Friendship* scripted below — was the same image affixed to the wall in front of him, but this time it was much bigger and in three dimensions. Nobody was behind the reception desk. More choral harmonies accompanied him down the hall as he went to look for someone to take him to see Grant Jarvey, editor of *The Metro Sun*. The singing (or as Sam put it when he told me the story, "that goddamn wretched humming") was starting to annoy him.

More than an hour had passed from the time Sam had left his office at the Department of Transportation. He had to use the men's room. He remembered he had passed one in the hallway, so he backtracked to find it, but it was locked. Fortunately, he maintained relative certainty that as soon as he found the receptionist, he could borrow the key and eliminate the possibility of needing to squirm and cross his legs throughout his important and exciting discussion with Mr. Jarvey.

All the offices on either side of the long hallway had open doors, but as he passed one office after another, Sam saw they all were empty. At least they *appeared* to be empty. It was a curious scene: a newspaper office with no people. He assumed they were all in an editorial meeting elsewhere in the building.

Sam randomly poked his head into one office and saw a young man, about his own age, crouched in the corner, in a squat position, rocking back and forth slowly. On the wall above the man was that same drawing of the two hands around a ray of sun, and below that was the *Peace Through Friendship* tagline. The man looked up quickly, and just as quickly put his finger to his lips, pointed upward, then returned to his rocking. Sam stood still in confused silence. The man finally spoke. He said three words—"Peace through friendship"—and asked Sam if he wanted to join him. Then he stood up.

According to Sam, physically this man was a perfect specimen of the young urban professional: clean cut, thin, full head of well-groomed light brown hair, impeccably tailored suit without a single wrinkle. Sam told him he had a one-thirty meeting with Grant Jarvey. He gave the young man his name, said he was a freelance writer, and tried desperately to ignore the fact that he had just witnessed the guy huddled like a dapper bum around an invisible bonfire.

The man told Sam that it was Renewal Time. (The capital letters are my contribution to the story, only because it seems as if that's how the man had intended it.) He said that Mr. Jarvey would be available once Renewal Time was over. Grant Jarvey was very punctual, the young man said. Then he asked Sam if he wanted to Renew himself while he waited.

It may go without saying that what my husband really wanted to do was *relieve* himself, not renew himself. But Sam knew that wasn't the proper thing to say or the right time to say it—unless, of course, that's what the young man had meant. Sam wasn't entirely certain. So he simply asked about the meaning of Renewal Time. The man responded that Renewal Time meant meditation time. He explained that everyone at the company was required to partake of Renewal Time at that hour of the day.

The man apparently realized that he had not introduced himself, so he took a step closer to Sam and said that his name was Matthew. That's when Sam noticed Matthew had two little yellow balls in his hands. It wasn't clear right away if the yellow balls were solid like a golf ball or pliable like a Nerf ball. Matthew put the yellow balls on his desk and extended his arm to Sam. The men shook hands. Matthew repeated those three words—"Peace through friendship"—and thanked Sam for sharing a part of himself. Sam didn't know what that meant, either, but let it go for the moment.

On Matthew's desk were three neatly stacked piles of papers, each weighed down by similar yellow balls, larger ones this time; Sam suddenly realized that they must represent little suns, which echoed the clutched sunray figures on all the wall.

So he simply asked if those images were indeed little suns. Sam hoped to create a friendly repartee with Matthew just in case the man was someone with whom he might have to consult as time went on. I suppose it's pretty obvious, too, that Sam wanted to be friendly so that Matthew wouldn't mind pointing him toward the nearest restroom. The feeling — and I'm sure you know the feeling I'm talking about — was now urgent. Matthew explained that the little yellow balls were called Soors. Sam thought he said the word sewers and repeated it that way. So Matthew spelled it out: S, O, O, R, S. He said that Soors keep *Metro Sun* staffers focused on their work and help them accomplish their daily tasks. They must all earn their Soors, Matthew said. They must earn them through patience and sharing.

Sam nodded as if he understood all this, although what he understood was nothing at all. He told Matthew that he was not familiar with the term, Soors, and wondered if it stood for something.

Matthew explained it was an obscure word in an ancient Chinese dialect, and that it has many meanings, such as understanding, salvation, tranquility, and confidence. He said it was a marvelous word because of how many splendid meanings it had.

Matthew sat down behind his desk and questioned whether Sam had ever written before for *The Metro Sun*. Sam said he had not and explained that his wife (me, of course) had come across the newspaper just a few days before and thought it might be a good outlet for his freelance work. (Sam always gives credit where credit is due — although I wouldn't have minded if he left me out of the equation just to speed things along.)

Matthew assured Sam that *The Metro Sun* would indeed be a good journalistic outlet for him, and thanked him for having offered his ideas and his gifts. He said he knew Sam would soon earn his Soors. "When you finally earn your Soors," Matthew explained, "you'll know that you have arrived as a genuine writer, and that's when the rewards begin, financially and otherwise."

Sam was uncertain if Matthew was being silly or completely serious. If what he had just said was a joke, Sam didn't get it. If it was serious, he *still* didn't get it.

He asked Matthew about his job at the newspaper. Matthew said he was the company's accounts payable manager. Sam (who desperately wanted to believe that Matthew *had* been joking) made a lighthearted crack about how grateful he'd be if Matthew could add a few extra zeros to his first payment. But Matthew did not appreciate the silly quip. He implied that Sam should learn more about the organization before making such jokes. Sam apologized. (I'm sure that must have been very hard for him to do.) Matthew wanted to know if anyone had told Sam that in order to earn his Soors, he needed to donate his gift for one year. Sam had no clue what 'his gift' meant, so he asked. Matthew explained that his gift was his talent—his writing. In other words (as Sam had Matthew clarify), he would have to write a few articles first with no compensation at all.

Sam told him that when he spoke with Mr. Jarvey's assistant on the phone, the assistant said nothing about the group being a religious cult.

Bad choice of words, Sam!

His comment was a poisoned arrow that went right through Matthew's heart. (My description, not Sam's.) Matthew stood up brusquely and said that they were not a cult, that they were known as Peace Through Friendship, a former sect of the Unification Church, under the peaceful guidance of Swami Kar Khoom Yani, once a disciple of the Reverend Sun Myung Moon before they parted paths. (I have no clue how Sam remembered all that, but he did—and I wrote it down because if I didn't I would never have been able to repeat it just now.) Matthew said that the group represented a life choice, that *The Metro Sun* was a legitimate New York City newspaper that covered everything from politics and sports to entertainment and crime, that editorially they were an independent organ, and that corporately they were an operating division of Peace Through Friendship, Incorporated, a small but successful publishing arm of the family.

Yes, Matthew spoke that jumble of words, Sam repeated it to me verbatim, and I wrote it all down.

Being a little more composed now than he had been when Sam shot him through the heart, Matthew insisted that Grant Jarvey was someone who Sam would like because he embodies all that is good about their family. And then he repeated those words which had become quite tiresome to Sam: patience and sharing.

Sam (no doubt with difficulty) also repeated them, and suddenly realized just how much it sounded like a mantra. He asked if he should wait for Mr. Jarvey in the lobby down the hall. Matthew said that would be fine. Then Sam asked to borrow a key for the men's room, but Matthew informed him that all the bathrooms were locked during Renewal Time. He put his hands on the two yellow Soors on his desk. All Sam could do was smile and tiptoe out of the office. He was more than happy to leave Matthew and his Soors and the scary drawing on the wall and the spooky chorus in the air—

—only to bump into the drawing and the chorus when he returned to the hallway. He tried the bathroom door again, but it was still locked, as he had suspected it would be. The urge to go was stronger than ever and getting more painful by the moment. He debated going back to Matthew's office to beg for the key, but was certain it would be met with a lecture of some sort. Sam didn't think he could handle that. (I know Sam. He would've wanted to throw something at Matthew.)

He ran to the lobby at the other end of the hall. This time a young woman was there, and he asked her to please point him to the nearest unlocked restroom. He said he would be eternally grateful for the information. The young woman said she was sorry, but that only *Metro Sun* staffers have keys. Sam wanted to know why she wasn't considered a *Metro Sun* staffer (with a key) and she said that she was a temp. Sam asked if she came from a cult temp agency. The young woman looked entirely confused at that. (I can't blame her.) Sam apologized and asked if there was anyone at all to ask about a key to the bathroom. Why, he wondered aloud, was the place so empty? The temp said it was because this seemed to be the time that all the men in the company squatted down in their offices clutching their balls. Sam was certain he had misheard her, but she repeated it, this time specifying that what they were clutching were their *yellow* balls.

Sam explained to her that those balls are called Soors. She repeated it back to him, pronouncing it as sewers. Sam spelled it for her. The young woman shrugged her shoulders, then said that she had strict instructions not to bother anyone while they're squeezing their balls.

Sam asked if it would be okay to walk around in search of someone who had a key. The temp said that since he had already been allowed to come up from the downstairs lobby that it would probably be okay. Sam thanked her and went down another hallway. The chorus urged him on, and so did his own feeling of doom—liquid metabolic doom. (I'm pretty sure Sam came up with that phrase when he first told me this story and that it stuck with me; it doesn't sound like something I'd come up with on my own.)

At the end of the hallway was a large alcove filled with metal shelves and what looked like maintenance supplies. Sam went inside, trusting that there may be a utility sink that he could use to take care of business. On the shelves he saw boxes and folders and copy machine cartridges and rumpled paper bags and other assorted office items. All the boxes were open. Inside one of them were a dozen long, clear plastic tubes stuffed with dead single roses. There were hundreds of buttons and rolls of stickers in another box. A third box stored little collection cans that said *Patience and Sharing* with that now all-too-familiar sun-and-hands logo. At the back of the alcove, against the wall, was a framed poster of The Reverend Sun Myung Moon, but someone had drawn a black eye on him with magic marker. There were also several piles of playing cards, and Sam saw the cards had a picture of a white-bearded Asian man on one side. Sam assumed it was Swami Kar Loom Yani, or whatever his name was. (Sam said it a little differently each time he repeated this part of the story.) On the other side of each playing card was a photo of a yellow ball — obviously a Soor — though each card had a Soor of a different size.

But there was no utility sink.

Now in complete misery, Sam knew he had no choice but to leave the alcove and come up with another plan. But as he was about to walk out, he spotted party items stacked neatly on a little snack table in a corner of the alcove: white paper plates and tall red plastic cups, plastic knives and forks, napkins, that kind of stuff. It was a godsend. (Sam's word.) He peaked around the corner to see if anyone was in the hallway. The hallway was empty. He grabbed a red plastic cup and finally, gratefully, relieved himself with a tremendous sigh of gratitude. He filled the plastic cup almost to the brim. Mission accomplished. But then there was the problem of getting rid of the cup. Sam had to find a sink — even a water fountain or a plastic-lined garbage can would do. Anything! Time still was of the essence, although it was now less of a physical urgency and more a logistical one. He could have left the cup there, but three people knew Sam had been in the building and could easily have put two and two together. He didn't want that to be his reputation in the world of journalism, even at *The Metro Sun*. So he took the cup and started down the hallway as quickly as he could. He held the cup as steadily as possible so that he wouldn't spill any of the liquid on the floor (or on his hand). After all, it may have been yellow, but it wasn't a Soor. (That's my own humorous contribution to the story. Well, at least I *hope* it's humorous.)

Before Sam had traveled even ten feet, a dapper man with thick silver hair stepped out of an office holding a Soor in each hand. They were larger than Matthew's. He almost knocked into Sam.

The man asked Sam what was so serious that he felt compelled to rush. Sam muttered an apology, and the man told him that nothing can be accomplished in a mad dash that cannot better be accomplished in a thoughtful saunter. (I actually like that phrase, despite where it came from. I might use it myself one day.) The man asked Sam if he had patience. Sam glanced at the cup and said that he didn't have as much patience as he'd like. The man asked if he was inclined to share. Sam lowered his hand and said that in most cases, yes, he was inclined to share. The man nodded while he gently kneaded the giant Soors in his hands. He told Sam that the Peace Through Friendship organization was waiting for him, if he wasn't already part of the team.

Thinking quickly, Sam told the man that he was not part of the team, that he was just a messenger, and the man said that messengers were precisely what was needed—messengers of patience and sharing. Then he asked Sam if he wanted to learn more about the organization and find out how to earn his Soors.

Sam said he had already learned how to earn his Soors, but that he was expected home right away. The silver-haired man smiled and told Sam to drink up and slow down. He held his Soors at eye level, glared at them, then lowered his hands and continued down the hall toward the alcove. Sam walked in the opposite direction toward the elevators. When he got there, he pressed the 'Down' button. He looked at the cult temp a few feet away from him. She was reading *Elle*. Sam asked her who the guy was with the silver hair. She said it was Grant Jarvey.

Sam rode the nine floors down in terror. He prayed that nobody would get on. Nobody did. He ignored the receptionist as he passed her desk. On Broadway, he looked for the first available garbage can and saw one on the corner. He was certain there was enough filth inside for one little cup of urine to make no difference at all. (I'm of a different opinion, but that's not what this story is about, so I'll skip it for now.) He tossed it in.

When Sam arrived home, he looked like a defeated man. He told me the story. I felt awful that I had been the one to suggest *The Metro Sun* in the first place. I tried as hard as possible to make it as lovely an evening for him as I could. At one point, later on, I suggested that there were probably some regulations that forbade companies in New York City from locking their bathrooms. Sam agreed. I also broached the subject of the truly offensive practice of forcing people to provide articles for free. Sam agreed with that, too. My words seemed to spur him into action. He wrote a lengthy letter to the editor to send to *The New York Times*, *The New York Daily News*, even *The New York Post*, just for the hell of it. It was an editorial challenge he took seriously. He seemed to have developed a new focus, a greater understanding, a sense of salvation, more confidence, perhaps even some tranquility as he poured himself into this unusual literary endeavor. The letter was all about *The Metro Sun*. In it he railed against its reprehensible practices and less-than-honorable methods, and he called for an investigation. It was at least four times longer than an average letter to the editor. *The New York Times* and *The Daily News* turned it down immediately, but *The New York Post* agreed to publish it. The letter appeared in yesterday's edition. Being the *Post*, they ran a quirky headline above Sam's letter: "Piss Poor Performance at *Metro Sun* Newspaper."

There's more. Sam's letter was discussed on at least three television shows and three radio programs that morning because in the letter he talks about "men with yellow balls," which the hosts of all six programs found irresistible.

I joined Sam on his ride into the city today and we overheard a dozen commuters talking about his letter. Two people even mentioned Sam by name. He whispered to me that if this keeps up, he might actually start to feel like an actual writer.

While we sat in a small coffee shop near Penn Station, Sam emphasized it was just a letter to the editor and nothing more. And besides, he added, it was in *The New York Post* (or as he specifically put it, "The putrid, puerile *Post*").

I told Sam that he *should* feel like a real writer because number one, his byline is in a New York City daily newspaper, number two, everyone's talking about it, and number three, with all the understanding, salvation, tranquility, and confidence he now possessed, he definitely earned his Soors without ever having to squeeze his balls.

Man of Clay

Percy was not a religious man, but he had faith. While he steered clear of houses of worship and found no value in the ritual of prayer or in the veracity of bible stories, he believed wholeheartedly in goodness, righteousness, conviction, even fate and destiny. To help raise his only son, he relied not on what religion instructed, but on what his own heart and mind commanded.

Tonight, he called his son Jeremy into the den and asked him to please sit on the couch. Jeremy sat on the edge of the cushion, signaling his unease. Percy was already on his favorite swivel easy chair beside it—Pop's Chair, as the family typically called it—which gave him the ability to sink down low or spin to the left if he felt the need to look away. Indeed, he might have to look away; after all, this was The Talk, the one he had been dreading since Jeremy graduated high school a few weeks earlier.

"Okay, son," Percy began. "You did well in school. You had many hobbies and activities. You have made us proud, your mother and I. And now you say you don't want to go to college. I want to tell you, Jeremy, that it's fine by me."

"You don't mind?" the strapping young man asked, backing up ever so slightly so that his torso was more fully relaxed on the couch.

"I don't mind, as long as you have a plan for yourself," Percy explained. "There have been plenty of young men and women over the years who, for one reason or another, decided not to go to college. I realize it's not for everyone. I do. Certainly it can save a lot of money. Time, too—if you're able to jump into something worthwhile. Some people have to wait four, six or eight years before they get a degree. If you begin a meaningful career without that, well—"

Jeremy was now fully inclined on the couch cushion, which sank down lower than normal because of his solid, exceedingly muscular frame. His broad right arm, up on the armrest, almost involuntarily rocked back and forth, not in fear or anxiety, but because of the growing confidence he was being given by this little chat with his father—'The Talk' that he had anticipated for weeks. He smiled. Percy did not see his son's smile, however, because he was glancing instead at his own lap, searching for his next crucial words.

"But here's the thing, Jeremy," Percy continued. "You'll notice I used the word meaningful when I was talking about a career. What you seem to want to jump into isn't quite what your mother and I had in mind as, shall we say, the safest or, frankly, wisest thing in the world." Percy finally looked up at his son. "Pottery? You want to be a potter? In a little one-man pottery shack? Up in the mountains somewhere? If I understood you correctly, that's what you said the other day. Jeremy, do you really think there's a future in that? Especially for someone with your gifts?"

Jeremy took in a breath, a slow one, to give himself an opportunity to search for the soundest and most respectable response.

"Pop," he began, "the way I look at it is that we have only one life to live. So we might as well live it in whatever way makes us happy. As long as I'm not hurting anyone, what does it matter that I want to open my own little pottery studio up in the mountains? I mean, I swear to God, I won't ask you or Mom for money. Ever. I'll build my existence around whatever money I'm able to earn on my own in the studio. I'll live within my means, and I'll make sure my means are frugal and smart. Believe me. I'm intelligent. And strong. I'll make it work somehow. Who knows—I may even give you and Mom some cute little grandchildren one day."

On one hand, Percy was enormously proud of the way his son addressed his concern and how he endeavored to make a compelling case. On the other hand, Percy still could not rationalize how anyone could see the practicality in devoting an entire career to running a diminutive pottery studio in a remote hamlet.

"Yes, Jeremy," Percy said, "you *are* smart. And yes, you certainly are strong. The strongest boy I've ever known. Not a boy anymore—the strongest young *man* I've ever known. The strongest young man *anyone's* ever known, for that matter. And I think that's the thing that bothers me the most."

"My strength?"

"And your abilities, yes. I have to believe that you were given that strength and those abilities for a reason other than making clay pots—"

"—And vases and ornaments and birdbaths and sundials..." Jeremy quickly added; he needed to make his father understand it was far more than just pots that he would create in his mountain studio.

"I know. I know," Percy said. "I get that, Jeremy. I really do. I'll admit to being a little ignorant about the whole pottery thing. The little one-person studio idea. The mountains. All that. But I'm *not* ignorant about how much help people always need. Our country needs help, Jeremy. Lots of help. We're in awful shape, son. Crime. Disasters. You name it. It's a mess out there. And with your gifts... well... like I say, maybe they're for a reason that has nothing to do with pottery. Do you see what I'm trying to say, Jeremy?"

"Pop," Jeremy said softly, "I never asked to see Maura naked by being able to look right through the door of the locker room at the pool before we started dating. I never asked to be able to open the locked steel door of the old Wilson warehouse when Maura and I wanted to make out on our first date. I never asked to want to try real Chinese food so badly that I found out how to fly from here to China in less than two minutes. I never asked to accidentally put my finger in the way of a spinning table saw in shop class without getting a scratch. The only thing I *did* ask for, Pop, was a pottery wheel, because that's what makes me happy. That's what I enjoy. That's what I've always wanted to do, ever since I can remember."

Once again, Percy was impressed with the skilled oratory of his son, if still not convinced that he was making a sensible career choice. But Jeremy was indeed an adult, not only in his eyes but also in the eyes of the law. He was bright, kind, moral — and Percy realized he should be allowed to make up his own mind. So, on the spot, there in the easy chair, he decided to let it go. That little silver capsule that he and his wife had found him in eighteen years ago could easily remain hidden for the rest of eternity. It was buried so deep in the ground behind the backyard shed that no one would ever find it. In fact, it was Jeremy himself, during the third year that he had been with Percy and his wife, who created that hole for the capsule merely by staring at the ground and making a powerful beam of energy come out of his eyes. Jeremy was only two-and-a-half feet tall at the time. The hole was eleven feet deep.

"Okay, son," Percy said. "You're right. You're absolutely right. I want you to do what you want to do. It's your life. I'll even help you find this little place up in the mountains."

"I'd like that very much, Pop," Jeremy said, reclining once more. He breathed deeply and sighed.

Percy smiled, too. Then he stood up, said goodnight to his son, went into his bedroom, closed the door, and prayed for America.

Molly in the Morning

Oh yes, all their kids are geniuses. No question. This one's son is the best soccer player that ever played middle school soccer. "You should see him use his head!!!" which is obviously always said out loud with not just one exclamation point, but three. That one's daughter is the best cheerleader that ever cheered for a varsity football team. "So personable! So popular!" (And when that one tells this story, she puts her hand over her mouth to make it seem as if she's embarrassed to have to admit how awesome her not-so-awesome daughter is.) All of their unbelievably gorgeous and amazingly handsome children are so damn gifted and talented—I swear to God someone really said this—that "the coordinator of the district's gifted-and-talented program doesn't even have to ask us for an application to be sent in. She just knows!" Imagine! She just knows! Want more? Okay. Jillian, or Ashley, or Meredith, or whoever, is so popular because of her amazing figure that boys "literally stand on their heads" to get a glimpse of her whenever she leaves the house in the morning." That's right, they "literally" stand on their heads. Take a walk down Jillian or Ashley or Meredith's block and you'll see a dozen pairs of legs sticking straight up in the air. Literally! Andrew, or maybe it was Mason, or Tyler, is so incredibly talented on stage that it won't surprise his mother if Steven Spielberg comes to the last performance of *Pippin* at school to offer him the lead role in his next movie. Olivia is such a wonderful singer that we'll probably hear her on the radio next year, right along with Taylor Swift. IQ scores? "Oh, my little Suzie doesn't need to take a formal IQ test because everyone already knows how smart she is. She aces every test she ever takes." I guess it doesn't matter that Suzie and her mother probably don't even have a clue what IQ stands for.

Don't you just love mothers these days?

Can I tell you a little about my own daughter?

Molly's smart. Not a genius, just smart. I have to get on her case every once in a while to study or to finish up a class project, but she always studies and she always finishes. I know she'll get into a good college. Not Harvard or Yale, but a good one. She's an excellent gymnast. She'll never make the Olympics—she doesn't have the body or the discipline—but that doesn't matter. She enjoys the workouts and the competitions and she's proud of the two or three trophies she's won over the years. My husband and I are proud, too. Molly plays the bassoon in the school band. Strange instrument—but I'm told it's very important to the band. She had a solo at the last concert, in a song called *Liberty Waltz*. It was good. The band instructor appreciates her dedication. He wrote something nice on the *Liberty Waltz* sheet music when Molly asked him if she could keep it after the last concert. I don't remember what he wrote, and I don't know what Molly did with it. But it impressed me that she even asked and that the band instructor complied without hesitating. Molly has no interest in sports (other than gymnastics). That's fine with me. She's busy enough. At school, she helped build the set for *Pippin* and had a blast. She even made a few new friends, which is great because she's always had a little trouble in that department. To tell you the truth, the set for *Pippin* was... well... let's just say it was very unassuming. Which made me realize our high school probably has a budget of about ten cents for its theater program. But that's okay. Molly had fun. That's what matters. Plus, it will be nice to add set-building to the list of activities on her transcript for college. Her list won't be a mile long, like Jillian's or Andrew's. But it will be fine.

Don't get me wrong. It's not that I refuse to brag. But I refuse to brag about every last thing Molly ever did or said in her life. If I want to say something nice about something she did or said, I do it without squeezing every last detail out of it and exaggerating it until it's almost unrecognizable from the truth. What's the point? So what if little Shawna or Ava have the world's most gorgeous green eyes? What does that mean in the grand scheme of things? You know what I like to brag about? I like to brag about the fact that Molly doesn't always need me to wake her up in the morning to go to school. Now *that's* something to be proud of! Today's a good example. When I woke up (a little late, I admit) I didn't see Molly, and I didn't hear her, either, which meant that she had gotten herself up and out of the house all by herself. I didn't have to pester her one bit. And this despite the fact that she was up late last night doing homework after gymnastics practice, and despite the fact that she doesn't like the chorus instructor who she has to see every morning before homeroom, and despite the fact that she's been dreading a biology test she has to take today. Despite all of those things, she apparently woke herself up, got herself ready, made herself breakfast, and walked herself to school. I smiled wider than I've smiled in a long time because I knew she did all this entirely on her own. I'll embrace honest smiling over fake bragging any day of the week.

Besides, there was no time to brag this morning, anyway. There were other important things to do. Like straighten up the house. You see, Molly and my husband make an absolute mess every morning. They both have a terrible habit of throwing their wet towels behind the bathroom door, which is why the bathroom door is always two-thirds closed whenever I go in there to clean up after they're gone. A mountain of wet towels behind it! That's why I always bump my left shoulder against the partially closed door whenever I try to squeeze through. My shoulder is always black and blue. That's my legacy. The black-and-blue-shouldered non-bragging mom.

On my way to the bathroom, I counted my blessings. Things were good (despite the sore shoulder). My husband likes his job and earns a good salary. Molly's a great kid. I even got to sleep late this morning. So instead of cleaning the bathroom, I went downstairs to the kitchen and grabbed a chocolate donut, which is like having a piece of cake for breakfast. I poured myself an extra large cup of coffee and put in more French vanilla cream than usual. I took the donut and the coffee into the den and watched *The Real Housewives of New Jersey*, even though I would never admit that to anyone in the world. A rare guilty pleasure. I sat and watched and drank my coffee and ate my donut. I felt I deserved it. When do I indulge? Maybe three or four times a year, at most.

Finally, after my decadent little treats with the donut and the housewives, I felt relaxed enough to go upstairs to tackle the bathroom. I pushed the bathroom door open in order to scrunch the wet towels behind it into a corner. They're easier to pick up that way. But the door hardly budged. It moved just a fraction of an inch. So I pushed harder. The door still didn't move. So I sucked in my belly (cursing the donut at the same time) and squeezed in through the small opening. The wet towels were actually up on the sink. And behind the bathroom door, on the floor, was Molly, fast asleep.

My Ass, Not Yours

TIME

September 2, 2008

On the morning of September 10, researchers at the European Organization for Nuclear Research (CERN) laboratory in Geneva will activate the LHC—the Large Hadron Collider— which is a $7 billion particle accelerator designed to send proton beams speeding around a 17-mile circular underground tunnel, crash them into one another in an attempt to duplicate the immediate aftereffects of what is commonly known as the Big

Bang, and then observe the fragments to learn more about the origins of the universe.

Critics of the LHC say the experiment may create a miniature black hole that could expand to disastrous proportions. On August 26, Otto Romsler, a German chemist, filed a lawsuit against CERN with the European Court of Human Rights arguing that creating such a black hole would violate the right to life of citizens throughout Europe. Last winter, two New York environmentalists sued in Federal District Court in Manhattan seeking to force the U.S. government to withdraw its participation in the LHC test. The lawsuits have led to disturbing headlines around the world, such as France's *Le Monde* newspaper, which stated: "World Expected to End in Eight Days."

GMail

To: WarpDriveBob@comcast.net
From: EdMcG@gmail.com
Subject: Large Hadron Collider
Date: September 2, 2008

Hi Bob old buddy. It's me, Ed. Just got to work after my weekly breakfast date with my good old Dad. He says hi.

As the only member of the old high school gang who knew the difference between a quark and a quasar, you must know about the Large Hadron Collider. I just read an article about it in Time Magazine. Are you following the news? If so, you know that they're gonna fire it up on Sept 10. Looks like it will cause some sort of black hole that will duplicate the original Big Bang and destroy the Earth. I told my father about it. He said I'm nuts, but he's been saying that since I was a kid. I'm not sure what I'm gonna do about the Collider news. Let's get together for lunch at least once before it happens! For old times' sake. Maybe at the Rainbow Diner in Hamilton. That's where I meet my dad once a week. Their portions are HUGE, and you know me! And anyway, what the hell's the difference if I turn into more of a blimp than I already am? Won't matter after Sept 10.

Your best friend from H.S. – Ed

P.S. I know you never got around to looking at the schematic for my little invention. I know you're very busy. If you have a chance, I'd love to get your impression, even though at this point nothing will ever come of it, for obvious reasons!

P.P.S. Nobody here at Jasper Innovations even knows that I've been inventing things on the side all these years. Christ — we help people coast to coast research patents and prepare patent paperwork, but some stupid-ass corporate rule says that employees can't patent things themselves. I just don't get this idiotic world. Do you? Will it be such a great loss on September 10? I don't think so.

P.P.P.S. Do you still read Leland Taibor's "End-of-the-World" blog? I do. Religiously. He mentions my name almost every time I email him a thought or an idea. My small slice of fame, right? Not bad for a guy who barely made it out of Colgate.

NEW TXT MESSAGE
9/3/2008
Text:
Kate, its me, Ed. FYI, I'm in the office now but will be leaving a little early today. Got a long list of personal things I have to do. All my work stuff is caught up, though. Thanks.
Ed McGuinn

NEW TXT MESSAGE
9/3/2008
Text:
Ed, ok on leaving early today, but in the future I need more notice if you are going to do that. As you know, we have a very full plate and need all hands on deck.
Kate

7 days of world left x 24 hours per day = 168 hrs.
Plans:
Try to see 8 movies (19 hrs).
Try to have sex a few times (12 hrs).
Eat some awesome meals (14 hrs).
Get some sleep (65 hrs).
Decide where to be for "THE END."

JASPER INNOVATIONS

Internal Memorandum

To: KATE SHAW
From: JOHN TILLMAN
Re: ED McGUINN
Date: 9/3/08

Kate, I was putting something on Ed McGuinn's desk this afternoon (he wasn't there at the time) and couldn't help but notice something a little disturbing on his desk — one of those little yellow Post-It notes. He doodled some strange stuff on it, all about devoting a certain amount of hours over the next 7 days to do things like eat a lot and watch movies and sleep (and have sex). Maybe it's just a joke? (I hope.) Weird. What should we do? Anything? Or just leave it alone so that we're not accused of invading an employee's privacy?

09/04/08

ED: Hi. Jodi. I have wanted to make love to you for years. How about 2nite?

JODI: Ed, should you be Instant Messaging stuff like this at work? I think Jasper has a policy about it.

ED: Fuck the policy. Besides, the world will end in 6 days, so who gives a crap?

JODI: I give a crap, Ed. I don't want to lose my job if the world DOESN'T end.

ED: If it doesn't end, it will be my ass, not yours. So don't worry. So... 2nite? Me and you?

JODI: Ed, I love you as a friend.

ED: Crap! I despise that line! I bet if I was 85 pounds lighter you'd make love to me.

JODI: Your weight has nothing to do with it, Ed. Besides, aren't you dating Mindy from HR now?

ED: Mindy? We had one date! That was it. I hate her. Do you know what she said to me? She said that anyone's replaceable.

JODI: She says that all the time, Ed. It's her favorite line. She didn't mean anything personal.

ED: I'm the only one at Jasper Innovations who knows how to fill out D5 forms. I am NOT replaceable.

JODI: I know that. Kate Shaw knows that, too, and she's the most important one who has to know it. Mindy doesn't have to know it. So stop this crazy talk now, Ed. Okay?

ED: Can't stop a speeding train, and what we have here is a speeding train.

JODI: I don't even know what that means, Ed. Hey--I hear my boss coughing in the hall, which means he may stick his head in my office. Gotta run. Talk later. Bye.

To: EdMcG@gmail.com
From: WarpDriveBob@comcast.net
Subject: Large Hadron Collider
Date: September 4, 2008

Hi, old friend. Sorry it took me so long to respond to your last email from two days ago, Ed. I was at a convention in White Plains. I'll tell you all about it when we meet. And we WILL meet, because I don't think the world will end when they turn on the Collider. Although, with the electric bill and the health insurance premium bill I just got in the mail, maybe that's not such a bad idea. Melissa says hi. Write back.

P.S. Your invention is interesting. We'll talk about it.

Kate /
Inadvertently saw some instant messaging
Ed McGuinn was doing yesterday with
Jodi Burns. Wasn't looking for anything—
just stumbled on it while doing system
maintenance. Nothing illegal, just strange.
End of world stuff. (Also asking her to have
sex.) Just thought you should know, in case
you want to address it.
Rocky, IT Dept.

"Leland's End-of-the-World Blog" By Leland Taibor
Posted by Leland Taibor on September 5, 2008, 11:38 AM
Email This Blog. Share to Facebook

Hi friends. I did some more calculations based on old theories which I compared to new data from the European Organization for Nuclear Research. It's never been clearer to me that when the Large Hadron Collider is turned on, its mini black hole will expand 436,000,000 times in 6.2 seconds... Kaboom!... Very rainy today. Wonder what the weather will be like on Hadron day. Has anyone researched what the weather has been just before cataclysmic events?.... A shoutout to Ed McG: I think your latest invention idea sounds marvelous. If the world doesn't end in a few days, I bet it will be very successful.

Document1 – Microsoft Word non-commercial use

September 6, 2008
From: Ed McGuinn
To: Every Jasper Innovations Client I Ever Did Business With
Re: You Should All Go to Hell
I am sending out this blast fax to say goodbye to all my former Jasper Innovations clients, and to say that I never really liked working with any of you. You all think you're hot shit, but you're cold morons. I am saddened that the world will end in four days, but the fact that you're going away with it is at least one small consolation. And to all you no-talent patent holders out there who call me the Fat Jasper Paper Pusher behind my back (I've heard it through the grapevine a dozen times), I'd rather be a fat paper pusher than a skinny asshole, like all of you.

"Leland's End-of-the-World Blog" By Leland Taibor
Posted by <u>Leland Taibor</u> on September 6, 2008, <u>10:44 AM</u>
<u>Email This</u> <u>Blog.</u> <u>Share to Facebook</u>

Hi friends. Looks like the weather will be beautiful on Hadron day. Anyone have any thoughts on that?..... Got an email just a few minutes ago from faithful reader Ed McG. He says he found nirvana, just in time for the end of the world: he sent a blast fax to all the clients he's been doing business with and told them what he really thinks of them. That was his nirvana. What's more, he didn't even get in trouble at work (at least as of this writing). Good luck, Ed.

9/6

Ed/

Right after lunch I received an email from Brian Higgins,

one of our clients in Oregon. Says he received a very

disturbing blast fax from you. Asked me if I wanted to see a

copy. Do I, Ed? Is this anything I need to be worried about?

Please come by my office at your earliest convenience.

/ Kate

09/06/08

ED: Jodi, I don't have time to chat. I'm leaving. I'm supposed to meet with Kate in a few minutes (her Post-It note didn't sound very happy), but I decided not to meet with her. I'm leaving the building instead, and I might not come back. In a few days there won't be any job to come back to anyway, so I'm leaving with some dignity. It took the Large Hadron Collider to make a man of me.

JODI: What??????????? What are you saying, Ed?

ED: Just want to let you know you're a lovely person. I hope there's an afterlife and that we get to meet there. (And maybe make sweet, sweet love!) First, though, I have some videos to watch, a few services to indulge in, lots of good food to take out, some liquor to buy, and a few awesome desserts to enjoy.

JODI: Ed, don't be hasty. What if the world DOESN'T end? Word gets around, and it might be hard for you to get another job somewhere else. Please don't do anything rash.

ED: Like I said, Jodi, if the world doesn't end, it will be my ass, not yours. Don't worry. Never felt better in my life. I'm getting a lot off my chest. Maybe that made me a few dozen pounds lighter!!!

JODI: Come to my office, Ed. Let's talk.

ED: Nothing to talk about. See ya.

JODI: Stop it, Ed.

JODI: Ed, are you still there?

JODI: Ed?

JODI: Ed?

From the desk of Ed McGuinn

Dear Mr. Robinson,

Just a brief note to tell you that as a landlord you are a reprehensible horse's ass, and as a person you are a reprehensible pig's ass. If you wanted to be a miserable, mean, unscrupulous, unlikable bastard, you should have gone into something other than a profession where it's important to try to get along with people.

If there is a hell, you will be its number one tenant.

— Ed McGuinn

September 7, 2008

P.S. You win. You get to keep the security deposit because once September 10th is over I won't be around to ask for it back. On the other hand, you won't be around to take it from me either!

From the desk of Ed McGuinn

Dear Mindy,

Hi. I'm in the building, but just to pick up a few things from my desk. I wanted to tell you that I still think you're beautiful and talented, but I didn't realize until you dumped me after our first date and told me that "everyone is replaceable" how clueless and self-centered you were. If by some miracle what's destined to happen on September 10 doesn't happen, I would suggest you try to think about something other than yourself at least once. But since September 10 <u>will</u> happen, I suppose it's a moot point. Bye bye D5 forms (which you stupidly claim anyone can fill out). Bye bye, Mindy (who for some reason I used to like).

September 7, 2008

Google Mail

To: WarpDriveBob@comcast.net
From: EdMcG@gmail.com
Subject: Large Hadron Collider
Date: September 8, 2008

Bob, sorry we didn't get to do our final lunch at the Rainbow Diner. I know you're busy. But after today there will be just one day left before THE BIG EVENT. Any chance we can meet, even for just a few minutes in a parking lot somewhere? A cynical person would say what does it matter if we meet or not at this point. But I guess I have a strong moral compass that will follow me into the afterlife. That moral compass wants me to see my best friend from the old days at least once before it all ends. –Ed

To: EdMcG@gmail.com

From: WarpDriveBob@comcast.net

Subject: Large Hadron Collider

Date: September 8, 2008

You're a riot, Ed. You should write for Saturday Night Live. You ARE joking, right? Because if you're not, and you're doing some of the things you once told me you'd like to do if the world was ending, it will be your ass, pal. I can't meet tomorrow. Melissa is taking me to some sort of salsa dance class. I promised her I'd go. (A big final kaboom wouldn't be such a bad idea after all! That's how much I want to avoid salsa dancing.) Let's meet next week, Ed. Don't do anything rash.

APPETIZERS

1a.	Spring Roll	1.35
1b.	Roast Pork Egg Roll (1)	1.35
1c.	Vegetable Egg Roll (1)	1.35
2.	Shrimp Egg Roll (1)	1.35
3.	Bar-B-Q Spare Ribs	(5) 6.45 (10) 11.75
4.	Boneless Spare Ribs	(Pt.) 5.95 (Qt.) 10.95
5.	Beef Teriyaki (4)	5.95
5a.	Chicken Teriyaki (4)	5.35
6.	Fried Shrimp (15)	5.15
New 6a.	French Fries	3.15
7.	Crab Rangoon (8)	5.15
7a.	Fried Biscuit (10)	3.85
8.	Shrimp Toast (4)	3.95
9.	Fried Wonton (10)	3.50
New 9a.★	Fried Wonton w. Garlic Sauce (12)	4.95
10.	Cold Noodles w. Sesame Sauce	4.95
11.	Golden Fingers (Order)	5.45
12.	Fried Chicken Wings (Order)	5.75
New 12a.★	Buffalo Wings (8)	6.50
13.	Steamed Dumplings (8)	5.45
14.	Fried Dumplings (8)	5.45
15.	Pu Pu Platter (for 2)	12.95

2 pork egg roll, 2 spare ribs, 2 beef stick, 2 shrimp toast,
4 fried wonton, 4 golden fingers, 2 fried chicken wings.

SOUPS *(w. Fried Noodles)*

		Pt.	Qt.
16.	Wonton Soup	1.60	2.90
17.	Egg Drop Soup	1.60	2.90
18.	Wonton Egg Drop Soup	1.70	3.10
19.	Chicken Rice or Noodle Soup	1.60	2.90
20.★	Hot and Sour Soup	2.15	3.95
21.	Chicken (or Pork) Yat Gaw Mein		4.70
22.	House Special Wonton Soup		5.35
22a.	Vegetable Bean Curd Soup	2.00	3.95

CHOW MEIN *(w. Rice & Noodles)*

		Pt.	Qt.
23.	Chicken Chow Mein	4.45	7.35
24.	Roast Pork Chow Mein	4.45	7.35
25.	Shrimp Chow Mein	4.75	7.65
26.	Beef Chow Mein	4.75	7.65
27.	Mixed Vegetable Chow Mein	4.25	7.25
28.	Lobster Chow Mein	5.15	8.85
29.	House Special Chow Mein	5.15	8.85

CHOP SUEY *(w. Rice)*

		Pt.	Qt.
30.	Chicken Chop Suey	4.45	7.35
31.	Roast Pork Chop Suey	4.45	7.35
32.	Shrimp Chop Suey	4.70	7.65
33.	Beef Chop Suey	4.70	7.65
34.	Vegetable Chop Suey	4.25	7.25

FRIED RICE

		Pt.	Qt.
35.	Mixed Vegetable Fried Rice	4.45	7.35
36.	Roast Pork Fried Rice	4.65	7.35
37.	Shrimp Fried Rice	4.90	7.65
38.	Chicken Fried Rice	4.65	7.35
39.	Beef Fried Rice	4.90	7.85
40.	Young Chow Fried Rice	5.15	8.35
41.	Lobster & Crabmeat Fried Rice	5.15	8.35

LO MEIN *(Soft Noodles)*

		Pt.	Qt.
42.	Vegetable Lo Mein	4.90	7.05
43.	Roast Pork Lo Mein	5.15	8.35
44.	Shrimp Lo Mein	5.35	9.05
45.	Chicken Lo Mein	5.15	8.35
46.	Beef Lo Mein	5.35	9.05
47.	Lobster Lo Mein	5.65	9.65
48.	House Special Lo Mein	5.35	9.05
48a.	House Special Chow Mei Fun		9.05
48b.★	Singapore Chow Mei Fun		9.05

CHOW FUN

48c.	Vegetable Chow Fun	7.70

CHICKEN *(w. Rice)*

		Pt.	Qt.
62.	Chicken w. Broccoli	5.35	9.05
63.	Chicken w. Snow Peas/String Bean	5.35	9.05
64.	Chicken Almond Ding	5.35	9.05
65.	Chicken with Pepper & Tomato	5.35	9.05
66.	Moo Goo Gai Pan (Chicken)	5.35	9.05
67.	Chicken w. Mixed Chinese Veg.	5.35	9.05
68.★	Curry Chicken w. Onion	5.35	9.05

SEAFOOD *(w. Rice)*

		Pt.	Qt.
69.	Scallops w. Mixed Chinese Veg.	5.85	10.15
70.	Shrimp w. Lobster Sauce	5.85	10.15
71.	Shrimp w. Broccoli	5.85	10.15
72.	Shrimp w. Mixed Chinese Veg.	5.85	10.15
73.	Shrimp w. Snow Peas/String Bean	5.85	10.15
74.	Shrimp w. Pepper & Tomato	5.85	10.15
75.	Shrimp w. Mushrooms	5.85	10.15
76.	Shrimp w. Almond Ding	5.85	10.15
77.★	Curry Shrimp w. Onion	5.85	10.15

EGG FOO YOUNG *(w. Rice)* *Per Order*

78.	Roast Pork Egg Foo Young	7.20
79.	Shrimp Egg Foo Young	7.95
79a.	Beef Egg Foo Young	7.95
80.	Chicken Egg Foo Young	7.20
81.	Mushroom Egg Foo Young	7.20
82.	Vegetable Egg Foo Young	7.20

SWEET & SOUR *(w. Rice)*

		Pt.	Qt.
83.	Sweet & Sour Pork	5.15	8.60
84.	Sweet & Sour Chicken	5.25	8.60
85.	Sweet & Sour Shrimp	5.25	9.05
85a.	Sweet & Sour Combo		9.05

(Chicken, Pork & Shrimp)

BEAN CURD *(w. Rice)*

		Pt.	Qt.
86.	Bean Curd Country Style	4.90	8.05
86a.	Bean Curd Chicken	5.55	9.05
86b.	Bean Curd Beef	5.80	9.35
86c.	Bean Curd Shrimp	5.80	9.35
86d.★	General Tao's Bean Curd		9.25
86e.★	Sesame Bean Curd		9.25

VEGETABLE *(w. Rice)*

		Pt.	Qt.
87.	Mixed Chinese Vegetable	4.90	8.05
87a.	Plain Broccoli	4.90	8.05
88.	Sauteed Snow Peas/String Bean	4.90	8.05
89.★	Broccoli w. Hot Garlic Sauce	4.90	8.05
90.★	Moo Shu Vegetable (w. 4 pancakes)		8.35
91.	Stirred Fried Mixed Veg.	4.90	8.05
92.	Snow Pea w. Mushroom & Baby Corn	4.90	8.05

SPECIAL COMBINATION PLATTERS

(w. Pork Fried Rice & Pork Egg Roll)

S 1.	Chicken Chow Mein w. Fried Noodle	7.60
S 2.	Shrimp Chow Mein w. Fried Noodle	7.60
S 3.	Roast Pork Chop Suey	7.60
S 4.	Roast Pork Egg Foo Young	7.60
S 5.	Pepper Steak with Onion	7.60
S 6.	Roast Pork w. Mixed Chinese Veg.	7.60
S 7.	Shrimp with Lobster Sauce	7.85
S 8.	Bar-B-Q Spare Ribs	7.85
S 9.	Sweet & Sour Pork (or Chicken)	7.60
S10.	Moo Goo Gai Pan (Chicken)	7.60
S11.	Shrimp w. Mixed Chinese Vegetable	7.85
S12.	Pork (or Chicken) Lo Mein	7.60
S13.	Beef with Broccoli	7.60
S14.	Chicken with Broccoli	7.60
S15.	Shrimp with Broccoli	7.85
S16.	Boneless Spare Ribs	7.60
S17.	Chicken w. Mixed Chinese Vegetable	7.60
S18.	Golden Fingers, Teriyaki Beef, Wings	7.85
S19.★	General Toa's Chicken	7.85

Village Malt Shop

HAND-DIPPED ICE CREAM
See our ice cream flavors on the board

HERSHEY'S Ice Cream
We only serve the best!

CONE OR DISH

Single scoop $2.12
Double scoop $3.35
Triple scoop $4.49
Kiddie cone $1.09

Special cones
Sugar cone: Add 15¢
Plain homemade waffle cone: Add $1

No-Sugar-Added Ice Cream and Frozen Yogurt available

The Casino Signature Sundaes
Two-scoop sundaes
$4.95
With whipped cream and cherry

PINK PANTHER
Cherry syrup

GROUCHO MARX
Heaping spoonfuls of walnuts

THE FONZ
Hot fudge, peanuts

SNOOPY
Chocolate syrup, peanuts

DOROTHY LAMOUR
Pineapple chunks

SCARLETT O'HARA
Strawberry topping

RUDOLPH VALENTINO
Chocolate syrup, walnuts

ELVIS (Dusty Road)
Chocolate syrup, malt

MAE WEST
Heavy on the hot fudge

MARILYN MONROE
Heavy on the caramel

I ♥ LUCY
Chocolate syrup

JOHN WAYNE
Hot fudge, walnuts

Marshmallow Sundaes
$5.25

W.C. FIELDS (C.M.W.)
Chocolate syrup, marshmallow, walnuts, cherry

ABBOTT & COSTELLO (C.M.P.)
Chocolate syrup, marshmallow, peanuts, cherry

Junior Sundaes

WIZARD OF OZ $2.79
One scoop, whipped cream, cherry

MICKEY ROONEY $3.50
One scoop, choice of one topping, whipped cream and cherry

EXTREME SUNDAES
All with whipped cream and cherry

THREE STOOGES BANANA BOAT
(Banana Split)
Three scoops of ice cream, strawberries, pineapple, chocolate syrup, with whole banana. $5.95

SHREK SUNDAE
(Brownie Sundae)
One scoop of ice cream served on top of a warm brownie. Topped with hot fudge. $5.95

GREEN MINT GRASSHOPPER
Green mint chip ice cream, hot fudge, crushed Oreo cookie, cherry. $5.75

BETTY BOOP-OOP-A-DOOP
Vanilla ice cream, strawberry topping, marshmallow, chocolate sprinkles. $5.75

MONKEY MEETS THE MOOSE
Moosetracks ice cream, chocolate sauce, whole banana. $5.75

BROWNIE BOMB
(Brownie Sundae)
Peanut butter sauce, hot fudge, over a warm brownie and peanut butter twirl ice cream. $5.95

PEANUT BUTTER EXPLOSION
Two scoops of ice cream (your choice), Reese's peanut butter sauce, Reese's Pieces. $5.75

MALT SHOP FAVORITES

TOWERING INFERNO
Eight scoops of ice cream, hot fudge, pineapple, peanuts, marshmallow, diced cherries, strawberries. $17.79
Beat the Casino record eating time of 1:09 min., set in 1986!

SUPERMAN
Ten scoops of ice cream, banana, strawberries, chocolate syrup, pineapple, peanuts, whipped cream, four cherries. $19.99

PIG'S DINNER
Five scoops of ice cream, whole banana, chocolate syrup, strawberries, pineapple, cherry syrup, caramel, whipped cream, cherry. $13.29

Finish this, and you'll earn our "Pigged Out" button!

I Pigged Out At Village Malt Shoppe

Emergency 911 Call Log
Zone NY687
Operator 332
September 9, 2008

OPERATOR	911 emergency. How may I help you?		9:03.24 pm
CALLER	I think I'm having a	*Transmission incomplete.*	9:03.29 pm
OPERATOR	Can you please repeat that, sir? What is your name, sir, and what is the — ?		9:03.32 pm
CALLER	Ed. Ed. I'm. I	*Transmission incomplete.*	9:03.36 pm
OPERATOR	Ed? Is this a medical emergency?		9:03.40 pm
CALLER		*No response.*	9:03.44 pm
OPERATOR	Sir, tell me where you are located, and we will —		9:03.49 pm
CALLER	Ar.... ta...	*Transmission unclear and incomplete.*	9:03:52 pm
OPERATOR	Can you give us a name and an address?		9.03.56 pm
CALLER		*No response.*	9:03.59 pm
OPERATOR	Sir?		9:04.01 pm
CALLER		*No response*	9:04.03 pm
OPERATOR	Supervisor 887, this is Operator 332. We need an immediate trace on this call.		

JASPER INNOVATIONS   Internal Memorandum
To: All Employees
From: Kate SHAW
Re: Ed McGuinn
DATE: September 10, 2008

It is with great sadness that we must report the sudden and unexpected death of our friend and colleague Ed McGuinn on September 9. Ed was rushed to the hospital from his apartment last night with severe chest pains but expired on the way. We have no further details at this time.

Nor do we have any details on funeral arrangements, but we are researching that now and will send another companywide memo as soon as we have more information.

Ed was a valuable member of our team and will be missed. If you have any questions, concerns or comments on this matter — including D5 forms that Ed was doing for you — please call Mike Webber and he will reassign the forms to either Frank, Bill, Sean, Rusty, Sarah or Laura, all of whom are more than able to help.

Thank you.

Tabernacle Tom and His Time Machine

I was standing outside the Jacob Javits Convention Center in New York City when I saw a guy across the street who looked interesting. He had long gray hair, wore moccasins, and was reading an oversized hardcover book. I mentioned this to my colleague Mike, who looked across the street to see what I was talking about.

"Interesting?" Michael asked. He sounded skeptical.

I told him I wanted to ditch the taxi line to go across the street and talk to the guy. That's when Mike looked at me with the same level of skepticism.

"Are you kidding?" he wondered aloud. "He looks like a seventy-year-old homeless bum."

"No he doesn't," I said. "Besides, I don't think the cops would allow homeless bums to be near one of one of the biggest trade shows in New York City. It's too important for the economy. They don't want to scare people off."

Mike stared at me pathetically. Maybe he knew more than I did about New York City. After all, I grew up in New Jersey, went to college in California, and work in Washington, DC; Mike has been a Manhattanite since the day he was born. Do I have the right to lecture him about New York City, about cops and homeless people? Probably not.

But I felt as if I had a right to lecture him on what looked interesting since my job as editor of *New Ideas Magazine* requires that very skill — to know what's interesting and what's not. Mike is the northeast advertising sales manager; he has nothing to do with finding, selecting, and editing stories for the magazine. I do not intend to disparage Mike, mind you; I'm merely trying to make a point. Not only did the man across the street have long gray hair and moccasins, but he also wore a long-sleeved T-shirt that said TABERNACLE TOM in stenciled letters across the front, which actually sounded vaguely familiar to me. My point is, if I tell someone that a man across the street seems interesting, they should damn well believe that he's interesting.

I told Mike to hop into a taxi to go back to the *New Ideas* sales office uptown, and that I'd catch up to him later that night to plan tomorrow's schedule. When the taxi departed, I crossed the street.

"Hi, Tabernacle Tom," I said. "What are you reading?"

Tom looked up at me.

"Hi," he said. "It's called *The Elements of Time Travel*. Why?"

"No reason. It's just that... well... it's curious to see someone reading an oversized book like that on a busy sidewalk in New York in the middle of a chilly afternoon. And since I edit a magazine about new ideas, which as a matter of fact is called *New Ideas*, I'm always looking for interesting stories. I was at the convention center across the street and saw you from the taxi stand."

"Do you believe in time travel?" Tom asked. He had been very patient while I made that long-winded explanation.

"Time travel? I don't know. Why do you ask?"

"Most people don't believe it exists."

"Do you?"

"I have a time machine at home."

At that moment, my interest in this man soared to an entirely new level.

Certainly I knew next to nothing about Tom, but was still convinced that he was worth getting to know, editorially speaking, if only to consider the value of writing a profile of an exceedingly colorful person on the sidewalks of New York.

"Can I see it?" I asked.

"My time machine? If you'd like to. We'd have to go to my apartment."

"Where's your apartment?"

"Tabernacle. In Jersey. In the Pine Barrens."

"Tabernacle?" I said. "I haven't heard that name since I was a kid. I went to camp there for a few summers. Do you have a car? I do, but if you also have one..."

"No," Tom said. "I don't have a car. I took the bus this morning to visit an old friend. But I think he's dead. So now I have to get home somehow."

I told him to follow me to the garage five blocks from the Javits Convention Center, where my car was parked. At first I worried it would be difficult for me to keep up a conversation with the guy, not just because he lagged behind, but also because it's not always easy to converse with a total stranger. Much to my surprise, that was not an issue at all, for along the way Tabernacle Tom asked me question after question and seemed to truly absorb my responses. In fact, there were no breaks in the conversation at all between the time we left the street corner where I had first spotted him to the time we arrived at the parking garage. The man was resiliently conversational. He asked when I was born, inquired about my hobbies, and wondered what I did for entertainment and what I remembered most as a little boy and as a teenager. He was interested in my friends and about my likes and dislikes. It was the most intriguing and confounding five-block walk I had ever taken. Tabernacle Tom was one hell of a character.

The drive to south Jersey was long, but not unpleasant. Tom and I continued to talk about many subjects. He told me how he came to be called Tabernacle Tom. (Briefly, he once drove from New York to Wildwood on vacation, got sidetracked by a fire in the Pine Barrens next to the Garden State Parkway, ended up in Tabernacle—and never left.) He told me about most of the jobs he had, including house painter, window installer, shopping center security guard, and "one or two others that I'd rather not get into right now." He also served two tours in Vietnam.

Tom's apartment comprised just two rooms—a tiny kitchenette and a bedroom that wasn't much larger. A short hallway into which was tucked a tiny bathroom separated the two rooms. His bed was a couch with a short blanket and a thin pillow. Next to the couch was a dresser, the top of which Tom seemed to use as a desk. He had it covered with newspapers, books, papers, pens, and a pair of binoculars. On the other side of the tiny room, to the left of the window, was an old-fashioned Seeburg jukebox, the kind I remembered playing as a kid in the dining hall at sleep-away camp. It had a transparent top through which you could see several dozen 45-rpm records and the motor-spring mechanism that delivered each disc to the turntable below it. It had a sweeping Seeburg logo on the front and logos painted on each side of the rounded Plexiglas cover. Colored lights inside the translucent cover glowed and twirled as if they were alive. It was a mesmerizing machine to behold— hypnotic back then, and equally spellbinding now.

"Make yourself at home," Tabernacle Tom said. Considering how difficult it would be for anyone to make himself at home in such a small space, I wasn't sure if he meant it as a joke. But it certainly didn't sound like he was joking, so I tried to make myself comfortable on the couch.

Tom went to the jukebox. He had it rigged so that he wouldn't have to put any quarters in it, as normally one would have to do to operate the machine; he just pressed a few buttons. Then he wedged himself between the jukebox and the corner of the room and slithered onto the floor. His face had the look of complete contentment. He remained silent as he glanced slightly to his left, toward the jukebox, waiting for the first record to drop and for the music to begin.

Then it began.

We listened to *Brandy* by Looking Glass, which brought me back to the beach in Sandy Hook, where my friend Bob and I slept overnight on a sand dune in search of shooting stars; we listened to *Another Day* by Paul McCartney, which made me think of a winter vacation in Florida with my grandmother and how she fed me so much that I put on five pounds in one week; we listened to *We've Only Just Begun* by the Carpenters, which reminded me of a girl I tried to impress and who eventually broke my heart; we listened to *Mr. Bojangles* by the Nitty Gritty Dirt Band, which was the first song I tried to turn into a short story; we listened to *Rocket Man* by Elton John, which reminded me of a memorable career day event at school that almost changed the course of my life; we listened to *Have You Never Been Mellow* by Olivia Newton-John, *It's Too Late* by Carole King, *Fire & Rain* by James Taylor, and a half dozen others.

After forty-five minutes, I glanced over at Tabernacle Tom. He had his hands clasped together in front of his chest, his legs crossed Indian-style, and his head turned slightly to the left, toward the jukebox, with an almost adoring look on his face. Other than that, not much had changed about his position and demeanor from the way it was when he first turned on the classic machine and slithered onto the floor. I cleared my throat. He looked my way.

"So," I said softly, returning to the topic that had brought me to his tiny Tabernacle apartment in the first place. "This time machine of yours, the one you say you have... Can I see it now?"

Tabernacle Tom smiled and turned his head slightly to the left again.

Riding on the Trees

The trip had been Lynn's idea. She said she saw it in a movie once: a guy and a girl who have to decide whether to commit to each other for life go together to a quiet bungalow in the mountains to see how they feel about their relationship after three days of seclusion.

I was all for it, for many reasons beyond the one that Lynn had in mind. For one thing, it would be nice to leave Reading, Pennsylvania for a few days, where Lynn and I live and work. For another; it would be a really nice way to celebrate our thirtieth birthdays, which are within a day of each other. Also, there would be a lot of lovemaking, which anyone would have to admit is never a bad thing. Finally, we'd be surrounded by an abundance of peace and quiet, which is always soul cleansing. After all, I was juggling classes at Albright College with working part-time at L.A. Fitness, and I was still trying to come to terms with the fact that I had already spent (or wasted, as it turned out) several years at another college studying for a field I ultimately determined wasn't for me. In short, I was looking back on a decade of trying to make sense of my life, which is precisely why an abundance of peace and quiet was what I felt I needed. At least that's what I hoped.

One other thing. I knew that going to the Catskill Mountains would be an emotionally stimulating return to a place that used to make me very happy. The bungalow Lynn had in mind for our three-day tryst was the one I used to visit almost every summer when I was a kid.

It was a therapeutic plan that Lynn came up with, and I thanked her from the bottom of my frazzled heart.

•   •   •

Lynn and I were on our way to the mountain town of Loch Sheldrake. We were going to stay at my uncle's bungalow, hidden deep in the woods. Uncle Phil lived in Nevada now, but held onto the bungalow partly because he knew I loved it so much, and I was his favorite nephew.

"My uncle is extremely liberal, and he'll love the fact that there will be some good ol' biracial nooky-nooky shaking the walls of his rickety old bungalow," I said when Lynn first brought up the idea two weeks earlier. "If I know my uncle, it won't be the first time!"

"Is that the only reason you want to go, Rob?" Lynn chided. "Sex? Does that mean we can only go to towns hidden in the mountains so that there aren't too many people around to make a fuss about a smokin' hot black chick and a skinny pasty white boy doing the wild thing?"

"No, sex is not the only reason, Lynn," I insisted. "Yes, it's a great one, but it's not the *only* one. You know that. And no, we don't have to stick to quiet places that not many people know about. Besides, the population of Reading isn't that small, and when have I ever shied away from publicly declaring my love for you, no matter where we are in town?"

Although Lynn was not sensitive at all about our romantic union, sometimes she had to wonder if I had any anxiety about it myself. She knew I loved her very much—that was never an issue—but she also knew that when you strip away the facade, my family (other than my Uncle Phil) was not nearly as liberal as they claimed to be. Lynn and I were involved in something that, even by today's standards, is not always easy for some people to accept. Lynn knew I had to deal with that from time to time.

"Listen, I know we live in a pretty progressive place in this otherwise backwards country," she said to me one day, "but I also know that our relationship may always be a bit of an uphill climb, no matter *where* we are."

"I'm ready to climb any hill with you, Lynn," I responded. "Anywhere. Anytime. You know I couldn't be happier. I've had a few girlfriends over the years, but you are by far the sweetest, smartest, hottest, most invigorating woman I have ever known, black or white, and I don't care who knows."

So the plan was made. Uncle Phil gave his permission for us to use his bungalow, and two weeks later we packed our bags, loaded my car, filled the tank — and off we went to Loch Sheldrake.

•   •   •

Lynn and I became engaged two years ago, but *dis*-engaged a few months later. I was a disk jockey at a rock 'n roll radio station in Reading back then. That's where I met Lynn. She managed a physical therapy center that advertised on my station. Radio had been my career goal since I was a teenager, but I came to hate the politics and the policies involved and the nomadic nature of the business. After receiving my B.A. in communications, I had to move to three different states for three different radio jobs. Reading was my third and last hometown, I decided. I worked at a station there for a few months and then quit and enrolled at Albright to study psychiatry, which had been number two on my original What-I-want-to-be-when-I-grow-up list. That's why I called off the engagement; it was only fair to Lynn. I didn't want her to hitch her wagon to someone who might end up being miserable all over again. I wanted to be comfortable with Albright, figure out if I'd stick with this new professional goal, and decide if I'd stay in Reading, all before asking her to commit to marriage. Fortunately, I was fairly confident that it would all work out. I least that's what I hoped.

Lynn, who endured a disastrous relationship with an auto mechanic named Kyle several years before she met me, said that she totally understood my decision to postpone the engagement and agreed to abide by it with hope and patience. Kyle turned out to be an angry and violent man, much to her shock and surprise, for he didn't start out that way. He was madly in love with Lynn, but his stubborn ways and exceedingly short fuse troubled her. One day, she mentioned she wanted to break off the relationship. Kyle didn't take it well. He grabbed her forcibly, shoved her into his beloved 1980 black and gold Ford Thunderbird, and swore he'd drive them both off a cliff. Even Kyle's dog, a vicious German shepherd who Lynn never liked, went along for the harrowing ride. At his owner's command, the dog bit Lynn on both ankles to stop her from trying to escape. But true to her strength and determination, she punched Kyle in the testicles and forced him to stop the car. She got out, slammed the door before the dog could escape, and ran away. She never saw Kyle again.

Lynn told me that story in vivid detail early in our own relationship, and I never brought it up again—although it remained with me all this time.

"If calling off the engagement means there's a gigantic possibility that we can be happy together for the rest of our lives, I'll gladly wait," Lynn said to me the day I had postponed the engagement. "I've been through a lot, and I'm pretty damn sure that you're the right one." She kissed me. I knew then that I loved her more than anything else in the world. "And that way, you can safely postpone the inevitable for another year. I bet that'll be a relief."

"Postpone the inevitable?" I asked. "What do you mean by that?"

"Well, now that we're no longer engaged, the skinny white boy doesn't have to worry about meeting the big black bear of a future father-in-law and the loud, sarcastic big black mama bear who's married to him. We can put that off for a while."

I reminded her I had spoken to her parents on the phone several times and had seen plenty of pictures of them on her cellphone. "They seem absolutely delightful, Lynn," I said. "I'm actually looking forward to it."

"Even though you once asked me if my daddy had a rifle at home?"

"I was joking, Lynn. You know that. And by the way, I'm also looking forward to the day when my gorgeous black chick finally gets to meet her whiney white future mother-in-law and the clueless white fool she's married to."

"Good," she said. "I'll bring my daddy's rifle."

•   •   •

We began the three-hour journey from Reading on a Thursday morning. I drove first. For the first few miles, Lynn and I repeated the name Loch Sheldrake so many times that it became gibberish.

"If you're as stressed and horny as I am, you'll let me drive straight through. We'll stop once to pee, as soon as we start riding on the trees," I said, once we ceased mangling the name of the town we were going to.

"No," Lynn countered strongly. "I don't want you to drive straight through. You were up almost all night studying for your finals next week. If you fall asleep on the road, we'll crash, you'll die, and then what's the point? We'll switch in about an hour and a half."

"*I'll* die? Just me? Not you?"

"Just you. This gorgeous black chick was made for living, honey, not dying."

"I see. But don't forget that you were also up a lot the last few nights."

Lynn admitted I was right. "But a little exhaustion is good for me," she added. "It puts me at the peak of my sexual energy."

"I'm not sure how to respond to that. But it's good to know."

I *was* exhausted, and Lynn knew it. So she kept me engaged with conversation until it was time for her to drive.

"What did you say before?" she asked. "Riding on the trees?"

"Yes," I chuckled. "When I was a kid, whenever we got close to the Catskills my mother would say, 'Soon we'll be riding on the trees.' I took her literally. I thought that somehow our car would actually be riding on top of a long row of trees, all bunched together. I was a dumb kid, huh?"

"No. You were cute," Lynn smiled. "And I can't wait to meet your mom, especially since she used to say adorable things like that."

"Seriously?"

"Seriously! Besides, I spoke to her on the phone once—remember?—just like you spoke to mine. She was very nice. I have a feeling she'll be very proud of you, Rob, no matter how many professions you have, and no matter what color your future fiancé happens to be. I'm looking forward to getting to know her."

"I wonder what you two will talk about."

"Well, speaking of trees," Lynn said, "I'll tell her how her little Robbie has his own little sapling in his pants that turns into a big ol' sycamore that *I* always end up riding on."

I didn't know how to respond to that, either.

•　　•　　•

"Let's switch now," Lynn said. "It looks like your eyes are closing."

"We'll stop in ten minutes," I insisted. "I'll pee, then you'll drive."

"Fine."

The radio was on softly. I considered turning up the volume to help keep me awake, but Lynn had more to say, so I left it the way it was.

"How do you feel?" she asked. "I don't mean physically. I mean about things in general. Leaving the radio station. Taking off your headphones for good. Not playing rock n' roll anymore. About Albright."

"Oh, is that all?"

I didn't respond right away because I heard an announcement on the radio about a traffic jam on the highway near the mile marker we were approaching. After turning off at the next exit, I merged onto a secondary road. I was familiar with the alternate route because my father used to do the same thing when I was a kid whenever there was too much traffic. Right after I turned onto the secondary road, I noticed a sign that said Rest Area Two Miles Stay Right, so I edged the car into the right lane and stayed there.

"How do I feel about all those things?" I said, picking up Lynn's conversation from before. "Well, I'm just a little mad that it took me eight years to decide what to do. I could have been doing it by now. But what's done is done."

"Just thank God it took only eight years and not *twenty*-eight years."

"You're right, Lynn. Sometimes I wish we can live our lives one time before we live them for real. That way, we can make all the mistakes the first time around."

"Dream on."

"It's just that life is so damn short," I said. "It could be over tomorrow. And I know what you're gonna say: that's why we have to make the most of every day. I'm trying, Lynn. I am. But it's not easy. I mean, everything we do has an effect on so many other things and on so many other people. It can get sticky. Messy. Complicated. Like with us, for instance. I'm making this big life change for me, but it affects you, too. It's a puzzle. Up can be down and down can be up. Like an amusement park, where you pull a gigantic lever that's supposed to make something drop out of the ceiling, but the floor opens up instead. That's why life isn't easy."

"Wow!" Lynn said. "Did that come out of your psychology class, or is it from your own crazy Caucasian brain?"

"It's actually a dream that someone shared in one of my psych classes. We talk a lot about dreams in that class, which I find fascinating."

Another sign came up that said Rest Area One Mile Stay Right.

"What are some of the things you discuss in your dream class?" Lynn asked.

"Mostly about what they could mean," I said. "Nobody knows for sure, obviously. Like trains, for instance. A lot of people think that if you dream about getting on a train, you're either worried about dying or about where your life is headed. Other people think that if you dream about juggling, it represents making decisions, and if people are laughing or throwing things at you, then you're questioning whether you've made the right ones. Fascinating stuff. "

Lynn was a good listener, and because of my own state of affairs, I valued having someone like that in my corner. That's another reason I loved her so much.

"We also talk about how dreams are made up of hundreds of little pieces of thoughts and memories and doubts and plans that get all jumbled together while we're sleeping."

"Do you believe that?"

"Absolutely. I wish you could hear my professor explain it. Dr. Willoughby. I mean, with that salt-and-pepper goatee and his polka-dot bowtie—I swear to God, Lynn, either he's the weirdest professor I've ever had, or the most mesmerizing. You'd enjoy him."

"Well, he's not here, and he's not the one I need to screw in about an hour, so *you* explain it to me."

"Okay. Dr. Willoughby says that every single idea, recollection, or anxiety you have is on what he calls little post-it notes in your brain, stored in a big metaphorical jar. When you go to sleep, the jar gets shaken up and all the post-it notes get mixed up. Then the jar gets turned over and a dozen post-it notes fall out and line up to create a single story, regardless of how senseless that story may be. That story is your dream!"

"Interesting," Lynn said. "But I'm dreaming about peeing now. So pull over."

•　　•　　•

Lynn took over the driving once we left the rest area. The GPS provided continuous directions to the bungalow, so she insisted I relax and not worry about a thing. We had about an hour to go.

"I'm in your strong, capable, sensual black hands," I yawned as I turned up the volume on the radio. Then I closed my eyes.

A few minutes later, I felt the car rise and fall, as if Lynn and I were driving on extremely bumpy terrain going up a steep hill. I looked out the window and saw giant boulders below us.

"What the hell…" I muttered. "Lynn, did you make a wrong turn?"

She told me not to worry.

"I guess it's a detour," I conceded. "Maybe they're building a new road or something. I'm sure it will level off in a few seconds."

But the road did not level off. It continued to be an uphill trek. Lynn, still the picture of confidence and composure, stopped the car. She looked at me with a mischievous grin, and then her eyes darted past me, through the passenger window, which seemed to be a clue that I should also look that way.

I couldn't believe what I saw. It was an amusement park. There were dozens of rides, each one swaying, twirling, rising, lowering, and wobbling, although no people were in sight. Merry-go-round music emanated from the sky.

"Maybe it's not open yet," I shouted to Lynn.

I heard someone calling out to me to pick a ride, but it wasn't Lynn's voice. It was much lower than hers. But I felt the need to respond.

"There are so many to choose from," I shouted back.

"Get on!" the voice said.

The ride I selected was in the shape of a giant pair of headphones. I hopped on. Each headphone cup grabbed one side of my body, and then the entire contraption lifted me into the air and spun me around. Everything became a blur. I saw a man with a goatee and a polka-dot bowtie pull a giant lever that made the headphone spin even faster. I felt sick and called out for Lynn.

"Over here!" she yelled. She was at the other end of the amusement park.

I jumped off the ride and searched for a path that would bring me closer to her, but all I saw was an oversized checkerboard with sticky black and white squares. I hated the feel. Each square had a picture of a girl's face. All the faces looked familiar.

"What the hell?" I said.

Walking across that sticky checkerboard was more strenuous than the most strenuous piece of gym equipment at L.A. Fitness. Every muscle in my body ached.

Lynn was on the other side of the gooey checkerboard when I finally arrived.

"You won't believe this," she said. "Look." She was standing beside a shiny railroad car. Black and white steam blew out of a smokestack on the locomotive next to it.

"It looks so real," I said.

We stepped onto the platform and stood inside the gleaming, luxurious railroad car. I spun around slowly to take in the entire scene. I saw my Uncle Phil on a checkerboard square eating an apple. By his feet was a crate full of other apples, which he started to throw at me. I could hardly breathe. My entire skull throbbed. I wondered if I had hit my head on the roof of the car while Lynn and I were driving over those boulders. But Lynn came over and hugged me tightly, and suddenly I felt safe again, safe and loved and protected, and I closed my eyes. I knew the pain and confusion would pass. At least that's what I hoped.

• • •

When I opened my eyes, Lynn was pulling off the highway to take a long country road that led to Uncle Phil's bungalow. She said that the past fifteen minutes on the road had been grueling, with a lot of bumps and potholes, and that I had seemed distressed during my nap.

"Nap?" I asked. "But the amusement park—"

"What amusement park?"

I shook my head and sighed. I didn't know what else to do.

"According to the GPS," Lynn said, "this road goes on for twenty-one miles. I'm hot and horny and I want to get there as soon as possible, so just shut your eyes again and keep quiet. No more crazy talk about amusement parks. Understood?"

"Understood."

I closed my eyes. A moment later Lynn repeated her command, word for word: "I'm hot and horny and want to get there as soon as possible, so just shut your eyes again and keep quiet..." Though I heard the words, when I looked to my left, Lynn's mouth wasn't moving. I just accepted it and looked out the passenger window. I was astounded to see that the car was actually riding on top of a long row of evergreen trees.

That's when we pulled up in front of Uncle Phil's bungalow.

"Let's get inside right now," Lynn said. *"Right now!"* Once again, her lips did not move.

"Aye aye, sir," I smirked.

I followed Lynn into the bungalow. As I pushed the front door open, I noticed it was covered top to bottom with post-it notes, each one filled with shapes and squiggles. Once inside, within seconds Lynn had her clothes off and helped me remove mine, and right there on the wood-plank floor of the living room we began to make love with some hasty yet passionate foreplay. As I prepared to consummate our lust, the front door opened and in walked my mother and Lynn's father, each holding two rifles. They juggled the rifles between them while staring at us naked on the floor and shouting "Hello, hello…"

"Leave us alone!" I shouted back.

"You say stop and I say go, go, go," the two of them cackled in unison.

"What?"

"You say goodbye and I say hello."

I felt Lynn's right hand on my shoulder. She was shaking me aggressively. We were still in the car.

"What are you doing?" I asked, "Why are we still driving?"

Lynn didn't answer. She kept her head straight ahead with her eyes on the road. A disc jockey on the radio said, "That was the Beatles with 1967's *Hello, Goodbye*. And now —" The car went under a stone overpass and the disc jockey cut out for a few moments. When we exited the overpass, *Brown Sugar* by the Rolling Stones had just begun.

"Jesus," I muttered. "This is crazy. This is absolutely…" Still reeling, it was hard for me to complete a simple sentence. I just closed my eyes to try to make sense of it all.

"We'll be there in fifteen minutes, but I gotta pee again, really bad," Lynn said. "Between my bladder and whatever's going on in your head, I think we should get out and stretch one last time. Let's run into that gas station over there."

She pulled off the road and parked.

"Come in with me," she pleaded. "It looks kind of creepy."

It did, though I had to admit to myself that creepy had been part of the journey for quite some time by now. The gas station was in terrible disrepair and seemingly on the brink of collapse. An old, battered, black and gold Ford Thunderbird was parked on the side, and tied to its chrome bumper was an old German shepherd who, even though lying down, was drooling buckets of saliva.

"Rob?" Lynn said. Normally she was calm about everything, but this time her voice had an exceptionally anxious edge to it. "Rob? Come in with me, okay? Please?"

"Oh, it's fine," I assured her, much more comfortable now with all the recent improbabilities. "I'll just relax in the car and wait until we're at the bungalow. For real this time."

"Rob—please!" she pleaded. "What's gotten into you? Come with me... Rob? Please?"

I knew she'd be fine. At least that's what I hoped.

Selective Emory

Emory Parker arrived at the Forked River service plaza off exit 76 on the Garden State Parkway at two o'clock on a summer midweek afternoon when the temperature was high and her expectations even higher.

Although a business meeting at a parkway rest stop was one of the least conventional requests to which the attractive graphic artist had ever agreed, her acceptance gave her an earnest sense of optimism, both about her personal life and her career. Perhaps that was because her straight red hair fell perfectly into place when she was getting ready this morning, which wasn't always the case. Maybe it was because she made it to the service plaza in her rented car in practically no time at all since traffic moved briskly between Jersey City and Forked River. Or the reason could be that her new, stylish leather briefcase, a gift from her parents for her twenty-eighth birthday, made a few heads turn when she walked into the rest stop.

She stood by the southbound entrance, her briefcase in one hand and her handbag in the other, searching the place for a man named Zach Gerber, owner of a new business called Gerber Associates. Gerber had advertised for a freelance graphic artist to design his company's internet newsletter. Gerber was also the one who suggested meeting at the Forked River service plaza since the company's new office was still under construction.

But the service plaza was crowded. As on most beautiful summer days, hundreds of people from New Jersey, New York, Pennsylvania and elsewhere were traveling down the Jersey shore to go to one of its popular beach retreats.

Pedro Ramirez entered the service plaza from the northbound side. He had driven up from Atlantic City, where he was employed by the Caesars Entertainment Group as a corporate limousine drive. Pedro, a dark and handsome young man who was just a few years older than Emory, had been in this country less than a year, and he, too, was searching for someone. As opposed to Emory, though, he knew exactly who he was looking for. It was his wife, Rosa Miranda Ramirez. She was taking a bus from Newark Liberty International Airport to meet him in Forked River, and from there they planned to drive together to Atlantic City, where Pedro had an apartment.

On the southbound side, Emory scanned the room from left to right, and on the northbound side, Zach did the same. After a moment or two, Emory saw Pedro through a break in the crowd and had a flash of hope that he was the business owner, Zach Gerber, for whom she was searching. He looked the part. Late thirties, well-groomed, wearing a dark, impeccably tailored suit. In fact, it was more than a flash of hope; Emory was absolutely certain it was Mr. Gerber.

She walked over to him.

"Zach Gerber?" Emory asked.

She smiled somewhat more expansively than she was used to smiling. That sprung from the fact that Pedro was very attractive and had piercing blue eyes. She embraced her expansive smile, rather than mute it, since she felt as if her teeth were whiter than they had been in a long time. It was, for her, another little emotional bonus that merely increased her confidence about this upcoming business meeting.

"Zach Gerber?" she repeated.

Pedro looked confused.

"¿Disculpe?" he asked.

"Are you Zach Gerber? From Gerber Associates? We spoke on the phone last week. Remember? About your internet newsletter? I'm the graphic designer." She held out her hand. "Emory Parker! I'm the one you spoke to. Call me Emory."

Pedro shook her hand, although he wasn't sure why he was doing so.

"¿Emory?" Pedro repeated with a heavy accent.

Two families walked between them; each family member was of a different age, but all sported billowy, oversized, severely colored shirts over their bathing suits. Emory and Pedro found themselves temporarily lost in that shuffle. Emory moved closer to Papa John's Pizza, which was not crowded at the moment. A determined nod of her head told Pedro that he should follow.

"Yes, it's Emory," she said once they were in the clear. "I know, it's an unusual name. Emory. I had nothing to do with it. My parents named me after the college in Atlanta. That's where they met. That's even where they got married, if you can believe it—right there in the student center. One minute they were psychology students, and the next, bam!—husband and wife."

On Pedro's face, suddenly, was a flash of understanding.

"¿Wife? Sí. ¡Mi esposa! Estoy buscando a mi esposa," he smiled.

Pedro looked over Emory's shoulder, still searching for the person he was hoping to spot. Emory thought he had simply seen something unusual over her shoulder, which would be par for the course at a crowded parkway rest stop.

"Estoy? Buscando?" she said curiously. "I'm so sorry—I really don't understand Spanish. It *is* Spanish, isn't it? Of course it is; what a stupid thing to say. I studied Spanish in middle school but then switched to Mandarin Chinese in high school. Like I'm really gonna need Mandarin Chinese on a daily basis, right? My mother said it would look good on my resume. I should've stuck with Spanish. Don't you think? Is your newsletter gonna be in English and Spanish? It doesn't really matter for the design. I was just wondering."

"Estoy buscando a mi esposa," Pedro repeated.

"Esposa?" The word sounded funny to her—funny and vaguely familiar. "What do you mean by esposa? Are you saying you're 'supposed to' meet someone? Is that what you're saying? Supposed to? I wish I was a little better with accents. Sorry. But if that's what you're saying, then I think it's me you're supposed to be meeting. Or did Zach Gerber send you here to meet me? Was Mr. Gerber not able to come? That must be it. I think I get it now." Emory pointed to Pedro. "But you *do* work for Gerber Associates, right? For Zach Gerber?"

When Emory pointed to him, as if by reflex, Pedro pointed to himself.

"Yo soy Pedro," he said. "Yo no soy de aquí."

"Pedro?"

He shook his head.

"Si. Pedro Ramirez."

"Well, whatever you're saying, you're obviously not Zach Gerber, and I'm guessing that he didn't send you here to meet me," Emory acknowledged. She was determined not to be upset about this slight interruption in her daylong streak of good luck; she remained confident that the day could still be in her favor— just like her hair and her teeth and the ride down the Garden State Parkway. "Oh well," Emory smiled, "I'll just keep looking for Zach Gerber, I suppose."

"¡Esposa, si!" Pedro said, having once again heard only the word he wanted to hear. "Estoy buscando a mi esposa."

"I wish I knew what you were saying. Obviously you're 'supposed' to do something or you're 'supposed' to meet someone. Because you keep saying it. Just goes to prove you should never listen to your mother. I wish I remembered a little more Spanish so that I could help you. I really do. Let me try, okay? I'd like to try. Now, who are you looking for? Who?"

"¿Who?" Pedro repeated.

"Yes, who?"

Emory pointed to the two dozen people on line at Starbucks and then to the group of women on line at the ladies' room entrance, and she moved her arm in a wide arc thinking that would help Pedro visualize what the word 'who' means.

"*Who* are you supposed to meet?"

Pedro was fairly certain that he did indeed understand what Emory was asking.

"Ah," he said, nodding his head. "Who. Si. Busco Rosa Miranda Ramirez. Mi esposa."

"Who?"

It was Pedro who now used a sweeping hand gesture the way Emory had done a moment before. He tried to describe Rosa's hair and height so that Emory would understand.

"Ella tiene el cabello castaño como el suyo y su misma estatura," he said. He pointed to Emory and suddenly seemed quite animated. This movement flattered Emory, for she thought he was describing her.

"Oh, I get it!" she announced proudly. "You're hoping to meet someone who looks like me. Am I right? Someone who has my color hair, someone who's my height—is that it? Does that mean you think I'm pretty?" She blushed. "That is *so* sweet of you to say!"

Just that morning, as she was getting ready, something made Emory wonder when she would finally get into a relationship that would make her happy. A guy named Jeff was her last, and that was three years ago.

"I have to admit," Emory continued, "no one has ever approached me like that before. This is a first. It's almost magical! Not that I mind—it's just that it's a bit of a surprise, in the middle of a typical afternoon. Well, I guess it's not a typical afternoon, really, since we're at a rest stop by the Garden State Parkway, of all places. What's it called again—Forked River? That's such a weird name, isn't it? Well, anyway, it's perfectly all right. I'm not gonna get all bent out of shape, if that's what you're worried about. I like it when guys do things in new and different ways. Especially when they're nice, like you. It's better than the same old tired pickup lines I hear from other guys. You know what I mean, right? Well, where do we go from here— what did you say your name was? Pedro? Where do we go from here, Pedro? Can I assume that you're not married? Forgive me for asking, but you have to these days."

Pedro shrugged and shook his head. Emory took that to mean he was single.

"Good. I knew you weren't. I'm single too. I was almost engaged once, but the guy said I was too naïve, and he broke it off. Me—naïve! Can you believe it? I'd like to think I'm pretty worldly, if you want to know the truth. I mean, I have my own little freelance graphic arts business, I make a good living, I deal with people all over the country, I play the guitar and I sing at parties, I even teach graphic arts part-time at Columbia."

There was another flash of recognition on Pedro's face, an even bigger one this time.

"¿Colombia? ¡Si! Mi esposa y yo somos de Colombia."

"Yes. Columbia," Emory said. "Twice a week. It's called being an adjunct professor. It doesn't pay much, but it's interesting and it's good experience. It might come in handy one day. You never know." She arched her body to lean in closer to him. She felt confident enough to do that; it didn't hurt that Pedro's cologne was very comforting in this crowded rest stop which otherwise smelled of sweat and coffee. "To tell you the truth, I thought that by teaching at a college I might be able to meet someone," Emory said. "You know what I mean? That's why I decided to be an adjunct at Columbia in the first place."

"Colombia," he sighed. "Si."

"Oh, it's really not that impressive. I'm just an adjunct. Twice a week. I think anyone can be an adjunct professor if they've worked in their field for a few years and have some good references."

A large TV monitor on the wall behind Emory played a commercial for Match.com. She couldn't hear the sound but knew the lady in the ad was saying "Come find me!"

"Colombia…" Pedro said.

"Yes, Columbia," Emory repeated. She looked away from the monitor and returned her attention to Pedro. "But you're embarrassing me. It's really not that big a deal. I mean, it's not Harvard or Yale."

"Extraño Colombia—"

She wondered if that was her cue to be just as silly. So with an exaggerated comical wave of her hand, Emory said, "Oh please!"

"¡Si! La policia," Pedro announced, having heard yet another word he thought would come in handy—a word that to his ears reflected the imminent help of someone who could assist in his anxious search. "La policia puede ayudarme."

Emory felt that Pedro's response confirmed that he, too, agreed that being an adjunct professor at Columbia was no big deal. "Yeah, I know. You should see some of the other adjunct professors at Columbia," she smirked. "Nothing to get excited about. So now we can stop with all this adjunct stuff! I get embarrassed easily, anyway. It's really not that big a deal. I swear."

"¿Usted va a traer la policia para que me ayuden a encontrar a Rosa Miranda para regresar a Colombia?" Pedro said almost breathlessly.

"Oh!" Emory replied the moment he finished saying what he was saying. "I guess you're still impressed with Columbia, aren't you? Well, even though you're embarrassing the hell out of me, Pedro, I appreciate it. I really do. My last boyfriend had no respect for anything I did. At least you do. Jeff thought that being an adjunct professor was a stupid waste of time. He was a jerk, now that I think about it. But you don't think that. Obviously! I don't mind telling you that you're a very special man, Pedro. I'm glad I bumped into you—even if you're not Zach Gerber."

Emory grabbed his hand and shook it.

"Buscaré un policía ahora," Pedro smiled. "Gracias."

"Gracias? Now *there's* a word I remember from high school. But you shouldn't gracias me, I should gracias you! For everything you've said. For being so nice. I'll be honest with you, Pedro—I haven't had much luck meeting nice people lately. I may be a little worldly and very modest, but that doesn't mean I don't get depressed sometimes. I do. I get depressed at least once a month. I guess I'm just not really a fan of the singles scene. I don't want to work so hard. You know what I mean? That's why it's nice to meet someone like you. Someone different, but sweet. Someone who takes initiative—and is nice about it at the same time. Someone who knows how to do the right thing. I mean, I don't expect miracles. I just want to know that there's someone out there who I don't have to ask to bring me candy and roses from time to time—"

"¡Rosa!" Pedro announced, this time with even more animation than during the earlier Colombia discussion. "Rosa Miranda."

"Yes, I love roses," Emory smiled.

"¿La policia me va ayudar a encontrar a Anna Rosa? Gracias. Gracias."

"Gracias for what? I really didn't do anything."

"Policia. Anna Rosa."

"Are you asking if you can buy me roses? Oh my God! I can't believe it." Emory covered her mouth with her hand. She leaned against a booth that a family had just vacated; a few empty cups and food wrappers remained behind and little pools of ketchup, mustard and sugar spotted the tabletop. But Emory didn't see any of that. She sat at the edge of the outermost chair. "Every time I think you've been as sweet as you can be," she said, "you do something even sweeter!"

Emory took a pen and scrap of paper out of her pocket and scribbled on it.

"My mother would call me crazy, giving my address and phone number to someone I just met—but I think I'm mature enough to know when something's right." She handed the paper to Pedro. "And this feels right. It really does. Here. It's my name, address and phone number. For the roses."

Pedro looked at the paper and shook his head. He had expected it to say something recognizable related to his untiring quest.

"I'll look forward to it, Pedro," Emory continued. "Don't forget to include a note if I'm not home when you get there—just so that I know how and where to respond, if you know what I mean."

"¿No policia?" he asked.

"Whoops—you're right," she chuckled, with a grin on her face. "*Please*. Please include a note. Thank you for reminding me of my manors! That's so sweet of you."

Holding the little scrap of paper, Pedro backed away a few steps, slowly and uncertainly. He tucked the paper into his shirt pocket. When he was far enough away, Emory took her cellphone out of her handbag and speed-dialed her friend Claudia.

"Claudia? It's Emory. You won't believe what just happened. You just won't believe it. I met this cute guy. He's Spanish. He's handsome, and he's so sweet. I think he likes me... No, I was supposed to meet that newsletter guy I told you about, but.... Yes! Just by accident... Yes, and not only that, but I gave him my address and phone number... Sure I'm sure. I'm not an idiot, you know. I wouldn't have given it to him if I thought something wasn't right."

Pedro was now several yards away. Emory turned around. She saw him wave to someone in the distance. He sprinted toward that person.

"¡Rosa! ¡Rosa!" he called out.

"Oh my God!" Emory said to Claudia. "Oh my God! I think he just saw someone selling roses. About a minute ago he said he wanted to buy me roses, and I think he's gonna bring them over to my apartment... No, I really don't remember how it came up. He just suddenly said he wanted to buy me roses. Claudia, I think this is the beginning of something. I can feel it. I can really feel it this time. I feel it in my bones. Oh my God, that's so sweet! I don't know if this Zach Gerber is even coming. I mean, a business meeting at a parkway rest stop? What was I thinking? I guess I'll just return the rented car and go back to my apartment."

"¡Rosa!" Pedro called out to someone in the distance.

"I knew that something good was gonna happen today when I woke up this morning," Emory said to Claudia on the phone. "I need some good luck for a change. After all this time."

"¡Rosa!"

"He is just *so* sweet..."

The Bittersweet Ballad of Bobby Blu

"Four million toenails!"

Amy lifted a large, pastel-colored cushion off the living room couch.

"There are four million toenails in my beautiful couch, Bob," she grumbled once again.

I couldn't tell if she was genuinely pissed off or just mildly annoyed. Whatever it was, I wanted to figure it out quickly because that would determine how the rest of the evening would play out. I wanted to have a pleasant night. I *needed* to have a pleasant night. So I purposely tried to lighten the moment to see how Amy would respond. That was a little trick I had learned over the years. With some luck, that would give me a clue.

"Sorry, Amy," I said, my mental fingers crossed, "next time I'll cut only *two* million toenails."

"Very funny, Bob," she said, refusing to look up. "When I want Jerry Seinfeld to live with me, I'll invite him over for dinner. I love you, I love your toenails, and I love the couch, but your toenails *in* the couch is just a little much. Don't you think? So help me out a little more. Okay?" She began to Dust Bust the toenails away, along with at least half a pound of dust balls. And then with her hand she picked up four pennies, two dimes, a nickel and two quarters, six red and four green garbage bag twist ties, and two empty candy wrappers (KitKats and M&Ms). To me, the line about Jerry Seinfeld meant she was only mildly annoyed, and mildly annoyed is always better than genuinely pissed off. Had she been genuinely pissed off she would have said something stronger, or she wouldn't have said anything at all. Now at least there was a fighting chance to save the night.

I was on the mahogany rocker at the side of the couch, hugging my guitar. After Dust Busting for a few more moments, Amy sat down to rest. The couch was against the living room window and the soft, wispy material of the curtains framed her artistically. It reminded me of an album cover I had created in my mind when I was twelve (which was the last year real vinyl albums were regularly produced). I suppose it was the quintessential fantasy album of my youth. It was to have been a work of jazz fusion on which I would have sung a dozen songs while accompanying myself on guitar. I even designed the album cover — in my mind, that is — which pictured a beautiful woman beckoning an unseen stranger to join her on the large, white wicker chair upon which she sat, naked, her breasts covered by her flowing red hair. It was a damn good album cover, thanks to a damn good fantasy.

When Amy and I met in college, I gladly altered the fantasy album cover so that Amy, instead of the make-believe redhead, could be featured. The altered vision was now of a beautiful young woman with shoulder-length brown hair, in a silky silver negligee that was slightly parted in the middle, a thin silver belt draped loosely over her crossed legs. The fantasy picture captured Amy's wise expression, the long, vertical dimples in each cheek, and the confident green eyes. I am off to the side on this imaginary album cover, just about out of view, clutching my guitar, with an expression that confirmed how the brown-haired, green-eyed beauty beckoned no one but me. In fact, if I remember correctly (and that gets a little more difficult with each passing year), *Beckoning* was the name of that fantasy album, as well as the name of a song I had actually written for it in real life. But, alas, it was the album that never was: *Beckoning* by Bobby Blu. Or *Beckoning* by R. D. Blume. Or *Beckoning* by anyone other than Robert David Blumenthal, which is my real name. You can't cut an album if your name is Robert David Blumenthal. Not even a make-believe one. As it turned out, I never did.

·   ·   ·

I'll admit it: until a few years ago, I really believed that I could turn the fantasy album into a real one. I even had a plan: I would wait until I had written twelve good tunes and would then pound the pavement in Manhattan until my feet swelled to the size of a bass drum in order to get my songs heard by the record company executives who could actually make it happen.

By the time Amy was Dust Busting four million of my toenails out of the couch, I had written only seven songs with which I was satisfied, had written no new ones in almost two years, and was even getting a little rusty on my beloved guitar. For one thing, I was busier than I wanted to be at the Ferguson Bakery Supply Corporation of Nyack, New York, where I was the Quality Assurance Manager. For another, if I wasn't at the plant seeking new ways to eliminate impurities, then I was at home unclogging toilets and building furniture from IKEA. Things beckoned all right—but a career in music wasn't one of them.

Amy has said many times over the years that my dream will come true one day, that I have the talent and the personality to *make* it come true. Maybe she believes it a little more than I do— particularly on nights when I feel life passing me by without so much as a drop of adrenaline flowing through my desolate bloodstream. It occurred to me that night—that Dust Busting night—just how disjointed my life had become, chained as I was to the world of bakery products, yet still grasping at the dream of becoming a professional musician. Thanks to the Ferguson Bakery Supply Corporation, I had no time to work on new songs and barely enough time to practice the old ones. Why did I still want to pursue such a lame idea? I knew deep down that it would never happen. And anyway, apparently luck was not part of my genetic makeup. So why should I even bother?

Lazily, I plucked out the first few notes of the *Entertainment Tonight* theme on my upper E string.

"Really? *Entertainment Tonight*?" Amy asked at the end of a yawn. "That's not exactly *Layla*. Why are you playing that, of all things?"

"Maybe because that's something that's missing from our lives," I said, "entertainment — tonight, or *any* night. Unless you consider dirty limericks on the wall of the men's bathroom at the plant entertainment."

"Don't Abby and Lucy entertain you?" she asked.

"Yes," I relented. "They do."

Abby and Lucy were our curly-topped strawberry blonde twins. They were happy, healthy and active five-year-olds. Those little tornadoes trashed the house even when they didn't try to, and since I was at the plant so much of the time, it usually fell to Amy to return the house to livability. It is our hope that once the girls are in school full-time next year, the house won't be such a mess, and Amy might then relax, do more for herself, maybe even reestablish her freelance interior design business. And wouldn't it be great if Abby and Lucy can actually help around the house for a change to further lighten the load?

Maybe there will even be enough time to make love again.

That was another 'entertainment' missing from our lives. Making love. I never understood how other parents found the time for it. To be fair to myself, I never believed that Amy had lost the attraction; she just temporarily misplaced it due to the extenuating circumstances of home ownership and twenty-four/seven motherhood. Between the two of us there was shopping to do, laundry to fold, things to fix, bills to pay... It was our very own *Day in the Life*. A sad, sad situation. No wonder there was hardly any sex anymore; we were both too busy singing the Suburban Blues. Playful words rarely were spoken or suggestive moves made. Even Amy's appreciation of my music, which once upon a time she made known nearly every day, was now relegated to a kindly grin or a gentle nod every once in a while. "That's nice," she would say when I attempted a new tune, or "I've always liked that," when I played an old one. That was about it. Even though the house always truly felt like my home, if it weren't for toenails and other mildly annoying distractions, Amy and I might have run out of things to talk about in that homey house ages ago.

"How does such a small room get so much junk?" Amy suddenly announced. She placed the Dust Buster on the floor with a thump and sat straight up in the chair. "Toenails in the couch don't help. Don't be lazy, Bob. Please. And don't sit around playing your guitar when you know we're having company. Don't you remember that Mike and Mary Jane and their kids are coming over Saturday afternoon? I need help around here. And it's getting late."

I didn't bother to try to lighten the mood a second time because I didn't want to push mildly annoyed over into genuinely pissed-off territory. So I leaned my guitar against the chair.

"Okay," I conceded. "You're right. What should I do?"

"Well, I'm baking a cake for Saturday and I need a container of heavy cream," she said. "Go to Shoprite and pick one up for me. Okay?"

Amy went into the kitchen. I followed. An idea had just popped into my cloudy head. Not a song, heaven knows—just an idea.

"I'll make you a deal," I said. "How about instead of going to Shoprite, I walk over to that little Quick Mart joint over on Main

Street? Things are a little more expensive there, but the fresh air will be good for me. It'll also take a little longer for me to get back, but I bet I'll be a pussycat when I come home and maybe I'll even help you bake the cake."

"No thank you. I want it to come out actually looking like a cake. I don't need that kind of help. But okay — go to the Quick Mart. I have to finish cleaning the living room, anyway. Just be careful by the tracks. And don't get home too late. Don't forget — this is where you belong, not at some out-of-the-way Quick Mart."

"It's a deal."

"I'm sorry I got angry, Bob," she added. Perhaps she had a millisecond's twinge of guilt for sending me out into the lonely night. "It just gets very frustrating sometimes. That's all."

"Don't explain, Amy" I said. "I love you just the way you are."

"Is that you or Billy Joel talking?"

"It was Billy Joel in 1976. Today it's me."

"Good."

Amy didn't dwell on the reasons I wanted to take a walk by myself. I guess she already knew. She knew that every once in a while I needed to get slapped in the face by a blast of cold air to remind me that just because dreams don't always come true, that doesn't mean I'm a total failure as a person.

I opened the front door. The moon was bright and fuzzy. It was chilly outside. I slipped into my favorite sneakers, which were by the door, and put on my old Oswego sweatshirt, which was on the doorknob of the coat closet. My hair became a crazy black mop as I pulled the sweatshirt over my head. There was a mirror with a little shelf near the front door, and on the shelf was a pair of sunglasses. I put on the sunglasses and looked at myself in the mirror. "Hey there, how's it going, Bobby Blu?" I smirked at the retro-cool R&B reflection.

"What's that, Bob?" Amy shouted from the kitchen.

"Nothing," I called back. "Just talking to myself. I'm going now. See you in a few."

"Be careful," she said. "Don't be too late."

"I won't."

I put the sunglasses back on the shelf, opened the front door, and walked out of the house. I knew it would be a long walk, but at least my sneakers felt good because my toenails were so short.

•　　•　　•

I purchased a container of heavy cream at the Quick Mart.

On my way home, I saw that a freight train had just arrived on a westbound track that ran parallel to Route 59, which I had to cross to get back to the side street that led to my neighborhood. Now Route 59 was blocked, and the train wasn't moving. It was an extremely long train—thirty-five or forty cars—and the only other crossing was Devlin Street, about a quarter mile away, and that street was probably blocked, as well. It was one of those overused, underappreciated freight trains that still crisscross the country day after day, the kind Woody and Arlo Guthrie sang about so eloquently in songs like *This Train is Bound for Glory* and *The City of New Orleans*. There was a train depot a few dozen yards to the west, a small wooden shack, really, that was hardly ever used. The station where people actually got on and off the commuter trains that also used that track was a few miles away. Perhaps some worker at the little depot was there to count or log in products that were being transported on the train. I had been glancing at that depot for years, fleetingly, whenever I passed by in the car, simply out of curiosity. I knew it had a stairway and a footbridge that crossed over the tracks and descended to the other side. But I was leery of using that stairway because in order to get onto the bridge, you had to go into the wooden shack, and I wasn't sure I wanted to do that. I didn't know what I'd find inside; some ornery old railroad guys, maybe, who might be suspicious since I looked like a hoodlum with a brown paper bag that easily could have been hiding a bottle of Jack Daniels. And with the luck I had been having lately, it wouldn't surprise me at all if they held me at bay with a shotgun until the police arrived, no matter how well I pleaded my innocence.

The boxcar directly in front of me had a huge, metal sliding door that was open about a foot and a half. Through that door I could see street lights in the distant darkness, which meant that the door on the other side of the boxcar was also slightly ajar. By my calculations, it would take me less than ten seconds to jump onto the ledge of the door, slither in, sprint through the car, and jump off the other side. Then I could be on my way home. Simple problem, simple solution.

So I hopped up onto the floor of the boxcar. That was the simple part. I stood up and looked around but couldn't see what products were stored inside because it was pitch black. My eyes adjusted quickly to the darkness, though, and I saw the car was empty.

I walked across to the other side, and when I got there, the train suddenly jerked forward. I fell down. The train stopped again. When I tried to get up, the bottom of my sweatshirt caught on a splintered piece of metal that was bent up from the floor. I tried to work the material of the sweatshirt around the splinter, but all I did was wrap it around tighter. The train moved forward again, and this time it kept moving. The car swayed in the darkness. My sweatshirt finally came loose. I stood up, but had considerable difficulty maintaining my balance since there was nothing to hold on to. The train went slowly at first, and that at least allowed me to grab onto a metal side-beam along one wall. I held on tightly. Within moments, the train was traveling forty or forty-five miles an hour. Maybe more. I tried to think, but that just wasted precious time, and by the time I *stopped* thinking, the train was moving at fifty-five or maybe even sixty miles an hour. That's just a guess. It could have been going faster.

The bag of heavy cream was no longer in my hand. I had dropped it. I looked around and saw the bag against the back wall. That's when I noticed that there was no doorway there, no opening of any kind along that wall, nor along the front wall, either. The only two doors were the ones on either side of the boxcar. Both of them were still open about a foot-and-a-half.

Despite being made of metal, the car smelled of some kind of wood. (I had to wonder if it was Norwegian wood, although I have no idea what Norwegian wood is or what it smells like.) I thought of Amy, standing in our kitchen, lining up all the ingredients she needed to make the cake for Saturday's company (all but the heavy cream, of course) and wondering where the hell I was and why I was so late when I had promised to come straight home.

The train stopped about an hour later. At least it *seemed* like an hour later. I didn't have my cellphone with me, so this is just another guess. It actually had stopped twice before, the first time on a skinny bridge that was high over a creek (as I gleaned from peeking out the door), and the second time in a tunnel that was darker than the boxcar itself. When the train stopped a third time, I saw what appeared to be another small depot—a tiny brick building, with lights along the roofline. There was a Ford pickup in a two-space gravel parking lot at the side.

I waited a few extra seconds to make sure that the train wouldn't jerk forward unexpectedly and cause me to fall down again. I looked through the opening to make sure there was solid ground beside the track. That seemed to be the case, so I slid through and jumped down onto the ground. I had forgotten about the heavy cream and left it in the boxcar. I walked around to a side of the building where there was a bench on which two men sat. One man wore what appeared to be blue overalls, and the other wore jeans and a sweatshirt that I think was red. It was hard to tell.

"Excuse me, gentleman. May I ask a stupid question?" I said as I slowly approached them. "Where am I?"

"Tannersville," Mr. Sweatshirt responded.

"Tannersville? Where's that?"

"P.A. In the Poconos."

"Pennsylvania? *Those* Poconos? The Pocono Mountains?"

"Well, there ain't no Poconos anywhere else. You lost, son? 'Cause you look lost. You *sound* lost, too."

"Can I catch a train going the other way?"

"Nope," Mr. Overalls said. "It's too late."

"Carole King, 1973," I said. Both men stared at me. "It's a song. *It's Too Late....* Never mind. Not important."

"Want us to get a policeman?" Mr. Sweatshirt asked.

"I don't think so," I answered. "Maybe you could just tell me where I could make a phone call and find a bathroom."

"No phone here," Mr. Overalls said. "No bathroom, either. Try Stinkey's."

"I beg your pardon? What's Stinkey's?"

"The bar down the block. On the right. They have a pay phone and a bathroom. But sometimes the pay phone don't work and the bathroom got no door."

"Great! Thanks," I said. Then I started to walk down the road.

It was a rural road, more dirt than pavement, spotted here, there and everywhere with junk—old engines, chains, tires, rusted farm tools—all of it vaguely lit in the night by the lights on the tiny depot by the tracks and, to a smaller degree, by the fuzzy moon.

I soon lost the benefit of the building lights as I continued along the road; the moon, which grew fuzzier by the minute, offered little further guidance. For a moment, I thought I was lost for good. But then I saw light again, red light this time, from neon beer signs in a small window on a low, square structure up the road a bit. I walked over to the building, went around to the front, and saw a hand-painted sign (in script) above a wooden door. If Mr. Overalls hadn't mentioned it, I might never have recognized it as the word Stinkey's. It looked more like 8temkav'z.

I pulled on the wooden door, which opened effortlessly because it had no spring or brackets of any kind, and walked in. I closed the door behind me. The door bounced open again because it didn't have a latch, either — just a rusted hook-and-eye contraption that was currently off duty.

It was dimly lit and smoky inside. Frank Sinatra was singing *Young at Heart* from a jukebox near the door. Fifteen or maybe sixteen people were in the place. Half of them sat in booths along one side of the room. One couple danced slowly in the aisle. A small cluster of smokers kept to themselves in a corner. There was a pool table in the middle of the floor, around which two men lurked like prizefighters. A man in a black tee-shirt (at least I think it was black, and at least I think it was a man) approached the door, apparently on his way out of the bar. I asked him if he could please point me toward the men's room.

"Down that hallway," he said. "It doesn't have a door."

"Yeah, I heard," I said.

I found the men's room — which did not, in fact, have a door — and took care of business quickly enough so that I didn't have to worry about someone barging in. I returned to the main room. Just a few feet to the left of the front door was a pay phone hanging on the wall. I walked over to it and prayed that it was operational. It was. I called Amy, collect.

Before she asked me why the hell I was calling collect from a pay phone, I said, "You'll never guess where I am."

"Standing on a corner in Winslow, Arizona," she said without missing a beat.

"No, but I might as well be. I'm in Tannersville."

"Tannersville? Where's that?"

"P.A."

"Pennsylvania? Where are you really?" she asked.

"Believe it or not, Tannersville," I repeated gloomily. "I swear. In the Poconos. The Poconos in Pennsylvania."

"As opposed to the Poconos in Vermont? You can't be in Tannersville, Bob," Amy said. "You belong in Nyack. Abby and Lucy just woke up and want you to sing another song." That image merely added gloom to gloom; singing to the girls was one of my all-time favorite requirements at home.

"I'd love to, but I can't. Because I really *am* in Tannersville."

"There's no heavy cream in Nyack? You had to go to the Pocono Mountains?"

"It's a long story, Amy. Listen," I said, "the bad news is that this is one of the craziest, most pitiful things that ever happened to me in my entire crazy, luckless, mildly annoying life. I'll explain it all later. But the good news is that I'm still alive and feel like a new song might come out of it."

It suddenly occurred to me, as I spoke those words to Amy, that I had said the *same damn thing* four or five times in just the last few months alone—that a new song might come out of one new experience or another. But when all was said and done, there were no new songs. I'm sure that thought crossed Amy's mind, too.

"Anyway," I said, "I'll probably be able to get home pretty quickly. I don't think it's that far. Maybe three hours by car. I'll rent one somewhere. I have my wallet and my credit card with me. Just not my cellphone."

"Fine. But explain it to me *now*, not later," she demanded.

So I explained to Amy exactly what had happened. I admitted that every part of the damn story was unbelievable, bizarre, and incredibly stupid. I suppose I sounded a little frustrated by the ordeal. Amy, wanting to keep me calm (bless her heart), acknowledged that unbelievable, bizarre, and incredibly stupid things can happen to anyone, and to not blame myself.

"I won't," I promised. "I'm just gonna have one drink and then get on my way."

"Do you have to have a drink? Can't you just come home?"

"Amy, a little while ago, I was in Nyack, not far from the Hudson River, holding a bag of heavy cream. Now I'm in Tannersville, in the Pocono Mountains, listening to Frank Sinatra sing *Young at Heart* at a place called Stinkey's that doesn't have a door on the men's room. Yes, I think I need a drink."

•   •   •

"Luck be a lady tonight. Luck be a lady tonight..."

Sinatra had changed his tune while I walked over to the bar. The bartender, a tall, thin man with a bushy yellowish mustache and a bright blue bow tie, stood with his hands on the counter. I smiled and asked for a Coors Light. The bartender returned my smile, said "Yup," and walked away. I looked around. There was a barstool nearby, but I remained standing. At the other side of the room was a wooden platform placed on what looked like old railroad ties, with a chair in the center on which rested an acoustic guitar. There was also a microphone on a stand, and a small amplifier. For a moment, I thought it was a mirage.

As Sinatra continued his song, the bartender returned and placed a mug on the counter in front of me. He poured the Coors Light so that its head of foam stopped just short of the rim. He smiled again, a casual, indifferent smile.

"Looking for lady luck?" he asked. "Like the late Francis Albert?"

"Nope. Just plain luck," I replied. Then he disappeared.

After a while, Sinatra finished his song and Engelbert Humperdinck took over with *After the Loving*. I turned once again to take in the Stinkey's scene. But instead of drinkers, smokers and dancers, my eyes locked on a woman, and her eyes locked on mine. She was a pretty woman, her expression quiet and reserved, though her dark, piercing eyes spoke volumes. If I had to guess, I'd say she was about fifty-five. She had curly dirty-blonde hair and a red and white flannel shirt tucked into snug jeans. She was shapely, with muscular arms; the type of woman, it would seem, who could beat you in an arm wrestle in seconds flat and then seduce you before the blood drained back into your hand. She walked over to me slowly.

"You're not from around here," she commented as she rested her hands on the empty barstool.

"You don't know the half of it," I replied as I took a sip of beer.

She leaned over the counter to look for the bartender. "Howie!" she called out.

Howie reappeared from the back.

"What'll it be, Rosemary?"

"The same," she said as she nodded toward my beer. Howie the bartender left again, and the woman whose name I now knew to be Rosemary slid the barstool a few inches closer to where I stood, and sat down. I knew I was staring at her, and I knew she knew. "So, what's the story?" she asked. "I *know* there's a story."

"How do you know?" I asked.

"There's *always* a story."

Rosemary stared at me with an intensity I had not felt from anyone in years. It wasn't just her intensity, but also her interest and concern that struck me, that made me feel alive, vital, real. Suddenly I realized just how right she was: there's always a story, just like my songs always have a story. (The few songs that exist, anyway.) For a millisecond of wonderfully insane optimism I wondered if in this real-life story this nice, pretty woman would ask me to sing some of my songs, right there at Stinkey's, up on that little stage on the railroad ties with the chair and the guitar and the mic stand and the amplifier. I wondered if maybe this would be the crowd that would really and truly appreciate whatever talent I had and give me the spotlight, however brief and out-of-the-way, that I'd been craving for years. Stranger things have happened.

To speed things along, I told Rosemary the story about the heavy cream and the train and the two men at the depot. Then I took another sip of beer.

"That's a hell of a story. At least you didn't get hurt along the way," Rosemary said. "So what do I call you?"

"Call me Bob. Can I call you Rosemary?" Her eyebrows raised in surprise, for she hadn't yet told me her name. "I heard the bartender say it before," I explained. "As they say, love grows where my Rosemary goes."

"I beg your pardon?"

"It's a song. *Love Grows Where My Rosemary Goes*. Edison Lighthouse, 1972."

"Oh. I was never really into groups and who sang what and that kind of thing. Sorry."

"That's okay," I said. "I won't hold it against you."

"Then we're even."

"What do you mean, we're even?"

"Well, usually when I sit down at the bar," she said, "the man I'm with has the decency to sit next to me. You haven't. You're still standing. I won't hold it against you. Not yet, anyway."

It was a very cunning ice-breaker of a line, so I grabbed another empty barstool from a few feet away, pulled it close to Rosemary, and sat. She held out her hand. I shook it gently (although on her end it wasn't so gentle).

"You like music, huh?" she stated.

"Very much," I said.

"Have another Coors and tell me more about your little story. It could be the most exciting thing to happen in this town in the last twenty years."

"I'm not finished with this one," I said as I lifted the beer mug.

"You will be soon. Howie—" she called out. "Howie, get my musical friend Bob here another beer. This one's on me."

Howie left. I looked for a clock on the wall. Rosemary put her hand over my chin and returned my face so that I had to look at her.

"Looking for a clock?" she asked. "Forget the time, Bob. We don't have time for time around here."

"Sounds like a song title. No Time for Time. Mind if I borrow it?"

"Be my guest." Rosemary scanned me with her dark eyes, up and down, and then sat up straight which, intentionally or not, reconfirmed her attractive physique. "You can borrow just about anything you'd like," she added. I had a lump in my throat and quickly took a sip of beer to disguise it.

Howie returned with two beers. When he set them down on the counter, he put his hands on the inner edge and leaned in to join our conversation.

"So, musical friend Bob—you write songs?" he asked.

"Yes, I do," I said, pleased that the question had been asked, and not all that surprised that it was; I could feel my luck changing with every sip. "Unfortunately, nothing you would have heard."

Howie grinned. "Don't look so blue. It'll happen one day. Is that why you're looking for plain ol' luck, so that one day your songs can be heard?"

"You're very perceptive," I said.

"I'm a bartender."

A short man in a suit who had been drinking in the back with another man who had a ponytail made his way over to our section of the bar to order drinks. He was heavyset and red-faced, but the suit looked serious enough, which made me think he was a businessman on his regular nightcap stopover before heading home to his wife and kids.

"Bob here is a songwriter," Howie told the man, "and I think he may just write a song about us one day."

"He accidentally hopped on a train in Nyack, New York, and ended up just down the road at the depot," Rosemary added. "But Bobby's a little blue right now. He needs a pick-me-up."

"Is that right?" the man asked. "Are you really a songwriter?"

"Not professional," I admitted. "My ship hasn't come in yet," I continued. "In fact, I'm so unlucky, I can't even walk through a train that doesn't have a seat without ending up in a bathroom that doesn't have a door."

The little crowd, which now included the man with the ponytail, laughed in unison. Rosemary slipped her arm through mine as if to show them all that I was her discovery.

"Your songs got messages?" she asked.

"Some. Not all."

"Because I'll be honest with you, Bobby — I don't like all those highfalutin messages you gotta think real hard about to figure out. I just like to listen and enjoy. Simple things. You know?"

"Come on, Bobby," Howie grinned, "play a few tunes. Get rid of the blues, Bobby. We all want to hear something."

"It's funny that you said — get rid of the blues, Bobby."

"Why's that?" Howie asked.

"My last name is Blumenthal, and I used to think of calling myself Bobby Blu without the e at the end — B, L, U."

Everyone in the small crowd cocked their heads in curiosity, almost at once and almost all at the same angle. I probably would have laughed had I not been so intrigued by the image.

"That's interesting, Bobby B, L, U," Howie grinned, spelling it out dramatically. "So what do you say? Would you like to play a few tunes?"

"Are you serious?"

There was a buzz of agreement from the patrons near the counter. Even the others, those still at their booths or by the pool table, looked our way and listened with sudden interest.

"I haven't written a song in years," I said to Howie.

"But you got some old ones, I assume."

"Well, sure..."

"You play guitar?"

"Yes—and I see you have one right there."

"Just waiting for you," Howie concurred.

Rosemary took my hand. "This could be your lucky day, Bobby," she said as she led me to the makeshift stage. I looked at her, only too pleased to stare, not just because hers was a pretty face, but also because I needed something on which to focus so that I wouldn't have to deal with the anticipatory glares from the other patrons. I hadn't played in front of crowds all that much. One time in college, and another a few years later. They weren't great experiences. The first time was when I was a junior at Oswego. It was in a student lounge called Pot Luck, but there was no luck there that night. (Plenty of pot, though.) My fellow students were more interested in flirting and drinking than they were in listening to my songs. Except Amy, who was my girlfriend. *She* listened. The second time was at a small place in Nyack, two weeks before our wedding. But there was a hurricane on the way and only six people showed up. Amy was one of them. There was supposed to be a third time two years ago, when I had been scheduled to play at a club near the Ferguson plant. But I came down with the flu and had to cancel. Amy made me play the entire set for her that night at home. She made tea and toast for me to nibble between tunes.

Howie stepped onto the stage and fidgeted with a few controls on the amplifier. There was a crackle and a hum. The amp was ready and the mic was live.

"Hold on," Rosemary urged. She hustled over to the jukebox, which was now playing *Everybody Loves Somebody Sometime*, and silenced Dean Martin by yanking out the plug. "Sorry, Howie," she shrugged. "I don't know how to turn the damn thing off."

Howie nodded amiably, grabbed the microphone, and made an announcement:

"Ladies and gentleman, in his first Pocono appearance, Mr. Bobby B, L, U."

Howie went back to the bar and I took his place on the platform. After the light applause died down, I thanked the small crowd.

"This is very nice of all of you," I said, leaning into the microphone. "This first song is a sort of unconventional love story called *Lithograph*." I checked to see if the instrument was in tune and had to do a little work to get it right. Then I began to play. I tried to keep the vocals soft, clear and focused and the guitar work steady and simple. I put as much emotion into it as I thought was necessary without making the story seem contrived or overly melodramatic. It appeared to work. The patrons listened and smiled. Nobody left. Nobody talked. There wasn't a hurricane in sight. I didn't have the flu.

When I finished the song, the crowd at Stinkey's gave me a warm ovation. I began a second number, an up-tempo piece called *Breeze*, which went over as well as *Lithograph*, if not a little better.

"Would you like to hear one more?" I asked confidently. There were affirmative nods all around. Howie looked pleased. Rosemary, now sitting in a chair directly in front of me, looked proud. My throat was dry. "I'm not used to this kind of thing," I explained. "Let me just get a sip of something and I'll be back in a sec."

I put the guitar on the floor and hopped down to the bar. The man in the suit and the man with the ponytail were still there.

"Howie," I whispered, "can I have a glass of water?"

"Sure thing," Howie replied. He stepped aside.

The man in the suit tapped me on the arm with the back of his hand. "This *is* your lucky day, Bobby," he said.

"It is?"

"I happen to be an executive with Columbia Records," he said, "and I'd like to sign you up." My throat, already dry, became even more desert-like, and I was no longer able to swallow at all. Fortunately, Howie returned at that moment with a glass of water and I took a long sip.

"Excuse me?" I said at last.

"That's right, son. I think those two songs were fabulous. You've got more, I assume."

"A few."

"Ten, twelve weeks down the road," the man pressed on, "we can have a single on the radio, a CD, a couple of TV appearances lined up..."

"Holy shit," was all I could think to say. I was speechless and lightheaded.

One of the pool players called out: "Hey, Bobby, you got another love song?"

"Sure," I called back. I took a last sip of water.

"We'll talk later, son," the man in the suit nodded. "Go do your thing."

I returned to the stage, sat on the chair, picked up the guitar, and leaned into the microphone.

"I don't know what to say, ladies and gentlemen... You see... after this set I'm gonna meet with that nice man over there and we're gonna talk about signing on with Columbia Records. I can't believe I just said that. Columbia Records! When I was a kid, I used to doodle album covers with my name on them inside my notebooks, and I always drew the Columbia Records logo at the bottom of the page." I looked at the man in the suit and smiled. "And I owe it all to Stinkey's." I strummed a defiant chord on the guitar. "I'm gonna write a song about this place one day, and about all you people, as a thank-you present. And if I make some money with Columbia Records, I'll buy a new sign for the place that you can actually read, and I'll make sure you get a door for the men's room."

The room fell silent. Then I heard what I thought was a stifled cough. When I looked up, I saw that the man at the back of the room who had coughed wasn't really coughing at all; he was laughing with his hand over his mouth. With any luck, it would have been the lone laughter in the joint, the lone laughter of a tipsy old fool who doesn't know where he is or even why he's laughing. But there was no such luck that night. None. When I saw the faces of the pool players, I realized that they, too, were doing all they could to stifle their own laughter. They weren't successful; they could not hold it in. Their laughter got louder, more open, more honest. Almost instantly, it was joined by the high-pitched giggle of the man in the suit and the hoarse chuckle of the guy with the ponytail. "Columbia Records, huh?" Mr. ponytail said as he tapped his friend's arm. "Last time it was RCA. Nice one, Ralph." And then more laughter from the booths opened up like a poisonous mushroom. It infected the entire joint. Soon everyone joined in. Howie, too. Rosemary, who had gone back to the jukebox, merely grinned.

I stared at her, fully aware that tears were welling up in the corners of my eyes. I tried desperately to hold them in. Suddenly I felt as if I had been everywhere in the world and had done everything there was to do, yet was still nothing more than a nowhere man with nothing to show for all his empty worldliness.

The man in the suit smiled pathetically. "Sorry, kid," he said. He shrugged his shoulders.

I surrendered, even though I had already been judged, sentenced and pumped with the electric current that flowed through my veins. It zapped all my strength. That's why I had such difficulty putting the guitar on the platform and holding up my head as I moved away from the stage. I let my eyes follow the simple patterns on the floor to avoid all other obstacles along the way.

I reached the door without further incident and came face to face with Rosemary. She had left the stage area and was now standing by the pay phone. She put her hand under my chin.

"They're idiots," she said as she lifted my face to look at her. "But like I told you, nothing interesting ever happens around here. I guess they have to make their own excitement."

"I guess there's nothing unusual about it, when all is said and done."

"Now don't go highfalutin on me," Rosemary urged. "I don't know what that means. I don't understand deep concepts like that. Remember?"

"I won't hold it against you."

I reached for the door handle—but Rosemary put her hand on top of mine and squeezed.

"Hey," she said, softer than anything she had said before, "why don't you come home with me? To my place. We'll forget about these idiots. I hate most of them, anyway."

"Then we're even."

"Come on, Bobby. Those songs... they were great... they sort of make me wanna get out of here, away from these jerks, to get lost with someone like you." I looked at her, but said nothing. "I'm real good, Bobby. You'll never forget it. Maybe your luck *will* change tonight after all. For real. What do you say?"

"To your place?" I asked.

"To my place. Just you and me."

"I don't think so."

"I'm sorry to hear that, Bobby," Rosemary said. "I really am. Is there anything I can do to change your mind?" She gave my hand a final squeeze. "Anything at all?"

"Can you answer one question?"

"Sure. Name it."

"What would you say if you found four million toenails in your couch?"

"Well, I guess I'd say it was time for a new couch."

"That's what I thought," I said.

I pushed the door. It swung out with ease. I prayed that getting back to Nyack would be just as easy. I decided not to worry about it. I knew that one way or another, I'd get home where I belonged.

Funny, You Don't Look Dead

A man rounds one empty corridor, which is green, and walks down another, which is orange. He wears a black shirt and black slacks, has an oversized black cap on his head, and on his face sits a pair of black plastic toy Groucho glasses that give him Groucho eyebrows and a Groucho moustache. He saunters slowly down the orange corridor and takes off his cap, which exposes his short black hair, and glances at the seven or eight doors he passes along the way. Each door has a small sign— Reconciliation, Reincarnation, Library and so forth. For a man who appears to be in his late middle years, he is in fairly good shape, with decent posture, although under his eyes are dark circles which are visible even with the Groucho glasses on. Between the hair on his head, the clothes on his body, and the circles under his eyes, it is quite easy for us to refer to him—since we must refer to him for the purpose of this story—as Mr. Black.

Mr. Black looks around cautiously, apparently wishing to neither be seen nor heard. Then he sees a closed door, also with a small sign—this sign says Parole—and he opens it. He enters the room, closes the door behind him, and sits on a straight-backed wooden chair that is pushed up against an unadorned rectangular wooden table. He breathes a sigh of relief and stares at the surface of the table.

Simultaneously, another man, this one with a head full of white hair, enters the green corridor, then turns into the orange one. Despite being much older than the first man, and despite the crouch to his posture, there is a bounce to his step. He has on a white robe of indiscriminate material. The robe, in concert with his hair and bright expression, makes it very easy for us to refer to him—since he, too, must be referred to—as Mr. White.

Mr. White looks around stealthily, but not because he doesn't wish to be seen; in this case, he apparently does not know where he is at the moment. He approaches the closed door of the Parole room, opens it, and steps inside.

"Oh—hello there," says Mr. White, good-naturedly. "Sorry to bother you, young man, but I think I'm lost. Ain't that a kick in the head? You would think they'd make the signs bigger for old fellas like me who have been around the block a few times, if you know what I mean. Who can read those little signs? I think my eyes are older than *I* am, for crying out loud! Do you happen to know which room this is?"

"According to the sign, this is Parole," Mr. Black says as he looks down and maintains his stiff, nearly emotionless facade.

"Parole? How the hell did I get to Parole? I'm looking for a place that's supposed to be next to Separated Twins. Holy moly—I might be three, four miles out of my way."

Mr. Black looks up. His blank expression does not change. There had not even been the hint of a smile in reaction to Mr. White's quip about his eyes being older than him. "I don't suppose this is what some call Heaven," Mr. Black says curtly.

"Heaven is one flight up," Mr. White responds. "This is..." He searches for a word. "Actually, I don't know what they call it. *Pre*-Heaven, maybe. That sounds like a pretty good bet. Not that I'm a betting man, mind you."

"I doubt this is Pre-Heaven," Mr. Black says pessimistically, "only because I am certain there is no Heaven, either—despite your assertion that it is one flight up."

"Why would you think there's no Heaven?"

"Because this entire place is a joke."

"A joke?"

"Yes. Of course. On the way here I saw a sign that said Health Insurance Executives Only. Obviously a silly prank. Why would there be silly pranks in Heaven or in Pre-Heaven?"

"Oh, that!" Mr. White smiles. He tries to hide an embarrassed grin. "We get bored from time to time, so one day we made up some crazy names based on some of the baloney we see going on down there. But guess what?—someone actually went ahead and ordered the signs. Can you believe it? Not that it's such a bad idea, mind you—health insurance executives needing a special room to decide their fate. It's funny! Same thing with politicians. Not all of them, but many. So yes, you're right—it started as a joke, but... well... there you have it."

Mr. Black shakes his head warily. "I don't believe any of it," he says. "This is not Pre-Heaven, and there is no Heaven above. Neither exist. And I don't know who you are or where you're from, but I am more than certain that this is one big joke."

"Oh, there's a Heaven," asserts Mr. White. "I live there. Listen, if you're wondering why I came down one flight, I'll tell you why: I overheard someone say that they opened a new delicatessen on this floor, so I decided to take a look for myself. I got a few minutes to spare and I feel like a really good pickle. But now I don't know where the hell I am. Can you believe it? I guess you could say I'm *in* a pickle, huh?" Mr. White giggles at his own humor and shakes his head. He notices that Mr. Black neither chuckles nor shakes his head, so Mr. White stops doing both and clears his throat as a way to change the subject with no further awkwardness. "Well... anyway..."

Mr. White backs away but then turns around. "Can I ask you a question? Why do they make you wear funny glasses in Parole? Some kind of initiation or something?"

Mr. Black furrows his brow. "What?..." he says—but then remembers what he is wearing. "Oh—the glasses. Nobody told me I had to wear them. I just felt it was... shall we say... necessary... It's a long story."

"A long story?" smiles Mr. White. "If you want to know the truth, fella, time I got plenty. Well, not plenty, but I got a few minutes. Actually, in a little while I'm seeing a show. They're doing *Fiddler on the Roof* upstairs, but it doesn't start for another hour and a half. It's a new theatre company—Paradise Playhouse. You've heard of it?"

Mr. Black remains silent.

"Zero Mostel's in it. And three others from the original cast. I love that show, don't you? *Tradition, If I Were a Rich Man, Sunrise, Sunset.* And when Tevye looks up and says—"

Mr. Black interrupts him sharply, clearly impatient and dismayed.

"You're a Jew?" he asks, glaring at Mr. White's face.

"Hmmm..." says Mr. White, "why does it sound like you wouldn't be too happy if the answer to that question was yes? Although I'm not saying it is. Actually, I like to say I'm sort of—"

"Who are you?" interrupts Mr. Black once more.

"I'd rather not say, if you don't mind."

"Why not? There's no need for modesty now, old man."

"Modesty? It has nothing to do with modesty. It's just that—"

Suddenly, a look of comprehension crosses Mr. Black's face. "Albert Einstein!" he says with a smirk. He is proud of his deduction. But Mr. White shakes his head no. "Ben-Gurion, then?" posits Mr. Black. Another negative response. "Wait a minute... wait a minute. I know," nods Mr. Black confidently. "You're Simon Wiesenthal, the famous Nazi hunter."

"Listen, Mister—"

"Funny, I didn't picture you like that at all."

"How did you picture me?" asks Mr. White. "Like Gregory Peck, I should be so lucky?"

"No," Mr. Black responds. "I pictured you sad and miserable."

"Sad and miserable? That's very interesting. May I ask why?"

Mr. Black takes a deep breath, flashes a brief but knowing and satisfied grin, and puts out his hands in a gesture of pity.

"Why?" he repeats. "I'll tell you why. Because you lived a wasted life, Mr. Wiesenthal. Simple as that. And I should think that would make you sad and miserable."

Mr. White repeats the phrase: "A wasted life? If you don't mind my asking, why have I lived a wasted life?"

"Because for every Nazi you caught, there were a thousand others who got away. And what did their capture accomplish, anyway? Not much, in the grand scheme of things. All that work, and for what? You're dead. There is nothing you can do about that. How does it feel?"

"How does what feel?" asks Mr. White.

"Being here—whatever this place really is. This *joke* of a place. This fake Pre-Heaven."

"How does it feel? Like a vacation in Coney Island, if you want to know the truth. The *old* Coney Island, obviously, but don't get me started on that."

"But how does it feel to be here with *me*?"

"Like a vacation in Coney Island with someone who wears funny glasses and doesn't like Simon Wiesenthal."

Clearly irritated, Mr. Black shakes his head and sighs.

"Would you like to know who I am?" he asks.

"To tell you the truth, I'd rather have a pickle."

"I think you might like to know."

"Why?" asks Mr. White. "You think I might have a grudge against you? Listen, mister, I'd much rather watch *Fiddler on the Roof* and eat a good pickle than hold a grudge any day of the week. To tell you the truth, depending on what they did, I'd even be okay with a health insurance executive going to Heaven before I hold a grudge. Whoever you are, if you're not in hell, how bad can you be?"

Now, finally, Mr. Black knows exactly what he must do in order to deal with what he regards as a stubborn, addled old man. He uses the index finger of his right hand to gesture for Mr. White to step further into the room. Mr. White obeys, with decidedly small steps. The finger keeps bending back and forth, over and over, to coerce Mr. White even closer, and Mr. White complies. He is now fully in the room and closer to the table. When he is just a foot away from him, Mr. Black takes off his hat and whips off his plastic Groucho glasses. As Mr. White gawks, Mr. Black places the glasses on the table.

"I don't believe it," says Mr. White. "Adolf Hitler! How the hell did you get up here? You should have gone directly to—"

"I did. I *was* there. All these years I was there. But this morning I noticed something I hadn't seen before. A tunnel. A skinny little tunnel hidden in a corner."

"A tunnel?"

"A tunnel—like an elevator—that lifts you all the way up here, to this so-called Pre-Heaven. I asked around and was told that every eighty or ninety years they make a mistake, and a few people down there get to take that tunnel to the Parole room up here to discuss the situation. Some people say it's just a rumor. But here I am."

Mr. White scratches his head. "Well, I'll be!"

"There's usually a guard down there," Mr. Black continues, clearly on a roll, energized by this retelling of his marvelous discovery, "a guard by the opening of the tunnel. I'm told he is supposed to stop people from sneaking in. But I created a diversion, jumped in, and was brought up. It lifts you up thousands of miles in just seconds. I also heard that once you are in Parole, no matter how you got there, no one can tell you to leave. They are required to listen to you. It is not negotiable."

"Not negotiable, huh? That's one hell of a loophole you stumbled onto, young fella. I wish I could find a few loopholes of my own every once in a while. I was never a loophole kind of guy. I was more of a—"

Mr. Black, even more annoyed now, shouts, "Please! Be quiet!"

Mr. White hushes. He remains silent while Mr. Black collects his thoughts.

"It may be a matter of only a few minutes before the next Parole hearing starts," Mr. Black speculates. "I have to work quickly. I have to find a way to make the best case I can possibly make in front of the Parole Board, if such a board exists and if this really is, as you insist on calling it, Pre-Heaven. On the slim chance that actual decisions are made here, I need to make an excellent case for myself so that they send me one flight up which, as you contend, is Heaven. I don't believe it for a moment—but anything would be better than where I have been stuck all these years."

"So you want to go to Heaven," says Mr. White. "Even though you don't believe in Heaven, you want to go to Heaven... Interesting.... Well, I wouldn't bet the farm on your chances being too good, considering who you are—you'll forgive my bluntness."

"Normally I would say you're right. However—"

"However? There's a however?" Mr. White scratches his chin, even though it isn't itchy. "This is one situation where I don't think there's a however involved, to be honest with you."

Mr. Black remains unfazed. For a moment, he twirls the Groucho glasses on the table with his index finger. He has a serious look on his face. Then he stops and looks up.

"If I could get someone very special to speak on my behalf in front of the Parole Board, that could make all the difference. Maybe my chances for permission to stay here would be a lot better than they would be if I had to speak only for myself. Do you understand what I am trying to say?"

"I'm listening," says Mr. White. He shrugs his shoulders. "I don't know if I'm hearing what you want me to hear, but I'm listening. To tell you the truth, I'm also thinking about a terrific pickle."

"If I can get someone special—someone like you—to speak on my behalf, think of how the Parole Board would feel. They would have no choice but to listen with a collectively open mind. It could happen. Adolf Hitler up here—instead of down there. Imagine."

"Yes—even though you don't believe in it, Heaven is a lovely place; that I know. I can certainly see why you're so anxious to stay. Gorgeous weather all year long. You never need a sweater. Nice music, too, no matter where you go. Not harps—everyone thinks harps. Probably from all those paintings. But it ain't all peaches and cream for me, if you want to know the truth. Everybody knows who I am, so I get bothered with questions all the time. Sometimes I just want to see a good show where no one bothers me. *I* should wear the funny glasses, not you! Which reminds me, I should really get back. I'm starving, and I want to digest before the show. I don't want to miss the first number, *Tradition.* Such an interesting way to start a show. Don't you agree?"

Mr. White begins to back out of the room. When he reaches the doorway, he turns around and puts his hand on the handle of the door.

"You won't help me?" asks Mr. Black.

Mr. White stops and pivots around to respond.

"It's *Fiddler on the Roof,* for crying out loud!"

Then Mr. White apparently has a thought. He lets go of the door handle and takes a step back into the room.

"Tell you what, fella," he says. "You help me find my way to the new delicatessen, and maybe, just maybe, I'll consider sending a note to the Parole Board with a few nice words."

"You're a very smart old man," Mr. Black says, quite pleased with the reply. "You see — we can help each other. We'll rejoice together."

"Rejoice? Hold on there, mister. I said I'd send a note, not take a stroll in the park with you every Tuesday afternoon. Besides, I don't even hold out much hope that a note will do much good."

"Why not? I already told you why I think it's a great idea."

"You told me," says Mr. White, "but I'm not convinced. Would you like to know why? Number one, if God has his eye on everything — and I have it on very good authority that he does — although he may have missed it when you slipped into that tunnel down there, he'll catch on soon enough, maybe even before the Parole Board gets here. Number two, despite the fact that once or twice I myself have toyed with the idea that everyone has at least one molecule of goodness in their souls, helping you would go against everything else I believe. So I'm afraid that whatever I would write in your defense might not be the best I got. You know what I'm saying? It just wouldn't ring true. Understand?"

Mr. Black lets it all sink in as he formulates a counterclaim.

"I see," he finally says. "Let me respond. Number one, God apparently is very busy at the moment. I've been absent from down there for quite a while now, and not a word from anyone. Number two, I know Jews, and despite everything else, they are committed to be the best they can be and they are uncompromising. Whether or not you really want to, Mr. Wiesenthal, you *will* do a good job for me. It is not in you *not* to do a good job on my behalf. It is in your blood to do a good job."

"'Not in me not to do a good job.' That's a double negative, right? Because I gotta level with you, fella, sometimes language drives me nuts. Double negatives, misplaced modifiers, clichés. It's sort of a pet peeve of mine. I avoid double negatives like the plague."

"The Parole Board wouldn't even have to think about it," Mr. Black continues, undaunted. "Just the fact that you wrote the note would be enough. They would ask themselves, Why would a great man like Simon Wiesenthal, the famed Nazi hunter, help defend Adolf Hitler, unless there was a damned good reason?"

"I've been wondering the same thing myself, to tell you the truth."

"There's a very good answer, old man. Because you *do* believe there is a molecule of goodness in everyone." Mr. Black sounds almost zealous in his argument. "Maybe you also believe that everything is a learning experience — that everyone on Earth learned a valuable lesson or two because of who I was in life and what I attempted to do in my time, lessons that can be used to improve the world. Which means that my life served a purpose. *That's* why you'll want to help me. *That's* what the Parole Board will believe. It makes perfect sense."

Mr. Black and Mr. White stare at each other. While the man who is standing remains noncommittal, the man who is sitting looks eager.

"So? You will help me, yes?" asks Mr. Black.

"But what would you do if you made it to Heaven?" asks Mr. White, more as a rhetorical statement than a question requiring a response. "It would be dangerous for you there. Not to mention that you'd be very lonely. No one would go see a show with you — I'm sure of it — not even a bad show. And forget about ball games."

"You think it would be dangerous? I doubt that. I'm willing to bet there is no violence at all in Heaven. Besides, you can't kill someone who's already dead. I'm also willing to bet that people in Heaven never get angry. That everyone in Heaven always forgives. You live there; I'm sure you know. Am I right?"

"You'd think I'd have these answers at the tip of my tongue, wouldn't you, since I've been up there so long? But to tell you the truth," says Mr. White, appearing both serious and eccentric, "I've been so busy lately, I hardly know who's who or what's what. But here's another thing: No matter what it's like in Heaven, you know who makes the rules. Am I right? The Big Guy. So you don't have to be a genius to know that he can break the rules from time to time. You see what I'm getting at?"

"No, I do not," says Mr. Black.

"Look. Even if you made it one flight up, who's to say the Main Man wouldn't make it very difficult for you once you got there, if he wanted to?"

"That's a chance I'm willing to take."

"I just don't know," says Mr. White. He thinks hard and looks somewhat pained with the need to do so. "The thing is, you were beyond explanation when you were alive. I'm having a little trouble with that, to tell you the truth."

"That's irrelevant now."

"Beyond comprehension."

"Irrelevant as well. Let me ask you this. If I was beyond explanation and beyond comprehension, how do you explain my luck in finding that tunnel in the first place, making it all the way here, and bumping into you, Simon Wiesenthal of all people, in a place where you can do me no harm? That says something about me, does it not? Maybe it is God's way of planting the seed of forgiveness and redemption. Don't you see?"

"Forgiveness and redemption... Interesting," smirks Mr. White. "You should have been a preacher. Or a lawyer."

"And here's something else to think about, old man. By helping me, you would feel truly blessed, as if everything you've gone through was worth the effort. To forgive and forget—that's the true measure of one's worth, is it not? To find that one molecule of goodness, as you yourself put it, that one molecule of goodness that is in everyone — isn't that what it's all about?"

Using his finger to jab exclamation points in the air, Mr. White says to Mr. Black, "To do right, to be moral, to educate, to be kind. *Those* are the real biggies, as far as I'm concerned. To forgive someone like you? — about that I'm not a hundred percent sure."

"Then I'm wrong about you. You are *not* a smart man. You are a stubborn man. A stubborn old man. The Parole Board may be here any minute. One last time: will you help me?"

There is a lull as Mr. White thinks it over.

"Well… you *have* made me think — I'll give you that. That's a good thing, thinking. Not enough people do it. Believe me, I know. You've made me go deep into my heart and mind, or at least what's left of it."

"And what does your heart and mind tell you?" asks Mr. Black.

"What does my heart and mind tell me? That I should listen to them more often. I wish I had better news for you. I hate to be the one who always brings bad news, but I'm afraid that's all I got, fella."

Mr. White takes a gun out of a pocket that was hidden somewhere in his substantial robe. It is a small black gun, and there can be no mistaking what it is against the radiance of his white garment. Still, it takes three or four seconds for Mr. Black to digest what he sees, and only another second to decide how to respond.

"You are a stupid, misguided old fool, my friend," he says. "Number one, as I said before, you can't kill someone who is already dead. Guns probably don't even work up here. And number two, you are Simon Wiesenthal, the Jew. You hunt and you judge, but on your own you never you assume the solitary role of executioner."

"*I'm* misguided?" asks Mr. White. "I don't think so, my friend. Number one, if guns don't work here, why do you think I have one? You think we need more useless junk up here? We got enough junk already. Games. Old coffee pots. And so many records, including 78s which we don't even have what to play them on anymore, and—"

"Enough!" shouts Mr. Black impatiently.

"Sorry. I tend to babble. And number two; I never said I was Simon Wiesenthal. *You* did."

Mr. Black glares at him and digests the words.

"You mean you're—"

"I'm afraid so. The Top Man. The Main Guy. The Head Honcho. The Big Cheese. You wouldn't believe what I've been called over the centuries."

"So you lied to me."

"No, no, no. I never lie. It's one of the Ten Commandments— which I'm proud of, but which I did *not* write, despite the book and all the movies. I gave Moses a fairly specific outline, however. No—I didn't lie. I just never corrected you. That's all. I never said I was Simon Wiesenthal. You did."

After another moment of reflection, Mr. Black's look of shock turns once again to confidence.

"Well—I'm glad," he says. "I'm glad you are who you are. Now I don't have to deal with some annoying middleman. I can appeal directly to The Big Cheese."

"That will be very difficult to do—especially after I use this." He raises the hand that holds the gun.

"What good will the gun do? Besides, even if it could accomplish what you seem to think it can accomplish, you wouldn't use it. 'Thou shalt not kill.' Remember? You said you are proud of those ridiculous commandments."

"Let's just say that particular commandment has a loophole."

Mr. White fires the gun. The shot is very loud and echoes in the tiny room. The bullet enters Mr. Black's chest and pushes him backward, which makes the chair tumble so that Mr. Black rolls up against the back wall.

"Now you won't be down there *or* up here. You'll be nowhere. You'll be really, really, *really* dead. Nonexistent. For good. Once and for all. Forever. End of story. Case closed."

Mr. White takes a step forward. He shoots again. This time Mr. Black's body convulses as if a bolt of electricity punched through it front to back, top to bottom. Mr. White shoots again. Mr. Black is now completely motionless.

Mr. White takes another step forward so that he is now against the front of the table. He leans over and shoots again.

"Funny," he says as he leans in, "you don't look dead."

He shoots one more time.

"There."

Satisfied, Mr. White shuffles backward toward the door, then stops, returns to the table, picks up the Groucho glasses and puts them on. He leaves the room singing "Sunrise, sunset, sunrise, sunset, swiftly fly the days..."

The Sea Glass Menagerie

Wednesday, June 8

Arrived in Cape May about 3 o'clock this afternoon. Had a late start leaving the house because Billie wanted to buy a new bikini first. She should have done that a few days ago, like me. But she's Billie. Said she didn't have time. Like I have a lot of time?

I like the Bonnie June. Very pretty B&B. First thing I did (after we checked in) was try on my bikini. (Should have done that a few days ago, but I REALLY didn't have time. Had 2 boring school papers to write over the last 2 weeks.) Anyway, the bikini looked okay. Not great. Just okay. Makes my hips look a little ~~fat blubbery~~ hippy. Billie says some guys like that. I think she said that just to make me feel better. Planning to get a bite to eat at Carney's for dinner. (Used to eat there a lot with my parents when I was a kid.) Maybe see a show at Cape May Stage after that. Will decide later. No rush to do stuff. Staying 6 nights (longest vacation of my life, I think!) Lots of time for amazing things to happen. Or not.

Went to the beach. Stayed an hour.

Thursday, June 9

Didn't go to Carney's last night. Went to Ugly Mug instead. Very nice. Had a Caesar salad. A little too limp, but not terrible. Billie had a turkey burger. Awesome dessert. Some kind of chocolate parfait thing with mocha sauce. It looked at my hips and said, You're mine, sucker! Billie flirted with the bartender. I'm not ready to do that yet. Want to feel more relaxed before I flirt. Maybe tomorrow. Or not.

Saw Butterflies Are Free at Cape May Stage after dinner. Small theater in an old church. It was ok. Not great. These actors don't make lots of money but seem to enjoy themselves. What a concept! Always wanted to play Jill in Butterflies. This Jill was pretty good. But the guy who played Don acted <u>TOO MUCH</u> like a blind person. The story takes care of that. The actor doesn't have to overdo it. But what the hell do I know? Sure, I know a lot about acting in Tennessee Williams plays (was in 3 of them before I switched my major), but what does it matter now anyway? (Can't believe I'm talking to my diary like it's a real person. Clue that I really need a vacation???)

Me and Billie (Billie and I?) sat an extra half hour at breakfast this morning talking to the owner of the B&B. Andy. Interesting guy. Used to publish a health magazine, then gave it up to run a B&B, which is what he always wanted to do. (Doing what you really want to do. What a concept!) Andy asked about our plans after college. Billie said she wants to be a vet and I said I want to be a teacher.

Got to the beach at noon. Sunset Beach, on the Delaware Bay. Not the regular beach by the ocean. I like it better. Quieter. No waves. Billie was laying (lying? Never knew the difference) on the towel and suddenly popped up and said Teacher? Wanted to know why I told Andy I wanted to be a teacher. She said, You switched from acting to sociology and now all of a sudden, teacher? I told her that teacher sounds better than sociologist, and <u>definitely</u> better than actress. Most people have no clue what a sociologist does, anyway. (Like <u>I</u> do?) Billie looked angry for some reason. Don't really know why. But didn't feel like talking about it, so I told her we'd discuss it later. Or not.

Friday, June 10

A little overcast today. Went to Sunset Beach. Saw something ~~strange~~ ~~odd~~ ~~bizarre~~ unusual. A man was walking on the beach picking up pebbles, shells and sea glass. He examined each piece, then skimmed each one into the bay, then wrote something in a tiny notebook. Looked like he was about 50. Curly yellowish hair. A little wrinkled. (A lot, actually.) Billie told me to stop staring and asked why I wasn't searching for hunks instead. I said it was a non-hunk vacation. She said there was no such thing.

Climbed the Cape May Lighthouse. 199 steps. Billie started bitching and moaning after 19. I didn't mind it. My hips thanked me. At the top I told Billie my idea for a romance novel that could be a movie. About a lady lighthouse operator who waits for her sailor-lover to come back from sea so that they can make passionate love on the beach. Billie suggested Bradley Cooper as the sailor. I said Brad Pitt. She asked who would play me. I didn't answer. Billie said she thought I'd say me — that I should play myself. I said, Did you forget that I switched my major? That it's stupid to try to be an actress, even though that's what I wanted for so many years? Billie laughed and said it's also stupid to be a sociologist because no one knows what that is. Argued about it 199 steps above Cape May. An old couple, tourists from Canada I think, heard our stupid fight and laughed. Yeah, real funny. Go back to Canada, ay?

Had dinner at Lucky Bones. Stuffed flounder. Delicious. No waiters, only waitresses. No single guys around, only couples and families. Billie was pissed! Kinda felt bad for her. I promised that the next place we have dinner would have lots of single guys. Hope I can make good on my promise. I really have no idea.

Went to Sunset Beach at sunset. Beautiful. They do a flag lowering ceremony for U.S. service people. Very moving. Plus, I like the fact that it's all families and couples. No gawking guys.

Billie was mad about that. Claims I didn't tell her it would be like that on Sunset Beach. But I did tell her. I think I remember specifically telling her. Or not.

Saturday, June 11
Andy's wife Deanna sat with us for a few minutes at breakfast. Deanna used to work on a cruise ship. Nice woman. Breakfast this time wasn't awesome. The French toast was over-toasted. Didn't tell that to Deanna.

Spent most of the day at Sunset Beach. Saw that man again. Still collecting and skimming and studying pebbles and shells and sea glass and stuff. He passed right in front of us. I said Hi. Billie looked mortified (right word?) that I said hi and turned around on the blanket to bury her face in the sand. The man said Hi back. I told him my name and he said people call him Auggie. I asked Auggie if he lived in Cape May. He said he used to be a wedding photographer but never liked it. He kept walking and collecting his stuff.

Finally had dinner at Carney's. Just got back to the room. When I was a teenager I'd stare at all the 20-somethings in Carney's who were trying to impress each other. Now I'm one of them!!! Met two guys who seemed nice. Nick and Al. They asked us to come over to the bar when they saw me and Billie (Billie and I? Billie and me?) at the table. Didn't really want to join them at the bar, but I could tell that Billie was ~~love-struck~~ ~~smitten~~ hot for Al and would hate me for the rest of my life if I screwed up a double date opportunity. So I said ok. The four of us are going out tomorrow afternoon. Maybe we'll have a good time. Or not.

Sunday, June 12
Just got back from our double date with Nick and Al. More like an interview than a date. But sort of nice anyway. Took a horse-and-buggy ride around Cape May. Probably would have been

more romantic at night. Maybe Nick and Al wanted to see what we really looked like in daylight! Horse pooped twice during the ride, but pooped in a pocket attached to its butt so that the poop doesn't go onto the street. Al said it's probably a patented invention. Said he's an engineering major at Cornell. Asked what I was studying and I told him I was deciding between elementary education and sociology and he said I didn't sound convinced. I said I didn't really care if he thought I sounded convinced. Actually I almost said something about once wanting to be an actress just to see the kind of face Billie would make. (My own private amusement?!) But I didn't. Nick said he's studying to be a landscape architect. Also at Cornell. Billie talked about becoming a vet. Nick told her she didn't seem the vet type, and Billie got really mad. She said, Hey, I know what I want! I think Nick was turned on by her ~~strongness~~ ~~toughness~~ self-confidence. Billie told him where we were staying. I have a feeling Nick will stop by to see her. Not Al. Not that I care.

Monday, June 13
Nick came for Billie after breakfast. He dumped his friend Al. Nick took Billie to a secluded beach called Higbee. Used to be a nude beach (I think clothing-optional is how you're supposed to say it) but isn't anymore. Billie and I read about it when we researched B&Bs months ago. Don't know if Billie would have wanted to be naked on the beach if that was still an option. She's unpredictable. Sometimes she surprises me. Told her I would NEVER go to a naked beach. She said, What would you do if you ever got a part in a production of Equus or Hair which have nude scenes? I said it was a moot point (never thought I'd use the word moot, but there you go!) because elementary school teachers always wear clothes, and that since I was going to be an elementary school teacher and not an actress I would never have to worry about it. Asked her why she brought up Equus and Hair when she already knew that. Didn't answer.

Went back to Sunset Beach. By myself at first. Andy and Deanna stopped me as I was leaving and asked why Billie wasn't with me. I told them where she was (Higbee still). Andy said he overheard the two of us talking at breakfast for the past few mornings and that our relationship reminded him of a sitcom. I wish he hadn't said that. Don't want to think about sitcoms.

Billie stayed with Nick at Higbee Beach for two hours. Then she went back to the Bonnie June. Deanna told her where I was (Sunset Beach) and gave her a lift so she could join me there.

At Sunset Beach Billie just laid (lay? lied?) face up on the beach while I looked around. Saw Auggie again. At first he was far away. When he got closer he said Top 'o the mornin' to you, lass, even though I don't think he's Irish. He had the most incredible collection of pebbles, shells and sea glass I ever saw, in a big plastic pail. He walked along the shore. So interesting to watch him, maybe because he looked so interested in what he was doing. He skimmed some rocks and pieces of sea glass into the bay, and every once in a while he jotted down a few things in his little notebook.

Went over to Auggie and asked what he was doing. And why. He smiled. Seemed like he had a story to tell but didn't want to tell it just then. That look and that smile — good character traits to use one day for ~~a part~~ something. Not that I'll ever need a character trait for any reason. Just saying. But then he <u>did</u> tell me his story. Said he's been studying pebbles, shells and sea glass and the way they skim in the water for ten years now only because it was something he always wanted to do. Doing what you want to do — what a concept!

Billie watched Auggie talking to me. I think she heard some of what he said. Or not. Don't know. Probably did, because a few minutes later she said whispered, Now <u>there's</u> someone who likes what he's doing. Asked her what she meant by that. She said that Auggie looked so happy about his sea glass and shells, like he had inner peace or something, which she said I don't seem to have. I told her that she doesn't seem to have inner peace either. What a stupid conversation! Don't think either of us knew what we were talking about. It was like we were completely wasted, which we weren't. Maybe it's from all the drinking we did back home. Or not.

Tuesday, June 14
Billie went out with Nick last night. Got back to the room a little past midnight. Told me it's over with Nick because he's more interested in himself than in her. They were in his hotel room, and she said he checked himself out in the mirror every 5 minutes.

Billie's still asleep. I'll go to breakfast alone.

Right before breakfast I went outside and called Mom. She said I had received mail from the sociology dept. at Montclair State. I know it's a bunch of boring stuff about classes and lectures and books and registering online and stuff like that. Blah blah blah blah blah. Mom said I also got a newsletter from the acting department because apparently they forgot to take my name off the mailing list after I switched my major.

Went back to the room after breakfast. Billie was up, but groggy. Drove to Sunset Beach alone. It was misty, but not too bad. Auggie was there! I wasn't surprised. Incredible the way he's always out there doing what he does. What he loves to do. Had his notebook in a bag that can be sealed (zip-lock?) so that his notebook doesn't get damp in the mist. Also had an umbrella that he stuck in the sand, and he sat under it to write in his notebook. I followed him as he moved from one part of the beach to another. He didn't seem to mind. I told him that I admired his perseverance (sp?) and his devotion to his work. (Billie would be soooo pissed if she saw me following Auggie around like a puppy.). He smiled and said it's not his work, it was his passion and his destiny. His words! What a concept.

Went back to the room. Time to pack. Billie was running out of steam anyway.

Got back mid-afternoon. Dropped Billie at her apartment, then went home. Mom said I looked good. Spoke to Billie on the phone. She went back to sleep after I dropped her off. I think I woke her. Oh well. She said maybe next summer we should try someplace else. Maybe Ocean City. Or Long Beach Island. Didn't tell Billie this (she hung up to go back to sleep) but I'd like to go back to Cape May. Maybe even to the Bonnie June. If I told Billie that, she'd say I just wanted to see Auggie again, even though he's more than twice my age and kind of odd. That's not the reason. Don't really know the reason.

Don't feel like unpacking right now. Too tired. Maybe later. I think I might log onto Montclair.edu first to look around for a few minutes.

Just turned off my laptop. Gonna try to take a nap. Don't know if I'll fall asleep. Too wound up because of what I just did. Switched my major back to acting. Will tell Mom later. If Billie calls, will tell her too. Or not.

One-Hundred-Fifty-Nine Pounds Max

On the first of July, a reporter from *The Washington Post* tracked down Max at the office of his real estate agent in Annandale to ask for a comment.

"A comment? Sure," Max said. "In three days it will be America's independence day, and in four days it will be *my* independence day."

Centauri III, with writer-turned-astronaut Maxwell Dean aboard, is scheduled for liftoff from Cape Canaveral in Florida at four-fifteen p.m. on Thursday, July Fifth. After thirty years of research, experimentation and testing among scientists at NASA and six private spaceflight companies, followed by fifteen years of national debate and discussion, and concluding with ten years of planning, the United States is ready to send Max Dean on a mission from which he will never return. On his lifelong journey into the celestial unknown, he will write whatever inspires him — what he sees, how he feels, what he comes to believe about life and the universe — and he will take photographs to accompany his literary musings. Despite the great distance Max will travel, people on Earth will be able to read his words and see his pictures every month through the use of powerful radio waves. These innovative waves will be boosted and rebroadcast every fifty million miles by miniature satellites that Centauri III releases into space as it travels on its eternal voyage.

Centauri III is the first space capsule that will employ a propulsion method that uses light itself to attain speed once thought to be unattainable. With this new technology, Maxwell Dean will reach Pluto and the edge of our own solar system by the time he turns forty-five, cross through a second solar system when he reaches the age of sixty-six, fly through the middle of a third solar system toward the end of his seventies, and most likely get two-thirds through a fourth solar system before he passes away of old age. He will travel hundreds of billions of miles. Between his current health and the exercises and medications that have carefully been planned for his time aboard Centauri III, Max is expected to live as long as one hundred years, and perhaps a few years beyond that. Not enough time to come home, but enough to see, absorb and describe in words and photos more about the universe beyond the Milky Way than most people can imagine.

"What have you done over the last, say, two or three weeks, Mr. Dean?" the reporter asked.

Max explained that he had signed papers, sent emails, said goodbye to friends and family, underwent countless medical tests and psychological screenings, settled his financial accounts, sold his car and his apartment (the money will go to charity), and hung out at the beach.

"The beach? Alone, or with someone else?" questioned the reporter.

"Alone, to the extent possible," Max stated. "Chesapeake Beach, on the bay. It's public — but more often than not, I'm able to find a secluded spot."

"Why alone? You'll be alone for the rest of your life!"

"Why alone? Because I don't know if I'll ever again find a place as special as a secluded beach," Max said with the utmost of conviction. "That's the kind of place where I spent a lot of my childhood. Those were very happy days for me. I had many personal issues as a child. I was a teenager when I first began to explore life as a writer, and I had many frustrations because of it. A secluded beach was my refuge. I enjoyed my time alone. So..."

The reporter urged him to elaborate, to talk about his beach visits when he was a child. Since it was just that one reporter who asked—a persistent yet relatively congenial fellow—Max complied with his request.

He told the reporter how he went to Chesapeake Beach almost every weekend in the late spring, summer and early fall when he was a boy growing up in Brandywine. His parents would usually go with him, but they always stayed in the distance to give him ample opportunity to explore his imagination without feeling self-conscious. As Max wistfully explained to the reporter, every time he went to the beach he took the following items with him: a plastic pail and shovel, a bag of pretzels, a Yoo Hoo, a bottle of sunscreen, a notepad and a pencil, a little astronaut doll named Captain Keith, and two beach balls. He rarely altered the inventory from visit to visit.

"A notepad and a pencil?" the reporter asked.

Max explained how he enjoyed writing essays and short stories about the beach, which he would try to sell (without success) to newspapers and magazines.

"A sort of preview of what you'll end up doing for the next sixty years or so," the reporter commented. "Writing."

"I suppose," Max responded. "Except that now, people will actually read what I write."

The reporter jotted a few words into his little notebook and smiled as he scribbled. Then he wanted to know about the astronaut doll.

Max described Captain Keith as his favorite childhood toy. It was a rubber plaything, not nearly as flexible as other popular dolls of the day, but to Max, that little astronaut was truer to life than all the rest. Captain Keith was indestructible, Max said; the toy astronaut could be buried in the sand, thrown in the water, or tossed off a cliff, and never suffer so much as a scratch. Also, by his inanimate nature, Captain Keith had to listen without complaint to Max's dreams about becoming a writer one day. Because he was just a doll, he could never lecture Max about the need to have something to fall back on. Captain Keith could not smirk when Max complained about being left out of games and activities because of how flabby and knobby-kneed he was. "He sure was a comforting little half-ounce friend," Max concluded without a trace of self-consciousness. "He always listened and he always understood."

The reporter enjoyed the account very much, and urged Max on. He asked about the beach balls.

The beach balls, Max said, were to throw into the ocean. He said he learned a lot about weight, mass, buoyancy and tides simply by throwing those balls in the water and then watching as they weaved and bobbed their way back—if they came back at all.

"Pretzels? Yoo Hoo?"

Max smirked at the reporter.

"I'm sure you think one was for eating and the other for drinking," he said. "That would seem obvious enough, I suppose, since everyone gets hungry and thirsty at the beach. And yes, I got hungry and thirsty, too. But there was more to it than that. I used the empty Yoo Hoo bottles and the empty pretzel bags to catch tiny sand crabs, which I would study and then release back into nature where they belong."

That's where Maxwell Dean ended his narrative. Only the pail, the shovel and the sunscreen were left out of the explanation, but he knew that these were the most logical beach items of all and assumed that the reporter required no further enlightenment. That may have been true—but the patient reporter was not quite ready to leave the real estate office. He wanted to know what Max had decided to take along with him on his everlasting trip to outer space.

"I heard from a source of mine at NASA," the reporter let on, "that you have a strict weight and size limitation on the personal items you can bring along with you. Have you decided what to bring, Mr. Dean?"

"No, I haven't," Max said, somewhat tenaciously — although he didn't mean for it to come out that way.

The reporter thanked Max for his time and left the office. A few moments later, Max said goodbye to his real estate agent and began his journey home. It was a three-mile walk; he had already sold his car and kindly refused the agent's offer to give him a lift. The reporter's final question reminded him of how he needed time to think about what he would bring with him on the trip. It was one of the most important tasks at hand, and one that needed to be completed as soon as possible. Max had always done his most serious thinking during solitary walks, so he used the walk home for that purpose alone — to try to decide what to bring.

During the walk, he ran through his head what the NASA people had told him regarding the collective size and weight of the personal items he could take along.

"I'm afraid it will have to be one-hundred-fifty-nine pounds maximum," mission control's assistant director had warned him.

"Excuse me?" Max had asked calmly. "Can you please repeat that?"

"Well," the assistant director explained, with a sympathetic look on his face, "we can't allow over three-hundred-thirty-eight pounds of cargo in the ship. You weigh one-hundred-seventy-nine. That leaves exactly one-hundred-fifty-nine pounds for anything you'd like to bring along. That's the best we can do. One-hundred-fifty-nine pounds, max. Sorry."

Max was aware of the assistant director's unintended name-related pun, but didn't wish to point it out. The man was having a hard enough time.

"Also, no one item can be larger than sixteen inches by sixteen inches," the assistant director continued. "I feel bad about it, but that's the best we can do, Max."

Those were the instructions. Just a few words, yet such a complicated task—and one on which Max had procrastinated for weeks. He could procrastinate no longer; one of the toughest decisions of his life had to be made in an excruciatingly short amount of time.

The Centauri III team had previously told him that the built-in equipment aboard the ship would accommodate any kind of video program or music he wanted to bring along. So as soon as he arrived at the house (which would no longer be his on July Fifth), Max looked through his massive collections. But what good was any of it, he wondered, without the ability to share movies and music with other people? He put it all on the front lawn with a sign alerting passersby they could take whatever they wanted.

He had many books, but they only reminded him of his own troubled history with publishing companies. It was a reminder he didn't want, so he put all the books in boxes to donate to the local library later in the day.

What about puzzles? He had about a dozen intricate puzzles—each with over five-thousand pieces—but to Max that was merely a reminder of time rather than an antidote to it. They were in shabby condition, anyway, so Max put them in a large contractor bag, which he deposited on the curb for the morning garbage pickup.

He had a few electronic games, but none had been modified for the ship's power sources. Maybe the new owners of the house would like them for when friends and relatives stopped by.

Those items put together weighed less than one hundred-fifty-nine pounds, and each measured less than sixteen inches by sixteen inches. He could take them all if he wanted. But Max was more convinced than ever that they would neither help him stay alert nor provide any sense of comfort. They would do nothing to soothe his heart and ease his mind on this unprecedented lifelong trip.

On July Fourth, Maxwell Dean hopped a chartered jet to Florida. He had with him just one paper bag. In it was Captain Keith.

Loony Linnie and the Palindrome Trio

My first day as a lifeguard at the Dolphin Motel started at nine o'clock in the morning. I sat there on the lifeguard stand looking around and I was like, Wow, this is boring. No one's here and there are only five cars in the parking lot, and, so, well, you know.

Back at school I had seen an ad for the lifeguard job in *The Tower*, which is the student newspaper at Kean University, which is where I go, obviously, and since I already had my lifeguard certification I applied for the job and got it. I live with my parents in South Orange, but the Dolphin Motel is in Wildwood, so I looked online and found a room in a private house on West Baker Avenue which is like just a few blocks from the motel. I also did a lot of research on Wildwood just so that I could plan a few things to do during my time off. Not that I expected to have like an awesome social life over the summer or anything like that, but I thought, what the hell. My lifeguard pay is $240 a week and my rent is $480 a month, so Mara, my roommate at Kean, said that I would be working for two full weeks just to have a place to live every month. I'm not exactly sure what she meant by that, but whatever.

Anyway, you might think that with my name, which is Linnie O'Malley, that I'd have red hair and freckles and that I'd have to be really careful in the sun. But guess what. My hair is black and I kind of always look tanned, and even though I use sunblock I don't have to worry about getting burned the way I guess lots of other O'Malleys have to worry about it.

So on that first morning at the Dolphin Motel, I hopped up on the lifeguard stand, took my sunglasses and the book I was reading out of my little carrying bag, wrapped the shoulder strap of my bag around the armrest, and prepared for a not too busy sunny morning. The book was *Fifty Shades of Grey*, which Mara gave me, even though I didn't ask for it.

Two old ladies stopped by at about eleven o'clock, but they didn't swim. They smiled at me. One of them asked me what my name was and I told her. Maybe she asked me my name just because she was just being friendly, or maybe she felt bad that I had to be there even though the two of them didn't even want to swim. I don't really know. Anyway, when I told them my name, they both said that I don't look like a Linnie O'Malley. I'm thinking, Oh really? Then they went back into the motel.

I mean, it doesn't take a genius to know that I don't look like a Linnie O'Malley. Right? I once told this guy at school that some people say I look Italian. His name was Andy. I met him when I was a freshman at Kean. I was majoring in psychology at the time. I'm pretty sure he thought I was good looking, but I think he lost interest in me because of some of the things I said. When I like a guy I guess I talk a lot. I don't know why. You know what I told him? You won't believe it. I told him that I didn't know if psychology was the right major for me and that I didn't know if I even deserved to be accepted at Kean in the first place because my SAT scores were so lousy. I even told him that I didn't know if I should stay a virgin until I got married. Can you believe it? That's just the way I am. I also told him that all the crazy things in my head usually drive me nuts and make me wonder if I should have myself committed. Obviously I was joking. I mean, come on. But I guess this Andy guy didn't take it as a joke. He said that I was obviously calling out for help and that I was really smart for trying to get it by talking about it, but that he wasn't the kind of guy who could deal with it. He stopped seeing me after a few days.

Okay. I have to talk about Ralph for a minute. Ralph is the assistant manager of the Dolphin Motel. He's skinny and he has a lot of pimples. That's not why he creeped me out, but I just thought I'd mention it. I'm pretty sure that Ralph likes me, and I'm pretty sure he came outside as much as he did just to talk to me. I mean, he had no other reason to be there. You know? He offered me Cokes and candy and stuff. I never wanted anything, but I didn't want to be rude, either. He came out one time and asked if I liked the book I was reading. I had read maybe one page or something like that so I didn't know what to say. But actually I didn't have to say anything because right away he started to tell me that he doesn't read books because he watches TV all the time. Even when he's behind the reception desk in the motel. I said that was nice and told him that I don't watch a lot of TV. He said that he was studying television production at Rider, at night, and could probably name every show that's ever been on and every new show that's coming out next year and stuff like that. I prayed that someone would come outside to swim just so that Ralph would have to go back into the lobby and stop talking about television. But guess what. That didn't happen. Ralph kept talking about television. He said that he liked *The Sopranos* and *30 Rock*. He said he likes game shows and reality shows like *Below Deck* and *Love Island* and stuff like that, which I know nothing about. Then a young couple came outside. Thank God, right? A man and a woman. They both had little silver necklaces with tiny Jewish stars. They sat on chaise lounges near the shallow end of the pool. Ralph went back to the lobby. I was happy about that.

Anyway, the Jewish stars reminded me of this guy I met when I was a sophomore. His name was Carl. He studied in Jerusalem for two semesters. I told him that some people say I look Israeli because of my hair and my complexion, and he said that he could understand why people would say that, but that my speech and my body language were a hundred percent New Jersey. I have absolutely no idea what he meant by that. Was it a compliment or an insult? No clue! Anyway, Carl was the handsomest guy I ever met at Kean. He asked me if I wanted to sleep with him, and I actually wanted to, but I heard my mother's voice in my head telling me that I shouldn't. So I turned him down because of that stupid voice in my head. Guess what. I actually told him about the stupid voice, and how it sometimes makes me want to check myself into some kind of loony bin. He told me that everyone feels that way from time to time and that I'm really smart for having the courage to talk about it out in the open, which he said a lot of people don't do. But he also said that it was too much for him to deal with. He said he dated someone in Israel with the same kind of problem. So he stopped going out with me after two weeks. I was really bummed about that. I mean, come on.

So my second week at the Dolphin wasn't much different from the first, to tell you the truth. There were four or five swimmers, tops. Ralph came out for a few minutes every day. You have no idea how hard it was not to be rude when he came out. I read two more pages of *Fifty Shades of Grey*, but it was really hard to follow. (I can't wait to give it back to Mara.)

One day Ralph came outside to ask if I had recently checked the chlorine level in the pool. I told him that I check the chlorine level four times every day, which he should have already known. (He probably did.) He said he was glad I knew all about pools because anything having to do with pools is Greek to him. I don't know where that expression came from or what it really means, but that's what he said. Then, out of nowhere, he described a bunch of ideas he had for television shows that he wants to try to sell to a producer. I was never so bored in my life. Believe me. Finally he went back to the lobby. But that thing he said about all pool stuff being Greek to him? Guess what. That made me think of another guy. Big surprise, right? There was this guy I met in my speech pathology class at the beginning of my junior year. That's my major now, speech pathology. His name was Eric. I told him that some people think I'm Greek. It came up because Eric came right out and asked me where my family was from. He said it was a hobby of his to guess where people came from, but that he couldn't figure out where my family came from just by looking at my face. After I said that some people think I'm Greek, I told him that my name was Linnie O'Malley, so he said that he was going to go way way way way way out on a limb—that's exactly how he put it, with all those ways—and make a guess that based on my name, I was Irish. That was kind of funny, I guess. Eric was cute. He talked a lot, and I had a hard time keeping up with what he said. Usually it was about astronomy, which he said was his passion. I told him that sometimes I get confused between astronomy and astrology and asked him if they're completely different. For some reason I felt really comfortable with him, so I told him that sometimes I feel like I'm from outer space. Like an alien. Like nothing seems right for me down here on Earth. Like I'm a little loony. Like maybe I should go back to my home planet or something. I thought I was being funny. One day Eric said that he loved how I always found a way to combine my world and his world, like when I talked about feeling that I was from another planet while he was talking about solar systems and stuff like that. I'm not a hundred percent sure I know exactly what he meant by that, but he said that I was really smart for getting his attention that way. Whatever. Fine. He said he had met a few people who actually believe in alien abductions and that those people really scare the hell out of him. He also told me that the word loony has something to do with the moon, and I said that the moon was one of the places where I'll probably end up having to live one day. I thought I was being funny again.

But guess what? I never saw him after I said that. I guess I became one of those people that scared the hell out of him.

Suddenly it was my third week at the Dolphin. How did that happen? Anyway, one day I saw two men in the parking lot, which is near the pool, past the fence, and I heard them talking. Good looking guys, I guess in their early thirties, and they were laughing. For some reason I wanted to yell at them to shut up— and I almost said it out loud. I was just so fed up with stuff. You know? With my life. With all those weird memories about Andy and Carl and Eric. With being so bored at the Dolphin. Plus, I never did get to go into Wildwood to do anything after work. I just felt so blah. I knew those two guys in the parking lot couldn't hear me, so in a kind of loud whisper I said, "Just go away. You have all of Wildwood to enjoy, you morons. Go down the Hippo water slide, or go whale watching, or fly on a parasail, or visit the doo wop museum, or pig out at a fudge kitchen. Why in God's name are you standing in a hot parking lot of a fleabag motel when you have the whole damn town to play around in? Okay, okay—you look like nice guys, but so did Andy and Carl and Eric. So what does *that* mean? I guess that means you're not the problem. I guess that means the problem is me. Loony Linnie. I shouldn't blame you two guys. I should blame myself. It's me. My life. Love and sex. Growing up. Going to college. My mother's voice in my head. Careers. All that."

Trust me, I know how silly it sounds to admit that I was saying all that stuff at the pool, sort of out loud. But it didn't seem silly to me at the time. It seemed a whole lot worse than silly. To tell you the truth, I felt like I was really going crazy. I mean, I was having the weirdest conversation in the world with myself right there at the empty pool! What I didn't know at the time was that Ralph had come back outside and was shuffling back and forth behind the lifeguard stand, really quietly, while I was having that weird conversation with myself, and that he apparently heard every word. I saw him sneaking back into the motel, which is how I figured out that he had probably been there the entire time.

I ended my first month at the Dolphin in a mood that I can't really describe. Don't even ask. Crappy is the only word that comes to mind. What made it really annoying was the fact that Ralph started to come out to talk to me at least twice a day now. Not just once, but twice. I didn't need that on top of everything else. Right? I mean, come on. I tried to listen to him, but mostly he talked about television, which I really don't care about, and it was just so hard to look interested. Believe me.

One afternoon, about my fifth week there, this guy came out of the motel. He was in his mid-thirties, I guess, kind of tall, salt-and-pepper hair, muscles, dimpled cheeks, straight white teeth. Really handsome. I mean, like extremely handsome. He had a 'Wildwood is For Lovers' towel and a novel by John Steinbeck, I think. Or J. D. Salinger. Somebody like that. I don't really remember. Anyway, he looked at me and said that he had been wondering where they've been hiding all the pretty lifeguards because down at the beach it's all guys there. And he says that now he knows where there's a pretty lifeguard. At the Dolphin Motel! That made me laugh. I didn't plan on laughing. It just came out. I also didn't plan on saying what I said next and have no idea where I got the nerve to say it, but I asked him where he's been all my life. I still can't believe I said that. You know? It's like a line from a movie, right? Anyway, he just smiled. (He had an awesome smile.) He said that Ralph told him that I went to Kean University, which he said is where he teaches. He said his name is Professor Nalla, but that I should call him Allan. Allan Nalla, which he said is a palindrome, which he explained is a word or a bunch of words that's the same backwards and forward. I had never heard of that before. He said he knew all about palindromes even though he's not an English teacher. He told me he teaches chemistry, and I said that chemistry is the one subject I never majored in at Kean. I don't know why I said that.

I guess I was sort of flirting with the guy. I mean, like I said, he was really cute. Anyway, then he explained how instead of teaching chemistry, what he'd really like to do is to be a chemist and invent new formulas. He started to describe this lotion he wants to invent, a suntan lotion that you put on once and it lasts all summer, no matter how many times you swim, shower, jog, or even make love. I mean, like, wow — he really said that. Okay? To be honest, I felt a tingle run down my spine when he said the words make love. I really did. Then he said that if he invents it he might call it Sum Lotion, which he explained is a play on the words summer and suntan lotion. Then Allan walked over to the edge of the pool by the deep end and dove in. He swam a bunch of laps (really well, by the way, which wasn't a surprise), then came out, grabbed his towel, wrapped it around his shoulders, and asked me if I'd be at the pool tomorrow. I said yes, especially if he wanted to talk about chemistry. I figured I already showed him that I'm not exactly shy. You know? So I just went for it. I told him that I can be interested in chemistry if I really want to be, and that if I had him for a teacher I'd really want to be. Can you believe I said that? I can't. But I did. Word for word. So he told me that I'm not only pretty, but also funny and smart. Then he asked for my name. I told him, and he said he'd see me later.

Now *that* was an interesting afternoon. Trust me.

The next morning, a fat old man came out to the pool. He had a Kean U. gym bag and sat on a chaise lounge by a little table near the shallow end. He took a lot of stuff out of his bag, and I mean a ton of stuff, like a can of prune juice, goggles, a bottle of pills, a tube of zinc cream, a magnifying glass, and two magazines. Probably more. I don't remember. He saw me staring at him and said that he knows his bag is like a 7-Eleven, and he apologized for it. I told him that he didn't have to apologize, and I asked him if he was from England, because he had an accent that sounded a little like Hugh Grant or Colin Furth, which are really the only two actors I can name who I'm pretty sure are from England. Anyway, this guy was so fat that the skin on his back pushed out the straps of the chaise lounge so that they practically scraped the cement. I was actually afraid the straps would snap. I was thinking, Hey, I don't want to be the one to have to scrape you off the cement, buddy. Anyway, he asked me if I'd like to know about the suntan lotion he wants to invent. I'm thinking, Wait—what? Suntan lotion? The handsome guy from the day before said the same exact thing. So this fat guy said it will be called Sum Lotion and asked me if I liked that name. He even called me Linnie, which is weird because I hadn't mentioned my name yet. Then he told me that his name is Neville Elliven, and he showed it to me written on his gym bag in really big black letters, which is when I realized that it's—now get this—a palindrome. Neville Elliven. He asked me if I know what a palindrome is, but before I had a chance to answer, he explained it. A word or a couple of words that's the same backwards and forward, he said. So I just blurted out the name Allan Nalla, because that name was still fresh in my mind from the day before. Remember—that really handsome professor? Allan Nalla? Anyway, this Neville guy said he was impressed with the fact that I was able to come up with another palindrome name so quickly, and he told me that I'm smart, that I'm pretty, and that I'm pretty smart. That's exactly what he said. You're smart, you're pretty, and you're pretty smart, except he said it with an English accent, which sounds even better than it does in English. Actually, it almost sounds like a pick-up line, doesn't it? But I know this guy isn't trying to pick me up. God forbid, right? I mean, not that I have anything against fat people, but, well, you know. Then he apologized. He said that it was totally inappropriate for him to say something like that, and he asked me to please not call the cops on him because he doesn't need any scandals at the university where he works. Now remember, he had a Kean U. gym bag, so I asked him if he happens to work at Kean University, and he said yes. Then I asked him if he teaches chemistry, and he said yes again. I'm thinking to myself, holy shit. He said that Kean won't let him do experiments on campus, so he might look for a new job somewhere else. Then he put everything back into his bag and went into the motel. I kind of just sat there for a long time staring into space. I actually started to wonder if I was hallucinating, even though I've never taken drugs and don't even know what hallucinating would feel like.

This morning a Chinese guy was standing by the locked gate when I got to the motel at nine-thirty. I'm the one who opens the gate every morning. He didn't have anything with him. He was just standing there. He looked at me and said that the early bird catches the worm. Or something like that. He said it's an old cliché that he's allowed to use whenever he wants because he's not an English teacher and no one can yell at him for using clichés. To be honest, I had no idea what he was talking about. But now that I knew he wasn't an English teacher I kind of felt like I had to ask him if he happens to teach chemistry at Kean. Right? I mean, if he said he teaches chemistry at Kean, I'd know for sure that I was right in the middle of loony land. Just like I suspected all along. So guess what. He said he teaches chemistry at Kean. But I didn't scream or have a major meltdown or anything like that. I held it together (which is something I heard someone say in a movie once). I got the key out of my carrying bag, unlocked the gate as calmly as I could, and tried to settle in on the lifeguard stand as if everything was normal. Which of course it wasn't. I mean, it was really far from normal. Billions of miles. I wrapped the strap of my carrying bag on the handrail. The guy sat down in a chair right next to the lifeguard stand and said Hello, Linnie. He told me that his name is Otis. Otis Sito. He said that he was born in Japan and that his real name is Otohiko or something like that, but when he came to America when he was little he asked his parents if he could change it to something more American. So he picked Otis. He spelled Otis Sito for me, so of course I told him that his name is a palindrome. He looked surprised and said that not only am I a sight for sore eyes, but that I'm very bright, too, and that he hopes I'm a quick responder, which is something I had never heard before. I guess he saw the confused look on my face. (You could've seen it from the moon!) He laughed and said that he has a fear of drowning and wants a quick responder nearby, which is when I realized that what he really meant was *first* responder, not quick responder. I asked him if that's what he meant and he laughed again and said yes, and he apologized for his bad English. He told me he doesn't swim, but just twirls around in the water on his feet. He asked me if doing that — just twirling around — is still good exercise, and I told him that it is. And then I started to cry. I can't say why, exactly. Well, I guess I can. I just felt like I was finally going totally and completely bonkers. Nuts. Insane. Out of my mind. Once and for all. Meanwhile, this Otis Sito guy did seven or eight twirls in the water and then went back to the steps and got out of the water. Even though it was early, the sun was strong and Otis told me that he's thinking of trying to invent a new kind of suntan lotion that lasts all summer long. I asked him if he'll call it Sum Lotion, and he said yes. That's exactly what he has in mind, he said. Sum Lotion. He asked me if I'd be at the pool tomorrow morning so that maybe I can give him a few pointers about not being afraid to drown. I mumbled okay, or something like that. I really don't remember. Then he went into the motel.

After he left, I sat on the lifeguard stand like a zombie for maybe fifteen minutes. Maybe more. I don't know. I mumbled to myself, Allan Nalla? Neville Elliven? Otis Sito? Chemistry at Kean? Sum Lotion? Seriously? Are you friggin kidding me? I just had to consider the fact that I was imagining all this. Hearing things that no one was actually saying. You know?

I started to cry. A lot. Who wouldn't?

I also decided at that moment not to finish out the summer at the motel. What would be the point? Right? First of all, hardly anyone swims anyway, but more than that, I need help. Mental help. A lot of it. As soon as possible. I'm certifiably crazy. I have to get out of there. I know I won't get paid for the whole summer if I leave early, and that I'll never get a good recommendation for another job. But I don't care. It's more important to get help. I mean like serious help.

So up on the lifeguard stand, I grabbed my purse from the armrest, but I grabbed it so hard that it opened up and all the change flew out, right into the pool. Nickels, dimes, quarters, pennies. I yelled FUCK so loud that I think everyone inside the motel must have heard me. I decided to leave the change in the water and just leave. I didn't want to say anything to Ralph, so I avoided walking close to the motel. I kept my head down and went through the gate by the parking lot so that I could go straight to my car. I looked up just for a second and saw Ralph walking toward me. An older guy was next to him, a man in a shirt and tie that wasn't tied. Ralph said hi when he was almost right in front of me. He told me that the guy next to him was Brad, and he said that Brad is a producer with Bravo, which is a cable network or something like that. Ralph said he called Brad a few weeks ago, right after he heard my crazy little speech on the lifeguard stand when I didn't know anyone was listening. Then Brad told me that over the last few days there have been hidden cameras and microphones all around the pool that recorded everything that happened, and that I'm going to be part of a new TV show called *Mind Games*. He said it will be a reality show that he thinks will be very popular. I really have no idea what a reality show is. Brad said there's going to be an episode all about me and about what he calls the palindrome trio, which he explained is Allan Nalla, Neville Elliven, and Otis Sito. Brad said that all three of them are actors who are just part of the show. Everything was planned. He says they have some great videos of me mumbling to myself, making weird faces whenever I heard something that sounded crazy (that's like a million things, right?), and even stuff they shot a little while ago when I grabbed my purse and all the change flew into the pool.

Brad suggested we go into the manager's office in the motel to talk. He told me that all three of those guys are there waiting to meet me, and that there's a lot to go over and a bunch of forms to sign and stuff like that. He also told me that I'm not crazy at all. I asked him if I can freshen up first in the ladies' room before the meeting. He said sure.

So here I am, freshening up in the ladies room. I'm picturing Professor Allan Nalla. He's the handsomest one of the three. Remember? I mean, he even used the words making love. I could swear that another tingle went down my spine just now as I said that. I mean like literally a second ago. I'd go to bed with a guy like that in a heartbeat and wouldn't even care about my mother's voice in my head. I'll find a way to get rid of that voice. I think someone like Professor Allan Nalla could be the one to help me do that, if you know what I mean.

I just combed my hair with a comb from my carrying bag, and now I'm straightening out my bathing suit. Fortunately it's one of my newer bathing suits that sort of shows off my figure. I'm glad I put this one on today of all days. In a second, I'll go to the manager's office. Guess what. I've decided to make the best impression I can possibly make on Professor Nalla. Then, when I get back to Kean at the end of the summer I'll switch my major to chemistry and get him to ask me out. I bet we'll hit it off. I know I can do it. I just know it. I mean, everyone I meet is either telling me that I'm completely loony or that I'm really smart. Normally I'd have to try to decide which one it is. But with this whole Professor Allan Nalla plan of mine, isn't it like completely obvious?

Old Rocker

Ray Deegan is an old rocker who likes to rock on an old rocker. The chair is one of two weathered but sturdy antiques on the rustic porch of Ray's Ocean Grove estate, which many years ago he had dubbed High Sea. The name is a play on words, based on two factors: when he was a famous rock musician he was lauded for his ability to hit a perfect high C in lyrics that called for a falsetto croon; in the fall, as the trees lose their leaves, when you look out of the guest room window on the third floor of his estate you can see the Atlantic Ocean. Hence, the name High Sea.

Three or four times a year people walk up Ray's driveway to ask him if his stunning, sprawling, three-story Dutch colonial is a bed-and-breakfast inn simply because it looks so inviting. Ray, who if prompted can get a little testy, is almost always tempted to growl, "Do you see a sign that says bed-and-breakfast? No? Well, gee wiz, Sherlock, there's your answer right there!" In fact, he said that very thing (or a close facsimile) on two separate occasions in the recent past only to regret it later on. Ray knows that most people mean no harm. So he tries to remember to smile and to tell those who inquire that there are plenty of B&Bs in Ocean Grove to be found just by driving around.

Ray's beautiful twelve-string Gibson acoustic guitar, just a short reach away between the two rocking chairs, leans against the white railing. Ray has a pad in one hand, a pencil in the other, and a look of contemplation on his wrinkled, windswept face. He had been struggling with a song. Even though Ray had proven himself years before as a skilled composer and lyricist, sometimes there is bound to be a dry spell. Working alone has been his preferred method of songwriting, but recently he began to toy with the idea of collaborating with someone to increase the chance for the right lyrics to find their way into the right tunes.

It is a beautiful Jersey shore morning in early autumn. The temperature is perfect for relaxing on the porch in comfy old jeans, a wrinkled Life Is a Beech tee-shirt, and a worry-free state of mind. Ray is in a charitable mood. He has no desire to be testy. That's the furthest thing from his mind.

He detects footsteps, thanks to the few crunchy leaves that have already fallen onto the pebbled driveway from the canopy of red oaks on either side. He hadn't been expecting any visitors. Could it be a neighbor? Probably not. Neighbors usually call first or leave notes in the mailbox when they need to borrow something or want to invite him to a party. But Ray refuses to be alarmed. He has been living at High Sea for almost twenty years now, alone, and it has always been safe. Even diehard fans, now that most of them are past retirement age, are respectful.

The unannounced visitor finally comes into view. It is a man, younger than Ray by about twenty-five years—mid-forties, he assumes—dressed in black jeans and a Just Do It tee-shirt. He walks slowly but decisively to the bottom step of the porch, stops, and looks up at Ray. He remains silent.

"Hello," Ray says. He tries to sound neither rude nor completely obliging.

"Are you... Aren't you Ray Deegan?" the gentleman inquires.

"I'm afraid I am," Ray responds. He uses that sardonic line— 'I'm afraid I am'—at least four or five times a year when answering that same question.

"Ray Deegan, the rock legend? From Ceramic Peacocks? And the Oxy Moron Quartet?"

"That's me," Ray acknowledges. "And don't forget the Dewey Decimal System, the group that started off the whole damn thing in July of '66."

"Oh—I know!" the man grins. The smile looks genuine, and that prompts Ray, who had already been calm, to relax even more. "I know all about your career, Mr. Deegan. Sorry to barge in on you like this…Wow—I don't believe it. I know all about the Ceramic Peacocks and Oxy Moron and the Dewey Decimal System. Dewey was really the first band to do folk, country and rock, even before Crosby, Stills and Nash. And Oxy Moron, in my opinion, was a hell of a lot better than Credence, who everyone used to compare you guys to. I have all your records, Mr. Deegan."

Ray smiles. "Records? You know what records are? I'm shocked! I may even pass out. Records!"

"Actually, I have most of them on my smartphone now—but yes, I know what records are. I look younger than I really am. I'm fifty-five. When I was a little boy, there were still LPs."

"Ahh, the good old days," Ray sighs, "when things could shatter into a million pieces."

"Wow!" the younger man repeats, ignoring Ray's attempt at humor. "Ray Deegan… I love the fact that you wrote all your own material. Every single song."

"Actually, I'm thinking of bringing on a collaborator for some new stuff. You see?—even inflexible old farts like me can change. Maybe the new stuff will even be better than the old stuff! You'll let me know, kid."

"Well, I don't have your entire catalog, I'm afraid. There are two or three Ceramic Peacock CDs that I could never locate, and I can't even find them online to download. I've tried. Some collectors have them, but they go for a ton of money, and I'm always strapped for cash."

Ray feels no need to put up his guard, even though the topic has taken a slight turn; he likes this young man's face and manner and gives him the benefit of the doubt.

"I'd love to give you a few CDs, son, but I don't have any. I swear to God, to Christ, Moses, Mohammad, Buddha, Hare Krishna — whoever your guy is."

"Oh — I wasn't fishing around for that. I'm sorry. I hope you don't think — "

"It's all right, kid," Ray adds quickly. "I'm the one who should apologize. I guess that kind of suspicious thinking just goes with the territory. Comes from a lifetime of being in the music business. Agents, managers, A&R people... A lot of deceitful, selfish sons of bitches."

"Yeah — I've heard that about the music business."

"Music is one thing, kid; the music *business* is something else. I guess that's why I like to be all alone out here. I'm surprised at myself for even considering a collaborator. But things change. I'm open to new things."

"It always makes me a little sad to hear that about the business," the visitor admits. "I don't want to believe it."

"It makes you sad?" Ray asks. "Why? — do you want to go into the music business?"

"Me? Oh, no. That's not for me. What I mean is, I love music and musicians and bands and all that, which is why it makes me sad. But no — I have no interest in going into the music business myself."

"Smart boy," Ray smiles. "What *do* you do, if you don't mind my asking?"

"I manage a bookstore," he explains. "Not one of those big-box chain store things. I hate those. It's just a little independent store in Northampton. Up near Amherst, where UMass is. That's where I went to school. I stayed there after I graduated."

"That's kind of far from here, son. Well, you picked a good place to visit if you like rock 'n roll bands. I mean, Jersey! You know?"

"I do know," the guest says. "Bon Jovi."

"For one, sure. Though that's a little past my time."

"Southside Johnny and the Asbury Jukes?"

"The E Street Band."

"Springsteen!"

"I actually sat in with the E Street Band a few times back in the day," Ray shares. "We once played at the Great Auditorium right here in Ocean Grove, years before I knew I'd settle out here. Crazy, isn't it?"

"I have a recording of that concert, although I don't think it's a hundred percent legal. It took a lot of research to find a copy. But I found one."

"Geez, kid—instead of working in a bookstore," Ray smirks, "maybe you should be a private detective."

"I don't want to just *work* in a bookstore, Mr. Deegan. I'd like to own my own place one day. Not just a bookstore, but a combination bookstore and café, with acoustic guitar players, people reading stories out loud, that sort of thing. Sort of like a modern-day version of what they used to have in Greenwich Village, way before I was born."

"Nice! Sounds like a fulfilling and worthwhile way to make a living, kid. Hey—you can trespass any time, son! I like the way you think," he says. "Welcome to High Sea."

"What *you* did was worthwhile, Mr. Deegan. You gave many people a lot of pleasure over the years."

"Maybe," Ray nods. "There were just too many distractions to make it *entirely* worthwhile. But thanks. I'll take any compliment I can get."

"Too many distractions? You mean too many drugs? Too much meaningless sex? Petty disagreements with the other guys? Crooked management?"

Ray's smile widens.

"Are you sure you're not a seventy-year-old acid rocker in a fifty-five-year-old bookstore body?" he asks.

The bookstore manager explains that he's read a lot of books about the old rock stars—books he says that were eye-opening and disturbing. "And relatives of the rock stars actually wrote some of those books," he adds. "Can you believe what some people will do for money?"

"Well, maybe some of us old rockers deserve it. To be honest, we did some pretty crazy stuff back then. Myself included. Wrecking hotel rooms, screwing around, threatening record company executives... I, for one, would *not* want to read a book about me, no matter *who* wrote it."

"It must be tough to think back on it," the visitor says. "I mean, on one hand, it was the music that was the most important thing, but on the other hand, you were young, free, impetuous, making a crap-load of money. It must have gone to your head."

"It really did," Ray admits. "Sometimes it was painful. Looking back on all the bullshit, the deceit, the crap, the selfishness—pretty painful stuff to remember. But you want to know something, kid? Every once in a while, someone like you trespasses on my property and makes all the pain go away... Hey, that was pretty damn poetic, wasn't it? 'You trespassed on my land and took away my pain...' Maybe I could write a song with that line. Or let a collaborator help me turn it into something. What do you think? "

"I like it, Mr. Deegan. It's really good."

Ray motions to the empty rocking chair. His guest sits and looks at Ray's guitar, which is now between the two of them.

"Gorgeous instrument."

"Thanks," Ray says. "I got it when I bought this place about twenty years ago. I lost it five times, right here in the house!"

The bookstore manager laughs. "Well, it sure is a big house," he says.

"And pretty messy, too, if you want to know the truth. But between you and me" — Ray leans toward the young man and pretends to whisper — "it cost two-point-one million to build and sits on five acres, which adds another quarter mil to the total value. So I guess I can afford to let it get a little messy from time to time. Huh?"

"Why not?" the visitor says. "You can hire someone just to find things when you lose them. You've earned that."

"Stop buttering me up, kid. I might have to adopt you."

Both men giggle like children. Ray likes the feeling. He doesn't giggle all that often.

"Just being honest, Mr. Deegan."

"You know what, kid? I believe you."

"You say that like you've run into other people who haven't been so honest."

"Like I said before, the *business* in the music business is a hellish monster. Makes people nasty. It's a devil, and sometimes it never goes away."

A look of recognition sweeps over the younger man's face.

"That reminds me of a song you wrote when you were with the Oxy Moron Quartet. *The Devil Is Here to Stay*. Remember?"

"Of course I remember. That's probably why I said it. Good goddamn song. But it brings back a shitload of bad memories."

"Really? I heard a bunch of the stories behind that song," the visitor mutters, "but nothing horrendous."

"There was a lot of crap that happened back then."

"You mean like a million people trying to get a piece of the action, and how you had to do some slightly questionable things to make sure you got your share?"

Ray nods his head and tells the young man that he calls it Evil Money. "Sometimes it hardly seemed worth the effort to write, record, and tour in the first place. Not when the result of all of it was all that Evil Money, if you ask me."

There is another look of recognition from the bookstore manager. "Wasn't that the name of a song you wrote when you were with the Dewey Decimal System? *If You Ask Me?*"

Ray acknowledges it was indeed the name of a Dewey Decimal System tune. He asks the young man if he knew that besides writing the song and singing it, he had also played the saxophone solo on that cut. The visitor says yes, he knows, and shares that he is also aware that Ray took saxophone lessons throughout his high school years in Edison, New Jersey.

"Holy crap—you *do* know a lot about me, kid. That's scary."

"Scary? Why? A lot of it is good. Especially the important stuff—the music. You really cared about the music, Mr. Deegan. You had a passion for it. You put a lot of thought into it. It wasn't just about shocking people, or being a star, or having sex and getting wasted. It was about the music. You're a very special man. I mean it."

Although he is not the one performing this marvelous oratory, Ray is breathless after having heard it from the mouth of this young-looking, middle-aged stranger.

"Very special *old* man is what you mean, kid," he says. "I only *wish* I can get laid that easily now. It's all in the past. But speaking of being special, after hearing that speech you just made, I think maybe you should become a writer. Instead of selling books, you should write them."

"Maybe if something important came along to write about, I would," he allows. "To tell you the truth, I'm actually more excited about the bookstore-café idea. That's what I really want to do. But it'll probably never happen."

"Why not? All you need is skill, a little patience, a little luck—"

"And a ton of money," the young man quickly tacks on.

"I wish I could help you out, son. I really do. But would you like to hear what my lawyer says about loaning money to people?"

"When's the last time you spoke to him?" asks the High Sea guest.

"Who?"

"Your lawyer."

"My lawyer? About a month ago. Why?"

"Well, you see… the thing is… I spoke to him yesterday."

Ray bites his lip. He actually gnaws on it for a few seconds.

"You spoke to my lawyer?"

The visitor nods.

"Why?"

Now it is the young man's turn to bite his own lip.

"Well… you see.. My name is Josh. Josh Sherman," he says. "My mother's name is Laura Sherman."

Ray can't quite place the name, though it sounds vaguely familiar.

"Laura Sherman?"

"You met her backstage at the Fillmore East. It was Oxy Moron's last live concert. You were on the bill with Steppenwolf… I was born nine months later."

Despite every conscious effort to conceal it, Ray smiles.

"Mr. Deegan," Josh says, "I just want you to know —"

"First of all, there's really no need to explain," Ray interjects. "I've been around the block a few times and nothing surprises me anymore."

"I want you to know that I'm not really looking to —"

"Also, maybe instead of Mr. Deegan you should just call me Dad."

Josh says he'd like that.

"But," Ray continues, "there's something that bothers me."

"What's that?"

"You're smart — that's a given. And you've done your homework. And I'm willing to bet you've heard or read almost everything there is to hear and read about me. That makes me pretty damn certain that you know I'm not the best role model in the world to have as a father. I more or less already admitted that to you myself. Frankly, Josh, that's gonna bother me a little bit. Hell — it's gonna bother me a whole lot!"

"Role model? Are you talking about the drugs and the sex?"

"For starters," Ray says. "On the other hand, like you said, a lot of the time it was just about the music. I hope you don't think your old man was just some sort of freaked-out acid king with an unquenchable need to screw." Ray chuckles after he says it. "Sounds like the title of a book, doesn't it? *Ray Deegan: The Acid King with an Unquenchable Need to Screw.* Geez — I hope no one ever writes a book like *that!*"

"You know, when people find out that I'm the only child of Ray Deegan, they're gonna ask me a lot of questions," Josh says softly. "They're gonna want to find out if certain things are true or not. They may even want *me* to write something like *The Acid King with an Unquenchable Need to Screw.* That's not something I'm eager to do. Unless, of course, someone offered me enough money to write it."

Ray leans back in the chair and rocks slowly on the High Sea porch for a few moments.

"Which means that *The Acid King with an Unquenchable Need to Screw* will never get written if someone offers you enough money *not* to write it. Is that what you're getting at, kid?"

Josh shrugs, almost like an innocent child accused of having done something naughty.

"Like I said," Ray continues, this time averting Josh's eyes, "that little bookstore-café seems like more than just a dream right now, doesn't it? I think you just found the key to open your front door. Am I right?"

Josh stands up slowly.

"I'd better get going," he says. "It's been a pleasure, Dad. Really. We'll be in touch. Your lawyer has my address."

Josh descends the porch steps.

"How does *Fillmore Surprise* grab you for the title of a new song?" Ray murmurs almost to himself.

"Catchy," Josh says. "Maybe I'll stop by again and we can write it together. What do you think?"

"What do I think? Let me ask you a question, son. Do you see a sign that says I'm looking for a collaborator? No? Well, gee wiz, Sherlock, there's your answer right there."

The One

The day I found out I was going to be a father, I joked to my wife that what I dreaded most was the day I would have to explain sex to whoever the kid ended up being. "*That's* what you dread most?" she said in response. "I'll make you a deal. *You* carry the baby inside of you for a couple of nauseating months and then go through excruciating pain to bring it into the world, and *I'll* explain sex to whoever the kid ends up being. Deal?"

I never mentioned it again.

One day, when the kid in question was four, Beth asked if she could come with me to the supermarket. Along the route to the supermarket is Grace Methodist Church, which has a massive crucifix on its small front lawn, with a sculpture of a writhing Jesus near the top. That's another thing I dread— passing the church with Beth in tow because I know that one day she'll ask me about the half-naked man who looks like he's in horrifying pain up on that cross. I don't know if that's easy for anyone to explain, but for a Jewish father with a smart and inquisitive Jewish kid, it can be quite the predicament.

It was late in the afternoon, and the day had been an extremely busy one. It wiped me out. I strapped Beth into the car seat and prepared for an eight-minute ride full of questions. I knew I'd be able to answer some and that I'd stumble around others. That was typical. No big deal. There would probably also be plenty of random comments and intriguing tangents. After all, she was four years old, and she was... well... she was Beth.

As we turned onto Middle County Road, we discussed a new playgroup friend of hers named Tommy, who had visited our house earlier that day. But Beth didn't answer me when I asked which of her toys Tommy liked to play with. When I looked in the rear-view mirror, I saw Beth staring at the crucifix on the front lawn of Grace Methodist Church.

"Kelly has one of those," she said.

"Kelly? Next door? What—a crucifix?" I asked. "A little one, like on a necklace?"

"Uh huh. Her grandpa gived it to her. He told her it was Jesus the Messiah."

"Oh," I muttered. I didn't know what else to say.

"What's a messiah?" she asked.

I really wasn't in the mood. I didn't have the patience. I didn't have the time. More than anything, I didn't have the answer.

As I pulled into the supermarket parking lot, Beth repeated her question.

"Daddy, what's a messiah?"

I kept the explanation as simple as I could and just hoped for the best.

"Well," I began, "the messiah is a man—or a woman, I guess—who God talks to."

"Why?"

"Because God is always looking for someone to be a very special person who can help the world become a better place."

"Why?"

"Because we need someone to help the world become a better place."

"Did Jesus make the world a better place?"

"Well, some people think so. Other people don't. That's why most people hope there will be another messiah one day. To try again."

"Who will the messiah be?"

"I don't know, sweetie. I don't think anyone really knows. God will have to find the right person."

"What will God say when he finds the right person?"

"I don't know. I guess he'll say, 'Hey you there. You're the one!'"

"Oh," Beth said—but it was the kind of "Oh" that other things often followed. I braced myself.

"You know what?" Beth asked.

"What?"

"God talked to me once."

"He did?" I prayed for a way to end this discussion as quickly as possible. "What did God say when he talked to you?" I asked.

"He said, 'Hey you there. You're not the one!'"

And then she told me which of her toys Tommy liked to play with.

Shirley & Morris's Personalized Ashtrays

Dad died. He didn't have to. He was only seventy-four, not overweight, walked long distances, had no family history of disease. But he smoked. A lot. Two-and-a-half packs a day for fifty-seven years. On his seventy-fourth birthday, he was told he had lung cancer and emphysema, was admitted to the hospital, and died a week later.

That was six months ago. Mom had lived in the same house with him in Springfield (the one in Massachusetts) since the year after they married in Springfield (the one in Ohio). Now Mom has decided to move. She no longer needs a big house, wouldn't be able to take care of it, and doesn't want the headaches. I helped her put it up for sale. I live two hours away, in Brewster, New York, and I have a wife and children of my own. But ever since Dad died, I've driven to Mom's house once a week to be with her. Twice I brought the kids along and spent a couple of hours with them at Six Flags New England, a few towns away from Springfield, before going to Mom's house for dinner. Mom stayed home because she doesn't like amusement parks, and since she stayed home, she said it was like we hadn't visited at all because we spent most of the day at Six Flags. She's a little ornery like that lately. Or perhaps I should say a little more ornery than she's always been. I guess it's understandable. So now I visit only by myself. Besides, there isn't a lot for my kids to do there.

My sister Claire moved to California three years ago. All of Mom's acquaintances moved away over the last two years. Until recently, she had never really been alone. For fifty years she had plenty of people around, mostly my dad, and a lot of friends, too. Now she needs help. She has to put her finances in order, decide between several senior condo communities, and prepare the house to show to potential buyers. There's a lot to do. I love my mother and I'm determined to do the right thing. I have plenty of patience, but my visits to her house have not been particularly enjoyable. Some are okay, but they are never wonderful. Emotions are still raw. I guess I'm still mad at Dad for having smoked so much, and also mad at Mom for being so stubborn. Whenever I try to help her make decisions about her future and about the house, it turns into an argument. What's more, the traffic I inevitably hit going back and forth between Brewster and Springfield is infuriating. What should normally be a ninety-minute trip almost always takes two-and-a-half hours.

●　　●　　●

This afternoon I am attempting to de-clutter her basement so that when real estate agents start to bring clients down there next week as part of the house tour, they won't be shocked by what looks like an underground warehouse. Mom isn't a hoarder, at least not by the common definition or in the conventional sense — but she has fifty years' worth of memories down there. Most of what she considers memorable are meaningless. At least to me they are. Things of all shapes and sizes. Mostly very old. The vast majority should be discarded. Mom won't have room for any of it in a small condo. I certainly don't have room to store anything in my own house. And who knows when Claire will be able to visit to decide for herself?

So I grab five heavy-duty plastic garbage bags and five empty boxes and go down into the basement. I'm determined to be ruthless.

Mom, always the willful woman, tries to obstruct my ruthlessness.

"If it isn't broken, don't throw it out, no matter what it is," she demands when she sees the plastic bags and the boxes. "Don't. You hear me?"

"I hear you, Ma, but we have to throw out a lot," I insist, in a tone I hope is just as willful. "We *have* to. What's down there is ridiculous. It will turn people off. Trust me." Even as the words come out of my mouth, I know I sound more whiney than willful.

"No!" she says. "If something's broken, throw it out. If it's yours or Claire's and you don't want it anymore, throw it out. But don't throw out any of my things. No matter what it is. No matter how small. Do you understand? I like all of it, even though..."

Mom has a habit of leaving sentences unfinished. Especially ones that have 'even though' near the end.

"Then why am I here, for crying out loud?" I ask, accepting the 'even though...' without further comment.

"To straighten up," she says. "To make it look neater. Do you understand?"

"Yes, Ma. I understand."

•   •   •

When I had arrived earlier today, I looked over a stack of Mom's mail, paid some of her bills, and discussed a few things over the phone with her real estate agent. After lunch, I went downstairs with the bags and the boxes. 'Let the games begin,' I mumbled to myself.

Just a quick glance around confirms what I already know — that the basement is indeed a subterranean depository. Here's an extremely abridged list — just a random sampling representing about a quarter of what's down there:

- Two Roaring Twenties Halloween costumes (one for a man and one for a woman)
- Four hula-skirted dolls from Hawaii
- Seven kazoos
- Soundtrack albums from *Bye, Bye Birdie*, *West Side Story*, *Oliver*, *The Sound of Music* and fifteen other shows
- A stack of seventeen framed photos
- A hundred or more *un*framed photos
- Two dozen empty picture frames
- Nineteen glass, plastic and pewter ashtrays from hotels, weddings, bar mitzvahs, Atlantic City casinos, and cruises
- Three old phones
- Six stuffed animals from the Forest Park Zoo
- Two curled-up South of the Border bumper stickers
- Twelve board games
- Two butterfly nets
- Two pairs of Mom's childhood ballet shoes
- Eleven wax apples and pears
- The front page from a novelty newspaper ("Fran Selig Wins Mrs. America Contest on Atlantic City Boardwalk")
- Six tall stacks of old copies of *Life Magazine* and six of *Reader's Digest*
- Five coffee mugs for Great Moms and four for Terrific Dads (one is probably still in his old office at work)
- Seven candy bowls
- Forty or fifty books
- Nine embroidered couch pillows with scenes of barnyards and skyscraper silhouettes

Naturally, I want to throw most of that stuff away. None of it is of use anymore. But every ten minutes, Mom yells down to make sure that I'm not throwing anything out. "Just straighten. No throwing out. Understand? I have my reasons, even though..."

I walk over to a wooden shelf that has five "Welcome to Aruba" trinkets from a long-ago vacation that Mom and Dad had won from Dad's employer. Three of the trinkets are on their sides and two are backwards. They're right next to six glass ashtrays, a few of which are from a cruise to Bermuda on which they had embarked for their twentieth anniversary. Two of the ashtrays are upside down. All of them are filthy. I take everything off the shelf, dust the shelf, dust the items, and then put everything back, facing the right way and neatly spaced. That's what I'm supposed to do. "Damn ashtrays," I mutter to myself. To me they represent the hundreds of thousands of cigarettes my father had smoked over the years. A symbol of unnecessary death. "Goddamn ashtrays."

"What?" Mom calls down.

I suppose my muttered comment was a little more than a mutter, since Mom had heard it from upstairs. Apparently her hearing is one thing that hasn't withered with age.

"Nothing," I call up.

"Everything okay?" she asks.

"Everything's fine," I respond.

"Okay. I made iced tea, if you want. Come up soon. I also heated up your leftovers from lunch, even though..."

I tried to figure out what was supposed to come after the 'even though,' but quickly gave up.

"You're straightening up, right?" she continues. "Don't break anything and don't throw anything out. Understand?"

Yes, yes, yes, yes, yes, I say—but in an exceedingly soft whisper that is impossible for her to hear.

I know that much of what is down there holds special significance for Mom, even if that significance is misguided. But what I don't realize until I start to find things *behind* and *under* other things is that dozens of items in the basement also hold special significance for me. My old Matchbox cars, for instance. My old magic kit. A deck of playing cards. A super-8 movie camera. My Humphrey Bogart poster. Wheels from a go-cart I built when I was ten. Those are the things I know I *can* throw out—with Mom's blessing, no less! They had been mine, not my mother's, not Claire's. So I grab one of the empty boxes and prepare to fill it with some of my own stuff. At least that will make a dent in decluttering the room. Every little bit will help. But something makes me sit down on the old threadbare couch (which also needs to be discarded). I need time to think. My mind is full of questions. How, I wonder, might my life have been different had I gone into filmmaking, which was a passion of mine when I was eleven years old? The super-8 movie camera made me think of that. Would I have married the same woman and had the same children had I pursued magic and juggling instead of the career I eventually went into? My magic kit put that thought in my mind. Magic was my obsession when I was thirteen. Then there were those two years in high school when I thought I'd win the Indianapolis 500 one day. Thanks for the memories, go-cart wheels! If I had I followed *that* dream, who might I be today? (And would I even still be alive?)

I stand up from the sagging couch and retrieve the magic kit. It's on the lower shelf of an old TV stand. There is an old TV on the top shelf. On top of the TV are three yardsticks emblazoned with the name of my father's old company. On top of the yardsticks are four upside down Happy New Year party hats, and inside three of the upside down Happy New Year party hats are two noisemakers, and inside the fourth upside down Happy New Year hat are three more ashtrays, each printed with the words "Shirley & Morris's 30th Wedding Anniversary" on the glass bottoms. I don't recall ever hearing about Shirley and Morris, but I assume that if they're still alive, they'd probably soon be celebrating their fiftieth or sixtieth anniversary.

Damn ashtrays.

I grab the magic kit from the lower shelf of the old TV stand and place it in the box. It reminds me of how my father used to be the only one in the family who seemed to take my interest in magic seriously. He always watched me patiently as I practiced levitating Claire or juggling tennis balls or making coins come out of his ear or guessing which card was his. Although he may have given me the make-sure-you-have-something-to-fall-back-on speech more often than I cared to hear it, never did he make me feel silly or small for having the magician notion in the first place. He said it was good to be passionate about something—so much better than being aimless and boring.

I didn't become a magician. Or a filmmaker. Or a racecar driver. I made the choices I made, and I am who I am. And right here and now, amid all this junk, I'm something else: a good son who, despite never having a good time making the trip, has once again journeyed two hours to help his aging, willful, widowed mother. The job is to straighten out and neaten up her chaotic basement without throwing out any of the countless memories down there—an impossible goal. It isn't fun. But here I am. I'm doing it.

With the magic kit in the box, I rip up the Humphrey Bogart poster and stuff it in the box next to the kit. Mom hears the ripping noise and calls down.

"What are you ripping up?" she asks. "Nothing of mine, right?"

"Nothing of yours," I confirm. I refuse to shout, since her hearing is apparently better than mine. "Just one of my old movie posters."

"Oh, okay. What are you doing with the pieces you're ripping up? Don't leave them on the couch, even though..."

"Don't worry. I won't."

I'm able to squeeze the movie camera into the box, too, on top of the ripped-up poster, which leaves just a little room for one additional small item. The playing cards, perhaps. They were part of my magic act. The memory makes me chuckle; I wasn't very good at card tricks. Despite how hard I tried, I never quite caught on. I never correctly guessed anyone's card. Claire never levitated, either. But I did once get five tennis balls to go round and round for twenty seconds nonstop. I was ecstatic about that when it happened. So was Dad. I'll never forget it. Could I still juggle? Now? Here in the basement? It was an intriguing thought. I'm not deluded enough to think I can juggle five balls anymore, or five of anything. But maybe three. I feel like trying. It's a sudden urge. But I need three balls and have seen none in the basement. I look all over. All that stuff down here, yet no tennis balls, softballs, volleyballs, beach balls—nothing round and bouncy. It's odd. Tons of junk and not a single ball! There's absolutely nothing to juggle with. I can't use the books because they'll flip open. It would be impossible. I can't use the ballet shoes, either; they're so delicate they'd fall apart in my hands and Mom would have my head. I look around. Yardsticks, party hats, noisemakers, ashtrays...

Ashtrays!

They're not round and bouncy, but at least they're small enough to juggle.

I walk over to the upside-down party hat and pick up the three ashtrays that are inside. Even though they had not been used as ashtrays for dozens of years, I can still detect the faint odor of tobacco on them and I don't like it at all. It's a smell I associate with cancer. With death. All three ashtrays were from Shirley and Morris's anniversary party, but they are all of different shapes—one round, one square, the third pentagonal. All three are nearly the same size, and each made of glass. Wow—Shirley and Morris were certainly ambitious trendsetters, weren't they? Multiple-shaped personalized glass ashtrays for one lousy party.

I begin to juggle the ashtrays. They stay in an airborne arc for five seconds, ten, fifteen. I toss them higher. Confidence reigns! Round and round they go. Higher and higher. It's magic.

And then I miss one. Then I miss another. And then a third. It all happens quickly. The three glass ashtrays shatter into dozens of pieces on the floor, from mid-sized chunks to tiny shards. Glass falling on glass. The noise is loud. But it's a wonderful noise. A spectacular noise.

"Goddamn ashtrays."

I hear my mother rush through the kitchen on her way to the top of the stairs. It sounds like an angry, nervous rush. I'm sure she'll yell down to me. Maybe even scream. But frankly, all I care to think about is how, after four long months, I finally found a way to have the most marvelous time at her house, even though...

Davening on Avenue Y

I have been a municipal judge in the southern district of Brooklyn, New York, for twenty-four years. If you'll accept an extra ounce of honesty (to go along with the thirty extra pounds I carry around), I am as fair and honest as they come. I never bend the law—though sometimes I allow good people to slip through a crack if they're good citizens and if the slipping through does not hurt anyone else.

I've seen it all in front of my bench: parents arrested for leaving their babies in the car while they shopped; teens caught smoking pot, drinking beer, or popping their parents' prescription pills behind the high school bleachers; senior citizens who stole merchandise on the street because they didn't realize it was part of an outdoor display; overworked and underappreciated husbands who temporarily go crazy and run through the park in their underwear, screaming obscenities.

I could write a book.

I know a lot of the people in this part of town. The cops who arrest or issue tickets to some of them are usually justified for having done so. Most of Brooklyn South's finest are fine.

Two or three are a pain in the ass.

One particular pain in the ass is Officer Rance Cunningham. You could say he rubs me the wrong way. (Though if you say it, you'd be understating it.) I've had a handful of brief conversations with Officer Cunningham over the six years he has been with Brooklyn South. A few times, I bumped into him at the commissary shared by the police station and the courthouse. He loves to hear his own voice. He's the guy who, when he talks to you, looks at the person next to you because that makes him think that two people are listening to him instead of just one. Also, he's far more interested in himself than he is in anyone else, and he's walked away from conversations that no longer serve his purposes. Officer Cunningham always slips into every conversation the fact that he's a proud atheist. Don't ask me why, but he wears it as a badge of honor. I'm not an atheist. I believe in God. I may not remember the last time I went to church, let alone confession, but I consider myself a spiritual man. That has nothing to do with why I can't stand Officer Cunningham and his atheistic self-righteousness. I have absolutely no problem with atheism; it's Cunningham's attitude I despise, his tone, the way he thinks he's always right and everyone else is always wrong.

Officer Cunningham issued a $125 traffic ticket to Rita and Marvin Greenbaum three weeks ago. The Greenbaums are in their late seventies. They have never been in front of my bench, but I saw them twice at the police station, the first time to report a break-in at their apartment and the second time to file a report about a menacing dog that seemed to park itself in front of their apartment building. Rita and Marvin appear to be good people. Very nice and decent, and extremely honest and kind. Officer Cunningham knows them, too, since he was the responding officer who went back with them to their apartment when they reported the break-in. I would bet a thousand dollars that Cunningham saw a mezuzah on their front door and maybe a Jewish calendar on their kitchen wall and boasted about being an atheist. That's just the feeling I have. I don't know if that's what actually happened, but it wouldn't surprise me at all.

When I saw the names Rita and Marvin Greenbaum on my docket that morning, something compelled me to conduct four or five minutes of research. I do that sometimes; once in a while it helps during the proceedings. I discovered the Greenbaums are on a fixed retirement income and have only limited savings. Marvin used to run a small hot dog, knish, and pretzel concession stand at the marina. Rita never worked because of fragile health. After doing my research, I realized their financial situation must have played into their decision to appear at the Brooklyn South Municipal Court to plead their case in front of a judge instead of simply mailing in the fine.

On the day of the hearing, the first question I asked Officer Cunningham was if the man standing to his left was the driver of the car to whom he had issued a traffic ticket. Cunningham confirmed it was the same man. Then I asked why he had issued the ticket and Officer Cunningham responded it was because Mr. Greenbaum, the driver, had ignored a stop sign at the busy intersection of Avenue Y and East 27th Street.

I turned to Marvin Greenbaum and asked him why he had ignored the stop sign. Mr. Greenbaum said that as he and Rita approached the intersection, it was completely devoid of cars in all directions — such an odd and pleasant surprise, he said, that it diverted his mind and he did not realize that he had failed to stop at the stop sign. He did, however, slow down significantly, he added decisively.

I asked Mr. Greenbaum if that was why he was fighting the ticket — because he was distracted and felt that slowing down significantly at the empty intersection was acceptable. I also reminded him that in the eyes of the law, slowing down is not the same thing as a full stop.

Mr. Greenbaum said no, that was not why he was fighting the ticket. The reason he was fighting the ticket, he said, was because the ticket had the date of September Fourteenth written upon it, whereas the day the incident occurred was September

Fifteenth. He said he was certain of that because September Fifteenth was the day of his grandson's bar mitzvah, which is where he and his wife Rita were driving to when they were pulled over by Officer Cunningham.

I had a copy of the ticket in front of me. I looked it over. The date Officer Cunningham had written on it was September Fourteenth.

I turned to Officer Cunningham and asked him to please check his ledger to see what date the offense had actually occurred. Cunningham took his thick black flip-book out of his back pocket and checked. He uttered a low "Hmmm," then acknowledged that the offense had indeed occurred on September Fifteen, not September Fourteenth, as he had written on the ticket. I reminded Officer Cunningham that such an error would legally void the ticket. I asked him how such a mistake could be made. Cunningham explained that he, too, became distracted while talking to Marvin Greenbaum because Mr. Greenbaum was rocking back and forth in the driver's seat of his car, in his sitting positing, and chanting a religious hymn that seemed identical to the hymn he had once heard in a Jewish synagogue to which he had been assigned security duty. Cunningham said it was one of the oddest things he had ever witnessed as a police officer.

I turned to Marvin Greenbaum and asked him to confirm that he had been rocking back and forth in his seat and chanting a religious hymn, and why he was doing it, if indeed that was the case. Mr. Greenbaum said that he was davening, which he explained is the Hebrew word for praying. I asked him what he was praying for. Mr. Greenbaum said he was praying that the police officer would write the wrong date on the ticket, which he knew would render it invalid. He said that God granted his prayer.

I looked at Cunningham's face. His expression was priceless. I can't explain it adequately. I don't think I can even try. (Maybe I *won't* write a book after all.)

So I voided the ticket and told Officer Cunningham that either he'd be fined $125 for violating Statute 10.3 of the Ticketing Religious Persons Code, or that I could dismiss his violation if he'd agree to give $50 to Mr. & Mrs. Greenbaum for their troubles. The officer reached into his pocket, took out his wallet, and handed Marvin Greenbaum two twenties and a ten.

Of course, Statute 10.3 of the Ticketing Religious Persons Code does not really exist. I made it up on the spot. I lied. Maybe I'll go to confession. Or maybe I'll just pray for forgiveness.

Kerplunk

"Hmm... Karen's Spicy Shit... "

That wasn't what it was called on the menu that was posted in the hallway just outside the cafeteria, but that's what Megan Gould called it when she saw it printed there.

Karen's Cajun Surprise was the featured luncheon item of the day. But Megan, who had been at the Simon Park School for eight years, believes that the names shown on the menu have little to do with the tastes left on the palate. So she gives everything that Chef Karen prepares a designation of her own making. Shrimp de la Karen becomes Shrimp Dull Like Karen. Monday Wafer Madness becomes Money Wasting Badness. It is just one of those traits that makes Megan Megan.

"Hmm... Karen's Spicy Shit," Megan said to herself out loud as she made her way into the cafeteria for a cup of coffee. She didn't think anyone would hear. She was wrong. The principal, Dr. Benjamin Tanner, impeccably dressed in a crisp brown three-piece suit, was off to the side, stirring his own cup of coffee.

"Megan, Megan, Megan..." Dr. Tanner said. He shook his head slowly, with the tiniest trace of a smirk. "Why do you play such a daring game?"

"Well, I'm afraid I believe that sometimes a little daring is the best way to enjoy yourself in life," Megan proclaimed.

"Do you really believe that?" Dr. Tanner asked.

"I do," she acknowledged. "Of course, most of my daring dreams never come true anyway, but that'll never stop me from wishing."

"Megan, Megan, Megan..."

"But until a few wishes come true, Dr. Tanner, please accept my apology for the disrespectful language I just used to describe Karen's Spicy Sh... I mean, Karen's Cajun Surprise. I didn't think anyone would hear."

Dr. Tanner accepted her apology, then walked away, shaking his head. Megan wasn't entirely certain if Dr. Tanner was angry, amused, mystified—or just concerned that one day he would have to terminate her employment at the Simon Park School. The fact of the matter is that Dr. Tanner had to discipline Megan twice in the last semester alone for indiscretions. The first time was when she wore a tee-shirt to school for a breast cancer awareness event—a slogan-laden tee-shirt she designed herself that said "Don't be a boob. Stay abreast. Good health is titillating. Get Screened." Several parents who had dropped their children off at school that morning saw Megan's shirt (which also had big brown dots to represent nipples) and complained directly to Dr. Tanner. The second time was when she emailed dirty jokes to all Simon Park staffers to underscore the dangers of using school computers for personal exploits. "It was time for Bill to come up with a new computer password," Megan wrote as an example of an inappropriate email joke. "So Bill typed *MyPenis* into the computer, but a message popped up that said *Not long enough*." One recipient of Megan's warning was Dr. Tanner.

Dr. Tanner always apologized for having to call Megan into his office each time he was required to talk to her about her indiscretions. He said he had no choice. He also apologized for having had to add comments into her employment record, and for his requirement to send her notes of censure on school letterhead. Although Dr. Tanner—who rarely smiled—had drawn tiny smiley faces in the upper left corners of both notes (she took that as a hopeful sign), the mere existence of the notes are serious enough to jeopardize Megan's future employment at another school, should future employment become necessary.

Megan is the Special Events Coordinator for Simon Park, a high school in Concord, New Hampshire for students gifted in science, math and technology. She enjoys and respects the students, and is always upbeat, even when complaining about what she calls her luckless lot in life. She often jokes about being single and unattached at thirty-six, and insists that marriage, or even an intimate relationship, is an unlikely prospect. Many of Megan's coworkers insist that's a foolish thing for her to believe. Everyone at Simon Park knows Megan makes fun of her own appearance, though most are convinced that beneath the drab clothing she wears every day is an attractive body. After all, even drabness cannot always hide curves in all the right places. She wears very little makeup, if any at all, though even without it she has a very pleasant face, with eyes that sparkle and an adorable dimpled chin. But Megan shrouds all that behind self-deprecating humor and silly expressions.

Megan lives alone in an apartment six miles from the school. On Karen's Spicy Shit day she left her apartment at seven o'clock, as she does every school morning, with a cup of home-brewed coffee in one hand, her keys in the other, and her pocketbook slung over her shoulder. The morning was beautiful, with a clear, blue sky and a crispness to the air. At school, after she muttered her indelicate comment about Karen's Cajun Surprise in the cafeteria hallway and then apologized to Dr. Tanner, she felt remorseful that the incident had happened at all. "Oh, what the hell," she mumbled to herself. "I am who I am. Goofy, luckless Megan." She knew there was no way to turn back the clock to avoid making that comment. All she could do now was purchase another cup of coffee, a bran muffin, sit alone at a corner table in the cafeteria, and hope for the day to get better.

Two students, a boy named Andy with a bottle of orange juice and a girl named Yvonne with a granola bar, asked if they could sit with her. Megan said yes.

"Never fails," Megan said to Andy when he and Yvonne had taken their seats opposite her. "When you know you're going to have breakfast with a beautiful young woman like Yvonne, your pimples magically disappear! Andy, your face is as clear as the morning sky."

Both students blushed.

"Oh, I can't embarrass the two of you, can I?"

"I guess you can," said Yvonne, who hid behind her granola bar. "I wish Dr. Tanner was more like you."

"What do you mean?"

"Well, he saw us kissing in the hallway before and told us we couldn't do that."

"Interesting," Megan said. "I bet that man kissed plenty of girls back in the day. And I bet they liked it. My wish is that one day he'll decide to be more of a primal man and less of a cautious bureaucrat. We'd all be better off. You think my wish will come true?"

"I hope so!" Yvonne said with obvious enjoyment. Andy looked at her, not knowing what to make of her delight. "Did you have a lot of boyfriends, Miss Gould?" she asked.

The question made Megan take a pause; it was a topic that wasn't easy for her to joke about, and equally difficult to discuss with any seriousness.

"I wouldn't say a lot," she offered. "A few, I suppose."

"How'd that go? Were you happy?"

"Happy? Let's just say they were relationships that neither of you should aspire to. Nothing heavenly. Rated NBD, for No Big Deal." Megan glanced around to see if Dr. Tanner was anywhere nearby. He wasn't. So she continued: "But here's the thing, kids.

When there's something you want, just go for it. You never know where it can lead, and you never want to regret not having done something you once upon a time considered very important to do. Time stands still for no one. And you can't turn back the clock... There—I'm completely out of clichés."

With the orange juice and the granola bar devoured, Andy and Yvonne said they had to go to class, thanked Ms. Gould for her advice, and departed. That lingering question—the one about her old boyfriends—lagged behind with Megan in the cafeteria. As she sat alone now, she thought about her three boyfriends, John in high school, Edward in college, and Sam at Simon Park. Loves lost. Loves never really found? For her, it was an open question—and a topic that sometimes made her cry. Still, Megan took a moment to think about all three boyfriends.

John, the high school boy, looked, spoke and acted far more mature than all the other seniors Megan knew, but she wanted to hold on to the tail end of childhood with a healthy dose of sarcasm and pranks. John thought she was pretty and fiercely bright, but saw no use in her immature attitude. He broke off the relationship.

Edward, a political science major at UConn, was the complete opposite of John—simple and childlike—with a penchant for fun and a carefree disposition. But Megan grew tired of trying to get him to be serious about anything at all. She broke it off.

Sam, a physics teacher at Simon Park, was the best parts of John and Edward. In the course of their five dates, Megan took to calling him Jes, which was an acronym created from the first letters of all their names. Sam wanted to know why she used the name Jes whenever she addressed him, so she explained it. He was upset at the fact that she often thought about other guys, and they argued about it. Soon, Sam avoided Megan at Simon Park, and then accepted a position at Emerson College in Boston.

Megan went to her office after she had finished her coffee and muffin in the cafeteria. There was a post-it note on the back of her chair. "Please stop by a.s.a.p. — Dr. T." She was fairly certain she knew what the note was about. No, not the spicy shit remark, but something else entirely. A few days ago she had blasted Bon Jovi in her office, at full window-vibrating volume, to protest a Board of Education decision that disallowed earbuds on school grounds. She was certain that Dr. Tanner needed to speak to her about that incident. It would be the third time she had to visit the principal's office this semester for disciplinary action. That did not bode well.

Megan went to the ladies' room to brush off any persistent muffin crumbs and to check her appearance in the mirror. "If I'm in for another dressing down," she said to herself in the mirror, "then I should at least look professional."

"I got a letter from Sam," Dr. Tanner said when Megan arrived at his office. "He's not happy at Emerson and may want to come back to Simon Park." Megan sat down in the chair in front of the principal's desk. "But he wants to know if that would be okay with you."

"That's why you called me down?" Megan asked. "Not the Bon Jovi thing?" She tried to sound neither sarcastic nor impertinent.

"It's one reason, yes."

Megan looked at Dr. Tanner and tried to pretend that he was Sam, to speculate just how she would feel about her onetime beau's return to Simon Park. But that didn't work. All she could see was handsome Dr. Tanner, and that made her blush.

"I guess things can get tricky when you've dated a coworker and it doesn't work out," Dr. Tanner acknowledged.

"Yes, it can get awkward," Megan allowed. "Embarrassing."

"You, embarrassed? I can't see that ever happening."

"Well, I love my job, Dr. Tanner. I love the students. I love my friends, though most of them have interesting social lives.

Romance and all that. Not me. I'm not one of the lucky ones. My wishes don't come true. So when it comes to my personal life, yes, I can get embarrassed. Blame it on unfulfilled wishes, if you must."

"I see," the principal said softly. "But the truth is, we really shouldn't be discussing this here. You understand, don't you? It's private. There's actually another reason I called you down here, Megan."

"What is it?"

"I need your opinion. Dominick in the Ecology Department wants to take a class to a stream about five miles from here, deep in the woods. I think he said it's called Cedar Meadow. He said it's very secluded. He wants the class to study rocks, plants, insects, that sort of thing. But no one's ever been there before — at least not from this school. You live around there, and I trust your opinion. Do you think it's a good idea? Do you think anyone can get hurt?"

"Well, I do know that area, Dr. Tanner. It's very remote. I've been there, but I don't really know how dangerous it is because I never really thought about it. But here's an idea. Since I don't have a social life to speak of, I'd be happy to check it out on my way home this afternoon. I practically pass it anyway. I can look around and give you my opinion first thing in the morning."

"That's what I hoped you'd say. Thanks, Megan. I appreciate it." Dr. Tanner's lips formed the closest approximation of a real smile Megan had ever seen on the principal's face.

Thirty minutes after the last bell, Megan went to her car and sat in the driver's seat for a few minutes before turning the key. "Well" — she said listlessly to her reflection in the rear-view mirror — "just another day, I suppose."

Megan drove to Cedar Meadow, which spans both sides of a twisty country road. She turned off onto a much smaller and curvier lane, which took her to a clearing in the woods, parked, got out of the car, slung her pocketbook over her shoulder and headed toward an area where she knew there was a dirt path. She found the path and followed it for two minutes before coming to the stream. The water was clear and sparkled in the late afternoon sunrays that pierced through the trees. The sight of it made her think back to when she was a little girl. Every time she was with her father and they passed a body of water—a stream, a lake, a birdbath, a fountain—he would take a penny out of his pocket and give it to her to make a wish and then throw in the water. If the penny hit the water and made a *kerplunk* sound, the wish was supposed to come true. As she grew up, she asserted to herself—sadly, but with a passive and stoic smile—that no *kerplunk* had ever resulted in a wish coming true, but she kept up the tradition for old times' sake. After all, one cliché that had become her favorite motto in life was Hey, you never know!

Megan took a penny out of her purse and then placed her pocketbook on the ground. She held the penny tightly in her fist, in front of her chin, while her face took on the countenance of deep and hopeful contemplation. Then she threw the penny into the stream. It made a tiny *kerplunk* and sunk to the bottom. Then, to her surprise, there was a second *kerplunk*. Could it have been a fish, or a frog, or a nut that fell off an overhanging branch? She turned around to see if she could determine the source of the second *kerplunk*—and saw Dr. Tanner standing there, still wearing his three-piece suit, though now his tie was gone and the tails of his shirt were untucked. Draped over his left shoulder was a large beach blanket. He had a bottle of wine was in his right hand.

"Megan, Megan, Megan. Did you make a wish?" the principal inquired.

"I did," Megan responded.

"Do you think it will come true?"

She smiled and kicked off her shoes.

Pidge

"You're Alex, for crying out loud. You'll think of something."

That—or something very similar—is what my mother says every time she asks me to complete a task that she could never accomplish on her own. It stems from the fact that throughout my adolescence, I used to solve all kinds of problems in the house through simple inventions and clever makeshift repairs. That was my skill.

For the third time this month, my mother asked me to visit Grandpa Moe in Manhattan, but this time specifically to make sure that he didn't watch the Tony Awards.

"How am I gonna do that?" I asked.

"You're a scientist, Alex. You'll think of something." (I'm not a scientist; I'm studying physics at MIT.)

According to my mother, the annual televised event, which bestows awards on Broadway's best, is an annual reminder to Morris Black, her father, my grandfather, of how successful he had been on the Great White Way from 1935 to 1949, and how *un*successful he's been from 1950 to now.

It's 2000 now. It's been half a century since 1950. You don't have to study physics at MIT to figure that out.

"His blood pressure goes through the roof and his heart starts racing like crazy, and he's ninety-three years old, for God's sake. He'll have a massive coronary just by *thinking* about that damn awards show, let alone watching it again," my mother fretted.

She had hung up the phone about ten minutes earlier; Grandpa Moe had called to tell her he couldn't find an important music book in his room and was convinced that one of his medical aids stole it. While he had her on the line, Grandpa Moe told Mom that if they do any more of those "stupid shtick production numbers" on the Tony Awards, he'll throw the damn TV out the window. "And I don't care if I kill somebody on the sidewalk," he added for emphasis.

"Stop worrying, Rhoda," my father said to her when she finally sat down at the dining room table to finish her lunch. My father is always the calm one when it comes to Grandpa Moe. "First of all," Dad said, "he can't lift the TV. Second of all, he can't open the window. And third of all, you can't change a ninety-three-year-old man who's been stubborn for the last seventy-three years."

"Jack, he still thinks he's gonna write a hit Broadway show. He's consumed by it. It's pitiful, Jack. Pitiful. And watching those idiotic Tonys only makes it worse."

"Kvetching makes him happy."

"Happy? Happy? You think that man is happy?"

"What a great title for a song, Ma," I said. "You Think That Man is Happy? By Rhoda Kasdan."

"You're not helping, Alex."

My parents live in Guilford, Connecticut, about a two-hour drive to Grandpa Moe's nursing home in New York. I visit my parents every other week, usually on weekends, and I visit Grandpa Moe about once a month. I've always wanted to visit more often, but between my classes at MIT and a part-time campus job, it hasn't been easy to get away to see him more than that. I feel bad about it. He was an enormous influence on me while I was growing up. I learned from him how to be passionate about the things I want to do. He encouraged me to follow my heart, told me all about Broadway, where he reigned supreme for many years, and about Montauk, where he summered and was a local legend, he took me backstage at many theaters in the city, and he always made me laugh. I was the youngest child of his youngest child, and even though there was almost a seventy-year difference between us, that never mattered. When he shared his stories, songs, jokes, philosophies and encouragements with me, the age difference somehow became inconsequential.

Until five years ago, Grandpa Moe lived in the Brooklyn apartment he had shared with Grandma Sally for over forty-five years. Grandma Sally passed away ten years ago. Then, when Grandpa Moe began to misplace things and raise hell with the landlord about one thing or another, Mom and her oldest brother, my Uncle Carl, moved him into a nursing home called River East, which overlooks the East River on the East Side of Manhattan, between Ninety-Third and Ninety-Fourth Streets. River East isn't far from the Ninety-Second Street Y, where in 1934 Grandpa Moe hosted a backer's audition for *The Family Tree*, a musical that became the hottest ticket on Broadway for two years in a row. Mom thought he would enjoy living close to the Ninety-Second Street Y. After all, there would be plenty of music clubs and opportunities to play the piano and tell old Broadway stories. But it didn't quite work out that way. When we took him to visit River East the first time, all he talked about was how times have changed, how people now were unimaginative, how no one at the Ninety-Second Street Y knows the difference between an overture and an overbite. He started to yell. But it was too late; Mom and Uncle Carl had already made all the arrangements and had broken the lease on the Brooklyn apartment. Living at River East was a done deal.

After *The Family Tree*, Grandpa Moe had two more hits on Broadway, *Pidge*, which ran a record 2,954 performances, and *Morocco Melody*, which ran a respectable 2,112 performances and had the most international touring companies of any musical up to that time. After *Morocco Melody,* he had two more shows that reached Broadway, though neither lasted more than five months. The last one closed in 1950. Grandpa Moe then spent a few years trying to mount another show, but to no avail. Between 1953 and 1957 he wrote sketches for Catskill resorts and parody songs for some unsuccessful television variety shows. After that, it was an endless series of plans, ideas, and meetings, all in search of another hit show.

There was never another hit show.

"Go, Alex. Go visit him," Mom said while I helped Dad clear the table. "It's early. Not even one o'clock. I don't mind that your visit here will be cut short—it's for a good cause. If Grandpa watches that damn show tonight, he's liable to jump out the window. You wouldn't want that, would you?"

"He lives on the ground floor, Mom."

"You're not helping, Alex. I called the place and asked if they can disconnect his television, but they said no. And even if they did, Grandpa would just walk out and go to an electronics store nearby and watch it there through the window."

"People can just walk out of River East? Nobody stops them?"

"If you're Morris Black, you just walk out. You know your grandfather, Alex. When Grandpa Moe sets his mind to something, he does it. Please, Alex. Go. I don't care what you do to stop him, but just make sure he Does! Not! Watch! That! Damn! Show! Do you hear my emphasis?"

"I think they heard it in Morocco, Ma. But how will I stop him? What if he really wants to Watch! That! Damn! Show! and there's nothing I can do about it?"

"You're an honor student at MIT, for God's sake. Nobody knows the things you know. You'll think of something, Alex. Take him somewhere."

"It'll be late, Ma. The Tonys are on at night."

"So? What are you, five years old? Since when are you afraid of the dark?"

Mom left the dining room to put a few things away in the kitchen.

"He's ninety-three!" I said to my father. "Didn't the doctor say he might have a year left, maybe less? If I take him somewhere, it shouldn't be too far. He should stay close to where he lives, just in case. Don't you agree?"

"That may be true," my father replied, calm as always, "but another way to look at it is that he's ninety-three, so what the hell?—anything goes."

"I'd rather not."

Dad knew I'd rather not, because he knew I didn't want to be the one to make Grandpa Moe unhappy. Dad understood I didn't want to be the one to force Grandpa Moe *not* to do what he really wanted to do. Grandpa Moe was old, admired, and gave the world a lot to enjoy. He didn't deserve to be tricked and lied to.

"Let's say I'm successful and I get him out of the building for a while," I posed to Dad, "away from all television sets. When we get back, someone's liable to say something about the Tony Awards anyway. Plus, it'll be on the front page of all the newspapers the next day. He always reads the paper. Then what?"

"You're Alex," Dad said. "You'll think of something."

•   •   •

There was no traffic going into the city, and River East has its own garage, so the entire travel-and-parking phase of the trip posed no problem at all. I considered that a good omen.

I promised my parents I would check in with them when I arrived at River East, so I called them on my cellphone from the garage. I didn't want to do it in front of Grandpa Moe because I didn't want to take the chance of inadvertently saying something that would give away the real purpose of my visit. Eloise, the lady who always is at the front desk when I visit, told me that Grandpa Moe had gotten a little crankier lately.

"Is that even possible?" I asked. She smiled.

Grandpa Moe was happy to see me, but it didn't take long for him to curse the city that gave him his life and career. That, of course, was the problem: the city also took *away* a big part of his life and just about his entire career. We sat in his room for a while. The television was on. I asked him if I could shut if off so that we could talk.

"I'll make it a little lower," he said.

After he adjusted the volume, he went to his desk, which was lost somewhere under countless newspapers, sheet music, and manila files. He found a clipping that someone had sent him about a revival of *Pidge* in Boca Raton that was very successful.

"You know how much I get for these revivals? About $300, tops. That's highway robbery. Crooks, all of them." I had heard the speech before — all about unions and rules and greed and lies and hypocrisy... He said it was always a little like that, but in the old days, when he was the Great Morris Black of the Great White Way, he made enough money so that even if he was bamboozled out of a few bucks, he still earned enough money. And if on one side he found nothing but greedy nogoodniks, on the other side he could always count on people who loved and adored him to pieces. It all balanced out.

"Broadway isn't Broadway anymore, Alex," he grumbled to me, even though no one had brought up Broadway. "Music isn't music. It's just talking, with a few notes stuck in. You can't put on a show these days unless you have nine-hundred producers and forty-five corporations behind you. And if you're old, they don't even want to hear from you."

I glanced out the window to see if I could spot anything I could use to change the subject. Luck once again was on my side.

A pigeon on the outside windowsill strutted and bobbed from one end to the other.

"See that pigeon, Grandpa? When I was a kid, before I saw a revival of *Pidge*, I thought that's what the show was all about, a pigeon. I was such a stupid kid."

"You, stupid?" he said. "You're Alex—the smartest kid I know. A genius. Those gizmos you used to invent..."

He walked over to the windowsill.

"This is my friend. I call him Pidge. Not too original, but to me it makes sense. He's here every day, my little Pidge." Grandpa tapped gently on the windowpane. The pigeon hopped a few inches out of fear, but remained on the sill. "Poor Pidge. When I kick the bucket, he'll have to find another friend. *Pidge* was a good show, Alex. Remember Sidney Blume, the main character? He identified with pigeons. That's why people called him Pidge, not Sidney. He was stuck in the city. He had to depend on crumbs from people who passed through his life. Just like a pigeon. The people who used to depend on him ignored him. He annoyed everyone. Just like old people today. Just like me. I've become Sidney Blume. I've become Pidge. A character in my own musical!"

"You don't annoy anyone, Grandpa."

"Poor Pidge," he said as he turned back to the window. "What lousy luck, huh? Having to live in this godforsaken cesspool of a city these days. Garbage on the sidewalk. New ugly new buildings blocking old pretty buildings. Where's his freedom, this poor pigeon? Look at him—so dirty. Hardly ever leaves that filthy windowsill because he knows that if he doesn't find something there, he might not find anything anywhere else. Just like me. Just like I'm stuck here. This is where I have to write my next hit show? This tiny room? This room is *my* windowsill."

The speech exhausted Grandpa Moe. He sat down on the edge of the bed, nearly out of breath. "The Tonys are on tonight," he said. "Channel two. You'll stay and watch with me?"

"Why don't we rescue him?" I asked. It was an idea that had popped into my head the moment Grandpa asked me to watch the Tonys with him.

"Rescue who?"

"Pidge! This city is no place for him. You said so yourself."

Grandpa Moe looked at me curiously. I wasn't sure if he was actually considering what I had just said, or if he simply thought he had misheard.

"Rescue him? What do you mean?" he asked.

"I mean, let's figure out a way to bring Pidge somewhere else. Montauk, maybe. Where you used to go. You always used to tell me how lovely and happy and clean it was out there."

"The tip of Long Island!" Grandpa Moe smiled proudly. "Another few steps, you're in the Atlantic. Fresh air. Clean sand. Beautiful lighthouse. Oy, how I miss it."

"You used to tell me a lot of stories about Montauk," I continued. "How there were a bunch of little cottages not far from the lighthouse, and how you used to rent the same one every summer. How you used to have to get a new piano every other year because the salty air from the ocean put it out of tune all the time."

"Three pianos I brought in Montauk!" he said. "I spent seven summers in a row there, in between *Family Tree* and *Pidge*. Of course, I could afford new pianos back then. Not now. Mary Martin used to visit me there. Ruby Keeler. Chita Rivera. We had such parties! I was interviewed at least once a week. *The New York Times*. *Life*. *The Saturday Evening Post*. All the big theatre people were there. Some just for the day. Others longer. Not a lot of tourists. Only one motel, I think. Most people went to the Hamptons back then. But a bunch of us theater people found Montauk. It was wonderful. Wonderful!"

"I'm sure it was, Grandpa."

"That's where I was respected. That's where I wrote some of my best material. And it was so beautiful—the air, the sea...

Don't get me wrong, Alex—I loved the city back then. But I got my rewards in Montauk."

"Let's do it!" I declared. "Let's bring Pidge to Montauk."

"Okay," he smiled. "Let's do it."

I considered ways to accomplish the task, and Grandpa Moe must have seen some gears turning in my head because he asked me what I was thinking about.

"I'm thinking about ways to do it without hurting ourselves, or hurting the pigeon," I said. "It might not be so easy."

"I'm not worried," he replied. "You're Alex. You'll think of something."

●　　●　　●

To create a safe and comfortable pigeon trap, I searched for anything I could find in Grandpa Moe's room. I found a small wooden box, a few little mirrors, some masking tape, an old clarinet reed, an even older trumpet mouthpiece, and a rusted harmonica. I left my grandfather for just a minute to go to the end of the hallway, where I opened the window to gather some sticks and leaves and feathers left there by another pigeon. I went back to Grandpa Moe's room. Then, with a little physics, a smidge of aviary knowledge, a pinch of Rube Goldberg, and an appeal to God for as much dumb luck as he could spare, I got Pidge from Grandpa Moe's windowsill into the box.

"Come on, Grandpa. We have to hurry. It's a long ride. Follow me and don't say anything on the way out. What if Eloise tries to stop us?"

"You're Alex. You'll think of something."

At the front desk, Eloise asked where we were going and what was in the box.

"Picnic dinner," I grinned.

"I hear a noise coming from your picnic dinner," she said.

"No. That's me," Grandpa Moe said. "Tapping my fingers. Thinking of a new song."

"Oh. Okay," Eloise relented as Grandpa Moe and I headed for the door that leads to the parking garage. "Don't come back too late," she called out. "The doors shut for good at eight-thirty."

Pidge stayed fairly quiet in the back seat as we drove east on the Long Island Expressway. Grandpa Moe, in the front seat with me, told some more stories from the old days about Montauk. He was entirely relaxed. He also told me some stories about New York City in more recent days, and when he recited those stories, he did not sound nearly as relaxed. In fact, he sounded quite miserable.

The two-and-a-half hours that it took for us to get to Montauk went by quickly. There was hardly any traffic. More luck! I gladly accepted it. I needed all I could get.

We parked on a side street that ended a few yards from the shoreline. It was an hour before dusk. We had driven around for a while before we began our search for the old cottage he used to stay in, but we couldn't find it. We considered the fact that the old group of cottages that he remembered may have been razed long ago; after all, the beach houses on the side streets all looked modern. We got out of the car. The lighthouse stuck up through the trees. We couldn't see the ocean because there was a sandy ridge between the beach and the side street.

I opened the back door of the car to get the box in which Pidge was waiting, and carried it with me as Grandpa Moe and I walked side by side toward the beach.

"I wrote a song called *Montauk Lighthouse,* but never used it," Grandpa Moe recalled. I didn't want him to talk about Broadway, so I quickly changed the subject by asking him if he remembered the name of the road that the cottages were on. "Name?" he chuckled. "You think that road had a name? Not in a million years. Heaven Lane — that's what I'd call it. Hey — you know something?" he continued. "See how the street curves around down there, toward the beach? There's no road past that point, but there's a path that goes through the dunes. I can almost make it out. I bet the path goes right to the old cottages. Let's take a look."

I followed him as he walked along the sandy ridge.

"When can we let Pidge go?" I called out, hoping Grandpa Moe would give the okay, because the box was getting very heavy

"Do it at the cottages, Alex," he said. "Not before."

It was a long walk. The ridge seemed to go on forever. Grandpa Moe was right — the road ended, but there was a sandy path that took off where the asphalt dropped away, and there were several cottages a few dozen yards in. He walked fast for a man of ninety-three. Even though I was seventy years younger, I walked slowly because I was exhausted from the drive and was now carrying a box with a restless pigeon inside. I was only halfway to the cottages by the time Grandpa Moe had arrived there. Through the thick expanse of bushes, I saw him standing among a small group of people. It took another two minutes for me to get to the group. Grandpa Moe was chatting with three old men and three old women as if he had known them forever. There were three weathered white cottages lined up in a row behind them.

"Alex, meet my new friends."

I grunted hello to the six senior citizens.

"Alex, they all remember *Family Tree* and *Pidge*, and they remember seeing me on *The Steve Allen Show* back in Fifty-Two," Grandpa Moe said excitedly.

"Speaking of Pidge..." I said as I put the box on the ground.

Grandpa Moe walked over to me. His new friends accompanied him.

"Okay, Alex. Let him go."

I opened the box. Pidge flew out.

"Wonderful," Grandpa Moe said. "Wonderful, wonderful. Free as a bird. Happier. Healthier. Out of that godforsaken city. Full of possibilities now. That's the way it should be. Am I right? So long, my old friend."

The pigeon flew in a handful of small figure-8s, then landed on the ground in front of us. He strutted around, sometimes in a speed-walk, sometimes with a hop, as if he didn't know quite what to do with himself. I must admit, he did indeed look happy.

One of the cottage men put his hand on Grandpa Moe's shoulder.

"Why don't you stay here with us, Moe," he said.

Grandpa Moe turned his attention from Pidge to the old man.

"What?" he asked, a curious half-smile on his face. "What did you say?"

"He said why don't you stay here," replied the lady next to him. "These cottages don't exist. Not officially, anyway. We just stay here. For eight or nine years now. You can stay with us. There's electricity, even. No one knows why. Everything we need, we get at a little convenience store about a mile down the road. We have no TV, no telephone, we see a newspaper maybe once a month—but we got so much more, Moe. We got each other. We got laughter. We got memories. We got hope."

"Stay, Moe," urged yet another man. "Forever. You'll tell us stories. You'll write new songs and sing them for us. What a beautiful place for a one-man show!"

Grandpa Moe looked from one cottage person to the other, and also to me, and he scratched his cheek and gently shook his head indecisively in all directions. Clearly, he didn't know what to think or what to say or how to react. And then, finally:

"My doctor says I got maybe ten months to live," Grandpa Moe said sadly. "If that. All my things are back in New York. My clothes, my papers, my doctors. All my medications. How can I stay? It's impossible."

"Nothing is impossible, Moe," one woman uttered gently. "All your medication is right here. With us."

Grandpa Moe looked at me.

"You know, Alex," he said softly, "maybe they're right."

My mouth hung open. It occurred to me I must have looked like a character invented by Grandpa Moe for comic relief in one of his shows.

"But..."

"No buts," Grandpa Moe demanded. He turned to the cottage group. "Did you know," he said, "that *No Buts* was actually the name of a song in *Morocco Melody*? It was a showstopper. Brought the house down every night."

"Yes," smiled one of the men. "We remember." Two others shook their heads in consensus.

"Alex," Grandpa Moe said, "they remember! They're my people."

Just then, Pidge strutted in front of us, then flew over to the nearest cabin and marched back and forth in proud militancy on the splintered wooden step.

"Okay, Grandpa," I relented. "You can stay. You can stay with your people. Forever."

"Thank you, Alex."

The cottage people smiled. Three of them clapped their hands and the other three gently patted Grandpa Moe on his arms and on his back.

"Thank you, Alex," he repeated. "You're a good grandson. The best — and I got five!"

"Just one thing..." I added anxiously. "What the hell am I gonna tell my parents?"

Grandpa Moe looked at me and smiled. I knew exactly what he was going to say.

Art of Deception

Evelyn, who is somewhere just on the other side of sixty-five, shuffles into the den of her Berwyn home in her favorite flannel bathrobe and settles comfortably in the big, old, faded light-blue easy chair that she's loved all these years. It is one of two matching easy chairs that she and her husband, Art, bought after they left Philadelphia for the suburbs. That was thirty-five years ago. Evelyn covers herself with the multicolored Afghan that is always there for her. She's had that Afghan for years, and sometimes she even forgets when she got it and where it came from. It doesn't matter, though. It's hers, and it's comfy, and she loves it, and with the old JVC television console it works just fine to help put another day in the past and get ready for the next one to arrive. The remote control is always on the armrest of the easy chair; for years she's heard horror stories from friends, relatives and neighbors about remotes that disappear for hours or even days. But Evelyn has always guaranteed its safe placement on the armrest. As a result, it is there whenever she begins her evening routine in the den, which precedes by about an hour her quick journey to the master bedroom to go to sleep for the night.

Evelyn turns on the TV, though she's really not interested in any particular show at the moment. She closes her eyes, ready to nod off for a while. A sort of pre-sleep sleep. That's been her routine for years, and it's always worked just fine.

Art arrives. He had been in his basement workshop patching together an old picture frame Evelyn had asked him to fix. He was glad for the task, for he needed time alone to think. To plan. He has something heavy on his mind which, had Evelyn been more alert, she would have seen on his face when he shuffled into the den. It was a decidedly different shuffle from his wife's; hers had been calm, his disturbed. Art, too, is in his bathrobe, and though he loves his as much as his wife loves hers, it does not look as comfortable or secure on him as it does on her because of Art's disposition and the body language that goes along with it. He tries, however, to appear relaxed, for ending the day in the den has also been *his* routine for many years, and he wants Evelyn to believe that everything is normal.

Art gazes at his wife for an extended moment before settling into the matching easy chair, two feet to the right of hers.

"Busy day?" he asks. He tries to make it sound compassionate.

"Mmm hmm..." responds Evelyn, almost involuntarily.

"Tired?"

"Mmm...

"Mind if I turn down the sound?" Art hasn't settled into the chair with the finality that used to accompany the act; he is still more off the plush cushion than he is on it.

"Fine..."

Art leans over to his left, grabs the remote from the armrest of Evelyn's chair, presses a button four or five times, puts the remote back on the armrest, then fully settles into his own chair. The volume is now so low as to be almost silent.

"So," Art says, "you say you're tired, huh?"

"Mmm hmm..."

"*Very* tired?

"Very..."

"That's good… That's good… Know why? Know why it's good? Because it's gonna be a hell of a night, Evelyn… A hell of a night… Wanna know why it's gonna be a hell of a night?"

Although Art looks at Evelyn, he also furtively glances to her right and to her left and above her head and below her chin, in tiny micro-second bursts of time, as if to probe for the right words to use, or perhaps to search for clues to help decipher Evelyn's own micro-reactions to the few words he has already spoken.

"Why?" Evelyn asks. But three seconds have already passed since Art posed the question, and he has nearly forgotten what Evelyn's 'Why?' is referring to.

"What? Oh! — why is it gonna be a hell of a night? I'll tell you why. It's gonna be a hell of a night because it's the perfect time for me to tell you something I've been wanting to tell you for twenty years. It's about time I got it off my chest, and tonight's the night. That's why it's gonna be a hell of a night…" He leans over to her. "You're sure you're really tired?"

"Mmm hmm…"

"Really tired, but still awake?"

"Mmm… barely…"

Art sees that Evelyn's eyes, which moments earlier had been half shut, are now three-quarters shut.

"Almost asleep, huh?"

"Yes…" Evelyn says.

That's precisely what he wants to hear. It's part of his plan. He'd tell Evelyn what he needs to get off his chest while she's so tired that the possibility exists for her to never remember in the morning. Meanwhile, Art would have the inner peace of knowing that he did indeed tell her. He was convinced it was an excellent plan.

"Okay, then!" he sighs. "Evelyn, I'm just a man… I guess that's not much of a revelation, huh?… The thing is, I've always wanted to be strong… I've always wanted to be different… Not weak, or common. Do you know what I mean by common?... Evelyn, do you know what I mean?"

Evelyn doesn't move. But after a moment, her mouth opens a fraction of an inch.

"Common..." she mumbles.

"Yes, common," repeats Art with a bit more exuberance than he had expected. "I didn't want to be just like thousands of husbands out there, with all the silly human male weaknesses that a lot of men have... For forty-five years I've worked so damn hard trying to be what I wanted to be, Evelyn—you know—a good provider, a great contractor, an encouraging father, a loving husband... Have I been? Have I been all those things, Evelyn?... Evelyn?..."

Evelyn's head moves ever so slightly to the right. Her eyes remain three-quarters shut, maybe even seven-eighths by now, and her mouth hardly moves at all when she responds. "Let's just rest..." she mumbles. It is almost as if she had learned how to be a ventriloquist within the past two minutes.

"No," he says. "I can't rest. I want to know. I need to know. Have I been all those things?"

"Mmm hmm."

"Good. Because I've tried... I've tried very hard, Ev, all these years. But twenty years ago, the common part came out. The weak part. I guess most men have that problem from time to time. I don't know; I'm only guessing... I was building that Pellicano house up there in Stroudsburg. Remember?... That's when we were going through those financial problems because of that idiotic lawsuit the year before. Remember? You were so angry because of that damn lawsuit. So was I. And you were also angry because of that silly, stupid fight I had with Brian and Brenda, just after they got married, when I didn't speak to them for a year... You were miserable, *I* was miserable. Both of us, miserable... It made me depressed, Evelyn... Depressed and...

well, vulnerable, I guess. You remember those horrible days, don't you, Ev? Twenty long, long years ago. Remember?"

Evelyn sighs deeply through her nose. A very weak "Mmm hmm" follows.

"And do you remember Loretta Pellicano? The woman who was building that house up there in Stroudsburg? That monstrosity she designed? Remember that Pellicano woman?"

"Big..." Evelyn murmurs.

Art looks directly at his wife now.

"Big? You mean the house?"

"No," Evelyn responds. She shakes her head so imperceptibly that Art may not even know she's doing it.

"Oh—" he chuckles, "you mean her chest, huh? That's right... Her chest, her hair, her bank account, her apartment in Philly... everything about that woman was big... including— how should I put it—including her come-ons. Her seductive ways. Everyone knew about her, although I was too busy building that damn house of hers to notice... Despicable, now that I think about it—the way she was."

"Big..."

"Yes, big... Who the hell knows why she came on to me? It's not like she needed me to give her a discount on the construction, for Christ's sake. She had more money than God, that woman. But before I knew it... before I knew what was happening... Evelyn, do you know what I'm getting at here?... Ev?... I was weak and miserable, and this big, blonde, rich lady was suddenly fawning all over me for God knows what reason... Maybe she was happy that I pulled off a few miracles by getting all those damn municipal variances to build that house—that monstrosity... Or maybe she was really touched that I made up for all those snow days by staying up there those two weeks in that crappy little motel, just so that I could work on the house whenever there was a break in the weather. Remember?"

"Snow..."

"Yes, snow! Lots of snow... That was part of the problem, Ev. You see? I was gone so much from home because of the damn snowstorms. Not to put any blame on you whatsoever, Evelyn, but you did insist that I stay up there in that motel so that I wouldn't have to drive back and forth in that awful weather... And that Pellicano woman was up there... and the variances... and the work... and the misery and the depression, both mine and yours... I don't know... I don't know how it happened, Evelyn, but it's bothered me for twenty years. It's been a heavy weight on my mind like... like... like I don't know what, Ev.... Ev — are you still listening?"

"Snowstorms..."

"Exactly. Snowstorms," Art says. "In fact," he continues, "that's probably what started the whole damn thing in the first place. One time she saw me up there at the worksite and she said I was — now don't laugh — she said I was adorable. Me — adorable! Can you believe it? And then we started talking, and she started to call me Artie — I hate that name, Artie — and one thing led to another... Do you know why she said I was adorable? Because during the second snowstorm, when I stayed up there the second time, I wore that crazy Goofy hat with the floppy ears because I couldn't find my regular hat here in the house. Remember that silly hat? I think Brian and Brenda bought it at Disney World on their honeymoon."

Evelyn's head-shaking is so slight as to be almost invisible.

"No," she sighs.

"No? It wasn't Brian and Brenda who gave us that hat?"

"Whitford," she says.

"Beg your pardon?"

Evelyn is quiet. Motionless.

"Ev, did you say Whitford? That Irish guy three houses down? What about him?"

"Goofy."

"Goofy? What about Goofy?... Wait a minute—are you talking about the widower with the white hair? *That* Whitford?... What about him?"

"Hat."

Although it still seems as if Evelyn has somehow learned ventriloquism, Art sees her lips move a tiny bit this time after the final t in the word hat.

"The hat?" Art asks. "The Goofy hat?... Hold on—didn't Whitford work at Disney World before he retired?... You mean *he* gave us that hat?"

"Mmm hmm..."

"Well, I'll be a... I didn't think he even knew who the hell we were... He didn't give us anything else, did he?"

"Pinocchio," Evelyn whispers; the multi-syllable, consonant-heavy word forces her lips to move more than they had in the last several minutes.

"Pinocchio? What do you mean, Pinocchio? The movie *Pinocchio*—the videocassette? He gave us the videocassette of *Pinocchio* that you gave to Brian and Brenda for the baby? Anything else?... *Snow White*, maybe?"

"Mmm hmm."

"You're kidding, right?"

"No."

"What about all those Disney World sweatshirts? Those too?" Art's voice gets a little harsher, louder, and shakier with every statement he utters.

"Yes," Evelyn says in a tiredly placid tone.

"When?" Art asks.

"Stroudsburg," Evelyn responds.

"When I stayed up there at the worksite? At the motel? Jesus, Ev, I was only gone for a few days each time! The first time only two days! Are you nuts? Are you out of your mind? That Whitford is a lunatic. Who the hell lives in Florida and moves to Pennsylvania to retire, anyway? Normal people do it the other way around. You shouldn't have let that idiot in the house,

Evelyn... How many times was he here?... How long did he stay? Ev?... Evelyn?"

"Hmm?.." Her brow furrows faintly.

"When was he here? During the first snowstorm? Was he just checking to see if everything was okay in the house?... Evelyn?... How long did he stay?... Did you give him dinner, too?... Did you have drinks?..."

Evelyn's face doesn't change at all.

"Did he... did he stay over?... Evelyn?"

Evelyn repositions herself on the easy chair.

"I'm tired," she whines.

"Evelyn!"

"Need to rest..."

Art pops out of his chair. He angles his tired torso to look at his wife.

"Evelyn!" he bellows, "I was gone only a few days, for Christ's sake. Each time only a few days at that lousy motel. There were snowstorms... She was a very strong-willed woman. She didn't want me to drive home, and neither did you. Are you gonna tell me what happened here with Whitford or not?"

Evelyn looks entirely composed in her easy chair. Art puts his hand on his hips, realizes how silly a position that is, folds his arms, but feels even sillier with that stance. He lets his arms drop to his sides.

"Ev?"

Evelyn remains quiet. Her eyes are shut.

"Christ Almighty, Evelyn.... How can I ever... Jesus, Ev. I just don't know what to... I don't know what I...." Art turns away from his wife and heads toward the opening between the den and the hallway, which leads to their bedroom. "I'm going to sleep. I don't want to talk about it." He stops on the threshold and turns back. "I can see it's gonna be a hell of a night," he grumbles. "One hell of a goddamn night..."

Dawn of a New Day

Greetings. My name is Professor Elliott Braydon Beckmond. Harvard University is where I have been teaching for nineteen years. I have three PhDs, one in English literature, another in political science, the third in urban planning & sustainability, and hold classes in all three subjects. Not much has changed over the years, at least in terms of the general nature of my general natural and the overall tenor of my overall tenure. To use a common cliché, I was known as a bit of a square peg regarding the way I look (always a tucked-in shirt and a bowtie), the way I talk (never an unsavory word), the way I conduct myself (exemplary manners), even the way I think (guarded optimism for the fate of humanity). If indeed a square peg, it has suited me fine.

Then a student named Dawn Nesbit enrolled at Harvard. Over the course of three semesters, she took four of my classes, stole my heart, and changed my life.

I viewed Dawn as one of the most remarkable young women ever to pass through this esteemed institution of higher learning. Her research projects and papers, our class discussions, the questions she asked and the comments and opinions she provided in class contributed to my deep admiration and respect. After the first semester, I was convinced that once Dawn Nesbit graduated, she would accomplish remarkable things.

Dawn is fiercely bright, quite fearless, wholly daring, and has an unshakable passion for the rights, dignity and potential of all people, regardless of race, creed, color or economic status. She exhibits a limitless storehouse of ideas. I loved to listen to her speak both in class and at the frequent unofficial teacher-student chats I had initiated at the Starbucks across the street from my campus office. After two semesters, I knew that if ever she entered politics, politics would never be the same. Before long, the pundits would say that Dawn Nesbit was the only officeholder who was in office for all the right reasons. They would say she was in the game not to be in the game, but to truly improve society, irrespective of how much people liked or disliked her. They would say that she was determined to give the job all she had, regardless of her chance for electability to a second term. Pundits would say that if ever there was a public servant who had the brains, guts, inspiration, and savvy to implement projects and plans that could make a difference, Dawn Nesbit was that public servant.

I feel compelled at this juncture to say that Dawn is quite beautiful. The word voluptuous is often used to describe her. This alone was the basis of my prediction that, despite all I just shared, many people would claim that her election success was based solely on the fact that so many men find her desirable. Despite that, I was certain that such an argument would be rendered moot once Dawn opened her mouth and spoke about issues, problems and solutions. Her looks would have nothing at all to do with her achievements. Of that I had always been certain.

I overheard a colleague one day call me Humbert Humbert while talking about me to another colleague. Am I a Humbert? A Svengali? No, I am not. First, Dawn Nesbit is an adult, not a child as in Nabokov's *Lolita*, in which Lolita and Professor Humbert Humbert are major characters. Second, I am just twenty-one years older than Dawn; those we call Lolitas are typically thirty or more years younger than their Humberts. Third, Dawn clearly has a mind of her own. She does not *need* anyone to take care of her or think for her—nor does she need anyone to look up to. She can change the world on her own.

I have been completely open and honest to this point in time and shall not stop now: I will admit without reservation that I fell madly in love with Dawn Nesbit. I desired her and was blessed to have her find in return some desirable qualities in me. Modesty forbids me from discussing how Dawn can turn the word pleasure into an inadequate descriptor.

What became particularly thrilling for me about knowing Dawn Nesbit, intimately or otherwise, is the fact that she is brutally honest. Indeed, that, too, has been quite a pleasurable attraction. So many people, when they speak with me, avoid certain sentiments and expressions, perhaps out of a sense of intimidation based solely on my position at the university and my reputation. But I do not enjoy being treated like that, for it can make conversations and relationships quite sluggish. I call it my Harvard Bubble. By contrast, Dawn holds nothing back when she talks to me or renders her opinions. She is incapable of seeing that bubble.

As soon as she graduated from Harvard, Dawn decided to run for councilwoman in Middlesex County, as an Independent. Together we formulated a fundraising plan and put together a marvelous staff of volunteers to handle everything from policy research to publicity. Her name provided the perfect slogan: "Dawn of a New Day." On the campaign trail she stayed true to the essence of what made Dawn Nesbit Dawn Nesbit: she spoke her mind. At campaign stops, dinner parties, conventions, union meetings, private affairs and elsewhere, she said what she truly believed, with no regard for how people might react. Indeed, in terms of Massachusetts politics, it *was* the dawn of a new day.

"Insurance companies are rogue institutions that need to be put under a microscope and punished severely for being so wicked and ruthless," she said at one campaign rally. A day later she added, "The ten-million-dollar-a-year CEOs at insurance companies should be made to live on the same salaries, pay the same monthly healthcare premiums, and receive the same level of care as their average policyholders. Only then should they be allowed to make company decisions." The insurance companies did not like those comments. Five of them took out full-page newspaper advertisements critical of what they saw as Dawn Nesbit's shortsightedness.

"Executives who earn millions of dollars a year but have to let go of employees because of poor financial performance should be ashamed of themselves. They should all be put on notice," Dawn said at another event. "They should add a few million dollars of their own back into the company coffers to save jobs. We should make *them* go to the supermarket on a tight budget and try to have enough money left over for gas to get home." One newspaper reported that two dozen top executives from the greater Boston region secretly convened to figure out a way to derail Dawn Nesbit's campaign.

"Teachers who don't know how to teach or who have lousy social skills should be kicked out of school, permanently," she said at a meeting of the Middlesex County Teacher's Convention. The union promptly threw their support behind Dawn's opponent.

"What the hell is the matter with the U.N.?" she yelled at a meeting of the New England Immigration Commission. "It employs thousands of people and spends billions of dollars, and what does it really accomplish for peace in the world? Not to mention," she added, "that too many U.N. diplomats do not obey our traffic laws, hotel room policies and many other rules of conduct. Let's make all foreign diplomats follow the same U.S. laws and rules that the rest of us have to follow, without exception, and throw them in jail if they don't comply." The

New England Immigration Commission disinvited Dawn to three more events at which she had been scheduled to appear.

"Three-quarters of all those in Congress are millionaires. They shouldn't be," Dawn complained at a campaign stop at an industrial park. "Congresspeople who serve the public should be Joe Schmos and Jane Schmos, and after their terms are over, they should just go back to their regular jobs. Also, politicians should never have closed-door meetings. Never! They are working for the people, and the people have a right to know everything that goes on. Everything! Politicians should be so transparent that you can see right through to their skivvies!"

"Skivvies?" called out an impertinent journalist in the crowd—a woman well known for the way she always tries to agitate whichever newsmaker she is covering. "Are you saying that you'd like to see what's under their clothes, Ms. Nesbit?"

"Brianna, obviously I was being both metaphorical and rhetorical. But since you enjoy being a cheeky reporter, I'll give you a cheeky answer," Dawn responded with a smirk. "Would I like to see what's under a congressman's clothes? Have you seen some of them? Definitely not. But some others? Sure! Why not?"

That got the most newspaper ink and the most radio and TV airtime of anything Dawn Nesbit ever said on the campaign trail—that one solitary remark. It had been noted that every daily newspaper and radio talk show in the country discussed that comment, mostly in a comical or contentious manner. It gave broadcast pundits and personalities what might be termed the Holy Grail for ratings. Asked to explain, Dawn refused to apologize for what came to be called her 'skivvies blunder.'

"This is all so silly," she said when asked about the story for the twentieth or thirtieth time. "Listen, we are all biologically, physiologically, and genetically predisposed to be attracted to the naked human body for purposes of mating. Propagation of the species. Don't blame me; blame evolution. Blame God. It's a fact. Why deny it? Why hide it? Come on now—most men's eyes light up when they see a shapely woman with big boobs. There's an instinctual reason for that. Most girls smile when they see a tight muscular tush on a guy. To deny that is to deny being human."

That was it. The game was over. After that response, there was no way for Dawn to continue on the campaign.

She had no interest in dropping out of the race (she was doing extremely well in early polling), but had no choice. Three weeks to the day it began, it ended. There were too many roadblocks put in her way, too many disinvites, rescinded campaign monies, late-night puns and gags, too many truths about her that, thanks to the press, were mangled into lies, which in the public's mind became indistinguishable from the real truths.

An hour after Dawn decided to drop out of the race—reluctantly, I should stress—I proposed to her and she accepted. There were the inevitable jokes about my marriage proposal being her consolation prize. I tell anyone who utters that quip that the true winner is me—that *I'm* the lucky one. The wedding is in three months. Dawn has been using her free time to arrange the ceremony, the reception and the honeymoon. She has been reorganizing my office, which she calls an unholy mess. She is finding new hobbies for me to explore, for she believes the ones in which I currently engage are uninspiring. She purchased new clothes for me to wear, asserting that they will make me more approachable. For the same reason, she is experimenting with changes to my hairstyle and eyewear, and is introducing me to new people with whom she wants me to become friendly—people she says will give me new ideas, perspectives, and emotional connections. She has taken to calling me by my first two initials, E.B., insisting it presents a more colorful and fashionable quality than Elliott Braydon, and she has obliged all of my friends and colleagues to do the same. Clubs and restaurants in and around Boston that I have never had an inclination to visit before are on our weekend agendas. She says she intends to find new things for me to talk about and new ways for me to talk about them. She says she has a complete plan of action for our future together as husband and wife.

My name is Professor E.B. Beckmond, and I have been teaching at Harvard University for nineteen years. Not much has changed in that time. Still, it is exceedingly clear that for me, it is the dawn of a new day.

Manhattan Moon

Although a simple guy, in the Army Jacob Kantor felt an air of nobility because he was from Manhattan. All the other young men in his barracks were from elsewhere in the country, and most had a sense of wonder about New York City. That's why they hung onto Jacob's every word about the tall buildings and the pretty girls, the gangsters and the Broadway shows, the speakeasies and Times Square, the bridges and the docks. But after seven months Jacob returned to his family's Lower East Side tenement, wedged between two long-vacant Vaudeville theaters, never having gone overseas. The war in Europe and Asia had begun to wind down just as he arrived at Fort Jackson, South Carolina, for basic training on his nineteenth birthday. When he came home, Jacob was just one of countless young men in the city who faced an uncertain future with a befuddled mixture of skepticism and hope. No longer could he tell exciting stories about the big city because everyone he knew back home had already heard them, and many had even more of their own.

Jacob had one advantage, though: in 1939 his father, Manny Kantor, wrote and recorded a song about New York City called *Manhattan Moon,* and for several months it was extremely popular on the radio and played in hundreds of jukeboxes thousands of times across all five boroughs of New York City. It sold more than a quarter of a million copies of the record and the sheet music. But Jacob was cautious about sharing that piece of distinction because if anyone asked, and they always did, he would have to admit that *Manhattan Moon* was Manny Kantor's one and only hit song. Manny wrote, recorded, produced, promoted, and distributed all of his own music, having been too distrustful of others to accept professional help. He ran his rudimentary studio out of his tenement apartment. Following the success of *Manhattan Moon*, Manny's plan was to write one distinctive song about all the big cities across America, and he did indeed write songs about Newark, Atlantic City, Boston, Philadelphia, Chicago, San Francisco, Miami, St. Louis and a dozen others. He had hoped that each one would be as successful as *Manhattan Moon*, at least in the cities in which each song took place. But only *Newark at Night* and *Atlantic City Serenade* received a smattering of airplay and a scrap of record sales — not even enough for a month's rent. The other songs failed miserably. It nearly compelled Manny to pick up and move to New Jersey to work at his cousin's paint store. But he didn't do that. He was too tied to New York City. Manny, who had loved music since he was a boy, refused to do anything else to support his wife Betty and their two boys, Jacob and Chet; creating music was the only thing that made him happy. He felt as if he made *other* people happy, too, and that was important to him. Music was his passion. His personal integrity — his intellectual honesty — disallowed him to do anything else with his life.

When he returned from the Army in 1946, Jacob knew he had to think about a career. He had many interests but could not identify a single genuine passion. He liked to work with his hands, to assemble models not just of ships and airplanes but also of buildings. Architecture was one profession he considered, but he didn't like the thought of returning to school. Furniture craftsman was another, but that reminded him of his Uncle Ted, a craftsman who suffered from so many work-related aches and pains that he ceased being able to work at fifty-two years of age. Jacob even thought about music as a career. But as quickly as he'd give it a thought, he would realize that his father's obsession with music forced the Kantor family to live in poverty most of the time, and that predictably soured Jacob to the idea. It wasn't money, or titles, or professional status that drove Jacob's search for a profession. Like the elder Kantor, he just wanted to be happy.

He also wanted to be in love.

Jacob had girlfriends throughout high school, and being in love seemed to him an admirable endeavor. His brother Chet, sixteen when Jacob came home from the Army, was as ambitious and arrogant as Jacob was discreet and modest. "Hitchhike across the county, get odd jobs, make love to girls in haystacks," Chet pestered his brother, who he considered a lazy and unexciting man. "Everyone thought *I'd* be the bum, but that'll probably end up being you, not me," Chet said one day to Jacob as the family sat in their tiny dining room for dinner. "If you ever meet a girl, she'd better have a lot of money, because you won't have a dime, and that'll be a big problem."

Even Manny and Betty commented on how difficult it would be for Jacob to find a girl to marry as long as he had no profession and no apparent ambition to look for a decent job. But Jacob tried not to let such comments bother him. He refused to allow these discussions to devolve into conflicts, and eventually his parents conceded he had a right to live his life the way he chose. "Well, Jacob," his father sighed a number of times, "we know you're a good boy. Intelligent. Honest. Respectable. That's important. Especially the honesty. The world is full of dishonest people. Trust me—you find that out pretty quickly in the music business. I'm proud of you, Jacob. So is your mother. So let's not fight."

In 1947, Jacob accepted a part-time job at a small lumberyard just a few blocks from the apartment. He used his free time to wander the streets of Manhattan in search of new inspirations. He went on a few dates, but the girls seemed to him to be images of what they dreamed they'd be instead of truly being those things. He spent time with Morty, his best friend, at Brooklyn soda shops where someone invariably would play *Manhattan Moon* on the jukebox.

Jacob was not unhappy, but neither was he fulfilled. Morty understood this. "Come with me to South Fallsburg, up in the Catskill Mountains," Morty announced one day at the soda shop. "Brickman's is having a singles weekend. Saturday morning to Monday afternoon. We'll schmooze our hearts out. And if you meet anyone, you can pretend you have a full-time job and a little ambition."

Jacob ignored Morty's comment but agreed to accompany him to South Fallsburg. It was at Hotel Brickman that Jacob Kantor met Rachel Melzner.

•   •   •

As a child, Rachel Melzner was not aware that her family was poor. This was a source of amusement to her extended family and to the parents of her friends, but her own mother, father and older brother failed to see the humor. Rachel was not foolish; quite the contrary, she was exceedingly bright, but believed whatever she felt, and what she felt about her childhood was that it was secure, privileged, and full of love.

Rachel imagined that poor families were ones in which the fathers had no job, became alcoholic and abusive because of it, and lived with their unhappy wives and bedraggled children in squalid tenements with neither heat nor running water. For that's the way poverty was depicted in movies and in books.

Sam Melzner, Rachel's father, worked as a janitor at a floor products factory in the Bronx. Her mother, Helen, had a part-time job as a packer at a toy company in Washington Heights.

With two incomes, how could they be poor? Their apartment was small—a tiny kitchen, narrow combination living and dining room, and two bedrooms, one of which she had to share with her brother Joseph—but it was tidy and comfortable. It was on the Upper West Side of Manhattan, where only rich people lived. That, too, is what Rachel had learned in picture shows and dime novels. Poor girls in stories could not take ballet lessons and French lessons and etiquette lessons. Through her mother's resiliency, Rachel could take all those lessons and more.

One day, when Rachel was eleven and her brother was sixteen, Joseph asked her, "Do you really need ballet lessons? Isn't there a dance club at school that's free? Mom and Pop could really use the extra money."

"Why? Despite what you and everyone else want to believe, we are not poor," Rachel said with conviction.

"Yes we are," Joseph contested, with more than a touch of irritation to his tone. "Rachel, why do you think Ma has to work? Why do you think that if I can't get a scholarship I won't be able to go to college? Why do you think we can never move from this lousy apartment? If Pop didn't work for the landlord, we'd be out on the street. And Pop—" Joseph added, seamlessly moving from one topic to another, "he's so damn honest that when his boss wants to pay him for an extra three hours of work, Pop tells him he only worked for *two* hours. His damn honesty keeps us poor, Rachel. It's crazy, but it's true. We'll never get ahead."

Sam and Helen had met in a Polish shtetl as teenagers and married at eighteen. At nineteen, as the eldest children in their respective large households, they journeyed to New York City to pave the way for their families to emigrate for a better life in America. They worked hard, but struggled. Sam was not known for his drive, but he was a good, honest employee. His boss trusted him more than any other worker at the floor products company, which is why the Melzners were given the opportunity to stay in the small Upper West Side apartment that was owned by the boss, when so many other families could never dream of living in that section of Manhattan.

With their combined incomes, Sam and Helen paid the rent and utilities, bought food and second-hand clothes, purchased a few goods to keep the apartment furnished and clean, bought school supplies for the children, and financially helped three of their less-fortunate relatives elsewhere in the city who were too sick to work. After all that, there were just a few dollars left every month. Sam thought they should save the extra money for their old age. Helen had other ideas. She wanted Rachel's future to be one of ease and prosperity. She did not want her daughter to struggle as she and Sam still struggled. Helen did not worry about her son Joseph, for he, too, was academically gifted and would probably become a doctor. But Rachel, despite her intelligence, was a simple girl who liked to dream and take walks and observe nature, and Helen knew that if she didn't meet and marry someone with means, she might very well end up poor. So, with the few extra dollars she had at the end of each month, Helen paid for ballet lessons and etiquette lessons for Rachel. Helen had two sisters and two brothers who had recently emigrated to America, each of whom had a skill they were more than happy to share with young Rachel, such as singing, painting, and speaking French. Her aunts and uncles enjoyed instructing their adorable niece because she soaked it up and was such an outstanding student. They also appreciated all that Sam and Helen had done for them; coaching Rachel was a blissful way for them to return the favor. Helen believed that all the lessons, both purchased and bestowed, would develop in Rachel a confidence that people would see as elegance. Men of means were attracted to elegance.

But then the family suffered a setback. Two of Joseph's fingers were severely mangled in the first year of World War II. He lost the use of both. Unable to become a doctor, he went to Queens College on a scholarship to train as a science teacher.

Rachel, meanwhile, graduated high school with honors. Her teachers said that she, too, could get a scholarship to college, but she chose instead to take a volunteer position with the New York City Parks Department for which she tended city-owned gardens. She also continued to live in the apartment with her mother and father. Since she brought no money into the house, she offered to make up for it by taking on all the cooking, cleaning and sewing that had typically been her mother's responsibility. She thought her mother would appreciate that. "I didn't raise you to cook and clean and sew," Helen chided her daughter one night after Rachel returned home from a Brooklyn park. "And why do you spend all your time with trees and flowers? How will that help anyone?"

"It helps *everyone*," Rachel said without further explanation.

When Joseph was in his first year as a science teacher at Queens College, he saw a flier in the hallway that advertised a singles weekend in South Fallsburg. He lived by now in his own apartment and spent almost all of his free time courting his fiancé, Marcia, who had no interest in travelling to the Catskill Mountains, especially since she no longer considered herself as being single. So Joseph told Rachel that he had some money saved up and wanted to give her a belated high school graduation present: he would pay for her three-day weekend at Brickman's Hotel in South Fallsburg. He insisted she needed to get away from the city for a while, to meet new people, to broaden her horizons. Rachel was resistant to the idea at first, but to allay her brother's concern about her well-being, which echoed her parents' concern, she accepted. She asked her best friend from ballet class, Sylvia, if she wanted to go along. Sylvia, an active man-seeker, said yes.

It was at Hotel Brickman that Rachel Melzner met Jacob Kantor.

•   •   •

Shortly after they arrived in South Fallsburg, Jacob and his friend Morty met Rachel and her friend Sylvia. Morty wanted to impress Sylvia. The four of them walked along a grove of stately birch trees behind the hotel. It was a beautiful and mild Saturday afternoon. Rachel identified several plants and flowers by name. Sylvia tried to change the subject.

Morty offered candy to the girls. He had several packets in his pocket. "Two sweets for two sweets," he said as he handed them the wrapped candy. Sylvia correctly deduced that Morty was a candy salesman and asked about his job and about his future prospects. Morty said he had no doubt he would become a vice president of sales for New York, New Jersey and Connecticut. "One day I'll earn fifty-thousand dollars a year, have an office in a skyscraper in Manhattan, and live with my family in a beautiful house out on Long Island," he said as he stared at Sylvia, whom he found very attractive. "I'll just have to spend a year or two as a salesman first, schlepping to little candy stores in the city, where I'll have to hear this guy's old man on the jukebox singing about a lousy Manhattan moon." He jabbed Jacob's ribs with his elbow.

Sylvia turned to Jacob.

"You're Manny Kantor's son?" she asked.

Jacob nodded, reluctantly. He also shot Morty a scornful look.

"How cute," Sylvia said to Rachel. "He's embarrassed by his father's fame! Tell you what, Jacob. I won't embarrass you anymore if you sing a little bit of *Manhattan Moon* for us."

As they continued to stroll around the lake, Jacob sang a verse of *Manhattan Moon*, but didn't enjoy having to do it. He didn't like Sylvia for asking, nor Morty for suggesting it in the first place. He did, however, admire Rachel, for she, too, looked embarrassed on his behalf, and her unsolicited comment about how well his voice blended with the natural surroundings intrigued him.

On Sunday morning, Hotel Brickman presented a series of coeducational classes and activities, including tennis, political trivia, bingo, and ballroom dancing. "Learn Something New While You Meet Someone New" the sign announced. Jacob and Morty attended the bingo game, Rachel and Sylvia took the ballroom dancing class. Although both were accomplished dancers, Sylvia thought it would be fun to dance with a stranger who depended on her to lead. Rachel simply thought it would be an easy way to pass the morning. In the middle of class, the teacher, Lady Emma, likened a certain ballroom move to a ballet step, and then demonstrated. Lady Emma enacted the move so poorly that Rachel and Sylvia had to work extra hard to stifle their laughter.

After lunch, on a grassy hill in front of the hotel, Rachel noticed a tree at the top with one long branch that stuck out waist high and horizontally. "Look! It can be a ballet barre!" Rachel gushed. "We can practice here on the hill, in the fresh air, without toe shoes or an incompetent teacher. Shall we?"

The two of them walked to the top of the hill, and both took turns using the branch as a ballet barre to do a series of classical dance moves. Sylvia went first, then Rachel. It was when Rachel was doing an arabesque that Jacob and Morty passed by at the bottom of the hill.

"She's spectacular," Jacob said breathlessly, almost in a whisper. "So graceful. So beautiful."

"The dame from yesterday? Ahh—she's probably a rich snob who came here just to show off," Morty countered.

"She's not showing off," Jacob insisted. "As far as she knows, no one is watching her. She's doesn't even know we're down here. She's not showing off at all, Morty."

After dinner there was a dance social. Jacob told Morty he wanted to stay in the room for a while, but he actually took a solo walk around the grounds. Rachel said the same thing to Sylvia; she, too, took a solitary stroll on the hotel's dirt paths.

It was a chillier evening than it had been the night before, so Rachel wore a stylish sweater that her mother had made for her to wear on job interviews—although Rachel had never worn it for that purpose. Its design hugged her figure, accentuating her allure a bit more than she normally would have allowed. The artificial pearls along the seams were so delicate and well-affixed as to look real.

"That's a very pretty sweater," Jacob said as he and Rachel were about to pass one another on the path near the tennis courts.

"Thank you very much. I wanted to wear something pretty in case you decided to sing a pretty song," Rachel smiled. "After all, you've already proven that you have a lovely singing voice."

"If Morty was with me, he'd say you're sweet and then he'd give you a piece of candy. I don't have any candy." Jacob reached into his pants pocket. "All I have are two chips from a bingo game. I didn't steal them on purpose. I promise. I guess I was just nervous."

"Why were you nervous?"

"Because I thought I might run into you again. And you're so beautiful."

Jacob and Rachel spent all of Monday morning together. They took their breakfast plates from the dining hall to the grassy hill. On the lawn, Rachel put down an improvised picnic blanket made from an oversized scarf that her mother had packed for her in case the evenings were brisk.

"That's a very fancy scarf," said Jacob. "Don't you think it will get dirty on the grass?"

"It could use a little staining," Rachel countered, "just to see how the other scarves live."

Jacob laughed.

By Rachel's request, they said very little about their families, just the simplest of details, such as how honest their fathers were and how capable their mothers. Also, by Rachel's request, they concentrated on talking about what made them happy and what they wanted out of life.

"I want to have a simple, relaxing life and live in a simple, beautiful house," Jacob said spontaneously. "That would make me happy. Not only that, but I want to build things for other people to make *them* happy, too."

Rachel thought that a charming sentiment and said so with her eyes and by placing her palm gently on Jacob's cheek.

"I'd like to build you a beautiful house one day, where you can dance your heart away," he said.

"I'd love a beautiful house," Rachel responded. "But not to dance in. All I want is a garden to... well, to garden in."

Rachel and Jacob decided to introduce their families to one another. They arranged to meet the following weekend in Manhattan to discuss it and make a specific plan.

"I will think of you and miss you until we meet again," Rachel said.

"Here's how to make that a little easier," Jacob advised. "Look at the moon every night. Wherever you are in one part of Manhattan, I will be looking up at the same moon in another part of the city. That will connect us — until we connect for real. And yes, I did steal that from my father's song."

Rachel smiled.

"My brother likes astronomy," she said. "He'll help me find the moon, even if it's cloudy. I just won't tell him why I need to find it. It will be our secret Manhattan moon. Our lune secrète ville. Everything sounds more romantic in French. Doesn't it?"

"It does now," Jacob said.

•   •   •

The next week, a customer at Jacob's lumberyard, impressed with his enthusiasm and helpfulness, asked Jacob if he would like to work for him. The customer owned a home construction company and was looking for an assistant project manager. He told Jacob he could pay him $100 more per month than he currently earned at the lumberyard. Jacob accepted.

"Is Rachel happy about your new job?" Morty asked him one night at the soda shop.

"Very happy. I told her on the phone last night. We're going to celebrate this weekend."

"Did you tell your mom and pop about Rachel?"

"Only what they need to know. No more, no less. Better that way. They'll meet her soon. We're all having dinner together two weeks from Saturday. At Rachel's house."

"It must be serious then."

"I'm going to ask her to marry me."

On Thursday night, Betty and Manny Kantor entertained friends from an adjacent building, the Turkels. Betty had known Annie Turkel for more than fifteen years. They were close. Manny and Marvin Turkel were cordial, though not as close as their wives. Marvin considered Manny a braggart, even though Manny never bragged.

"Jacob has a terrific new job and a wonderful girlfriend," Betty gushed to Annie as the two couples sat in the Kantors' small living room. "Her name is Rachel. I have a feeling this is the one. Mother's intuition."

The corner edges of two decaying rooftop marquees, from the two abandoned vaudeville houses on either side of the building, were visible from the living room window. Pigeons strutted across each marquee. The sight distracted Annie, though only for a moment.

"Mazel tov," said Annie. "I'm sure she's pretty, this Rachel. No?"

"I'm positive. And from what I gather, wealthy too. She lives on the Upper East Side, no less. She studies ballet, she sings, she paints, she speaks four languages. Must have gone to private schools. A princess, this girl. And she likes to take care of gardens in all the city parks, so she has a heart of gold to go along with all her money. Can you believe it?"

Manny, sensitive to Marvin's misplaced jealousy, did not add to the conversation in any significant way because he wished not to make it seem as if he were boasting about his son's good fortune. Marvin Turkel, whose own son was a poorly paid shoe salesman in the Bronx who was married to an obese woman with a bad temper, did not smile all evening. But Manny was delighted, as was Betty. After all, their son was marrying into wealth.

● ● ●

At a nephew's bar mitzvah, Helen and Sam Melzner sat at a table with their daughter Rachel, their son Joseph, and Joseph's new wife Marcia. Marcia was critical of most of the Melzner relatives and her behavior embarrassed Joseph. Rachel departed for a while to look at the gardens in the backyard of the catering hall in Queens.

"Did you hear about Rachel's fiancé?" Helen announced to the other guests at her table. She knew only what Rachel had told her—and Rachel hadn't told her much—but it was more than enough for the bar mitzvah table. "He's the son of Manny Kantor," Helen said proudly.

"Oh! The *Manhattan Moon* Manny Kantor? *That* Manny Kantor?" asked Cousin Rose.

"That's the one. And other songs, too—but the other songs are probably more popular in other states, I'm guessing."

"The son is a musician too?" asked Rose's husband, Harry.

"The son does something in real estate. What's the company's name, Sam? Rachel told us, but I can't remember."

"Island Properties," Sam said proudly.

"Ooo—sounds exclusive," said Cousin Rose. "Maybe he builds estates for millionaires. Maybe he and Rachel will live in one of his own estates one day. Have you met the boy?"

"Not yet. But if Rachel likes him, I'm sure he's very nice and very handsome. The two of them walk constantly—walk and talk about all kinds of things, Rachel tells me. Maybe they talk about having children, I should be so lucky. How could I not be happy about that? My grandchildren will be able to have what my children never had."

•　　•　　•

As Manny and Betty Kantor drove from the Lower East Side of Manhattan to the Upper West Side to dine with Helen and Sam Melzner, their excitement was unambiguous. Visions of opulence blossomed in their brains. When they saw the skinny brick apartment building wedged between two larger marble buildings, their smiles wilted, though their anticipation remained.

Betty saw the modest furniture inside the small Melzner apartment and wondered if somehow the Melzner affluence had vanished. She silently prayed that if it did, it was just a temporary disappearance.

When Manny queried Sam about his profession, he recognized the name of the company that Sam had mentioned — National Flooring. He wondered aloud when Sam had started the firm, and in what year.

"When did *I* start the firm?" Sam laughed. "That would be Peter Galante, not me. About twenty-six or twenty-seven years ago. I've been the janitor there since 1922. But I'm as honest as the day is long, and I gotta tell you, Sam — I know more about that factory than Galante does!"

Betty Kantor admired all the photographs that Helen Melzner had placed around the apartment: Rachel dancing, Joseph accepting a science award at school, the family in earlier days strolling down Park Avenue in the snow. "Fortunate family," Betty said aloud. She regretted it instantly, for she knew how easily it could be misinterpreted either as sarcasm or jealousy.

"We're all in good health, thank God," Helen said in response. "There's nothing more important. My Joseph is a professor. My Rachel is such a joy. Both my children have found wonderful people to spend their lives with. So yes, we feel very fortunate, Betty."

Rachel and Jacob arrived at the apartment. They had spent the day together. The six of them, the young couple and both sets of parents, settled in for dinner. Helen served pot roast and potatoes, carrots, wine, and Danish and coffee for dessert. It was a polite evening, though smiles seemed hard to find and silences came all too easily.

Back home, late that night, from his bedroom Jacob overheard his parents talk about the evening.

"No chandeliers? No fancy china? Their apartment is smaller than ours!" noted Betty. "I know," Manny agreed. "You take two steps, you're at the other end. The place is as long as one of his handyman mops. He's a janitor, Betty! A janitor!"

In his bedroom, Jacob ignored all the nonsense chatter that he had overheard. He trusted that his parents' anxiety would blow over before long. It had to. Love conquers all. In fact, when Jacob was a boy, his father had composed a song with that very title.

"And do you mind telling me where they get the money for all the lessons?" Manny continued. "The dancing, the French, the whatever... What—he's a counterfeiter, too? An honest janitor *and* a counterfeiter?" Manny sat on the couch wearily with a very quizzical look on his face.

· · ·

The next weekend, the Melzners drove to the Kantors for dinner. Sam knew immediately that the address Rachel told him to look for was nowhere near the Broadway theater district, as he had assumed it would be from a comment Rachel once made about two theaters being across the street from their apartment building. The Kantor address was much further downtown.

"What's that?" questioned Sam as he pulled up in front of the tenement building that displayed the proper address. "Marquees? Those buildings have been vacant for years! The only performances you'll see on this block are by fat rats and skinny bums."

Helen begged him to calm down; she was worried about his heart. He calmed down, though once inside the apartment it was Helen who felt the need for a sedative, for when she visited the bathroom she saw a music stand on top of the toilet and a massive reel-to-reel tape recorder in the bathtub. For a moment she thought she was on the verge of fainting. But she maintained her composure over the meal of roasted chicken and green beans that Betty prepared, along with Manischewitz wine and cookies for dessert. The dishes were chipped but clean. Likewise, the conversations were strained but amicable. Jacob and Rachel sat together and made sure their legs touched under the table.

Sam asked Manny what he was working on these days. Manny ranted about unscrupulous agents and greedy promoters and rotten producers and evil publishers. "I think I'm the only honest person in the entire music business in this godforsaken city," Sam said. "They say you have to lie a little and cheat a little to get ahead in this racket, but I refuse. Honesty is my middle name. But still, I plan on having another hit one day. You'll see."

Though Manny was the one complaining, it was Sam who suddenly had a headache.

On the ride home, Sam and Helen seemed to be lost—not on the roads, but within their emotional states. Rachel, in the back seat, was equally lost in her own blissful world. "Sam, there was a rusty music stand on the toilet," Helen repeated over and over from the front seat. "And a hideous tape recorder in their filthy bathtub!"

Rachel ignored all she heard from the back seat. She knew that before too long her parents would recognize and accept the power of true love. True love, like resilient plants and flowers, always finds a way to bloom. That thought had been in Rachel's mind because it was similar to the words on a large sculptured flower box she had tended to earlier that morning at the Brooklyn Botanical Gardens.

Sam looked at his wife. "You know what I think, Helen? I think they're poorer than we are," he said, with a very quizzical look on his face.

•   •   •

Jacob and Rachel Kantor hosted a thirtieth birthday party for their son Adam in August 1981 at their home in Roslyn, on Long Island. All of Adam's grandparents were there, along with his

Uncle Chet and Chet's third wife, Yvonne, and his Uncle Joseph, who had never remarried after his divorce from Marcia. Adam's younger sister Michelle, and Michelle's fiancé Mitchell, were also at the party, along with a few of Adam's friends and some of Jacob's coworkers from Island Properties, where he was the senior vice president ("through no fault of my own," as he liked to say).

The birthday party doubled as a celebration for Adam Kantor's second nonfiction book having made *The New York Times* bestseller list. The meticulously researched volume, called *Manhattan Moon: A Love Story*, was about his parents' courtship and marriage. It had eighteen chapters with such titles as "A Hideous Tape Recorder in a Filthy Bathtub," "As Long as One of His Handyman Mops," "No Chandeliers and No Fancy China," and "Fat Rats and Skinny Bums." One review called the book "chock full of endearingly quirky stories traceable to eccentric folks who are, by turns, droll, stubborn, loveable, and scrupulously sincere."

There was a *Vanity Fair* reporter at the party assigned to write an article about the book celebration. The reporter interviewed Adam, Jacob, and Rachel, and then asked to speak with Adam's grandparents. Jacob told him that the private car he had hired to drive them from Manhattan to Roslyn had probably hit traffic on the Long Island Expressway. They were already forty-five minutes late.

When the elder Kantors and Melzners finally arrived, the *Vanity Fair* reporter rushed over to them by the piano in the den, eager to get some quotes. Manny had a copy of *Manhattan Moon: A Love Story* in his hands.

"Your grandson's book is quite enjoyable, isn't it?" asked the reporter.

"I read most of it in the car," Sam said proudly. "Out loud so that everyone could hear."

"He has the best eyes of all of us," Helen added.

"And what did the four of you think?"

"A real *tummler*, my grandson," Manny nodded. He looked at the others. "What were some of those crazy chapters again?"

"'A Hideous Machine, a Filthy Tub,' something like that," Betty tried to recall.

"'No Fancy Schmantzy Chandeliers' I think," said Helen.

"Fat Rats, Skinny Bums," Sam added. "Such a funny novel my grandson wrote."

"Novel?" the reporter repeated. "No, no—it's on *The Times* nonfiction bestseller list. It's all true."

"Come on, fella. Impossible," Manny insisted. "Such crazy things! All made up. Every bit of it. Don't you think we'd know what's real and what's not? We were there."

"I'm starving," Sam grumbled. "An hour on the Expressway. Where's the food?"

And with that, Adam's grandparents left the reporter standing alone by the piano with a very quizzical look on his face.

About the Author

Joel began in journalism at age 17 as a stringer for his hometown newspaper on Long Island, and continued training in college as an arts reviewer. His first job was as an assistant editor on a trade magazine. He then moved into corporate communications.

He is the author of seven published books, including two novels, *Blowin' in the Wind* and *Almost Like Praying*, and a nonfiction book on the late singer Karen Carpenter called *Some Kind of Lonely Clown*. He has also produced CD compilations of the comedy music created by his late grandfather, Benny Bell, about whom he wrote a book called *Grandpa Had a Long One*.

As a journalist his work has appeared in dozens of magazines, and he has had several op-eds published in *The New York Daily News*, *The Hartford Courant* and other newspapers. He also writes the monthly "Off Ramp" humor column for *Connecticut Magazine*. The topics on which he writes—in books, magazines, blogs and newspapers—range widely, from the prospect of recording dreams, to married couples who meet for the first time on stage, to the joys of aging.

Joel and his wife live in Connecticut. Although his profession is also his hobby, he takes time out to empty litter boxes and create rock gardens. He used to play the guitar to relax, but arthritis put an end to that. That's not one of the joys of aging.

Note from the Author

If you enjoyed *Weinerface*, please leave a review on Amazon or any other book-related site of your choice. For authors, online comments are one of the most effective ways to spread the word. Who knows—maybe there's another book of short stories like the ones in *Weinerface* waiting to be born. Let the marketplace demand it by showing your support for the effort with reviews and comments.

Thank you very much!
Joel Samberg

We hope you enjoyed reading this title from:

www.blackrosewriting.com

Subscribe to our mailing list – *The Rosevine* – and receive **FREE** books, daily
deals, and stay current with news about upcoming
releases and our hottest authors.
Scan the QR code below to sign up.

Already a subscriber? Please accept a sincere thank you for being a fan of
Black Rose Writing authors.

View other Black Rose Writing titles at
www.blackrosewriting.com/books and use promo code
PRINT to receive a **20% discount** when purchasing.

CPSIA information can be obtained
at www.ICGtesting.com
Printed in the USA
JSHW020455170323
39064JS00001B/2